W9-DBG-797

Gamblers and Dreamers

Charlene Porsild

GAMBLERS AND DREAMERS

Women, Men, and Community in the Klondike

UBCPress / Vancouver

© UBC Press 1998

Reprinted 1999
All rights reserved. No part of this publication may be
reproduced, stored in a retrieval system, or transmitted, in
any form or by any means, without prior written permission
of the publisher, or, in Canada, in the case of photocopying
or other reprographic copying, a licence from CANCOPY
(Canadian Copyright Licensing Agency), 900-6 Adelaide
Street East, Toronto, ON M5C 1H6.

Printed in Canada on acid-free paper ∞

ISBN 0-7748-0650-8 (hardcover)
ISBN 0-7748-0651-6 (paperback)

Canadian Cataloguing in Publication Data

Porsild, Charlene L., 1965-
    Gamblers and dreamers

    Includes bibliographical references and index.
    ISBN 0-7748-0650-8 (bound)
    ISBN 0-7748-0651-6 (pbk.)

    1. Klondike River Valley (Yukon) – Gold discoveries. 2.
Dawson (Yukon) – History. 3. Yukon Territory – Population
– History. 4. Yukon Territory – History – 1895-1918.* I. Title.
FC4022.3.P67 1998   971.9'102   C97-910920-5
F1095.K5P67 1998

This book has been published with the help of a grant from
the Humanities and Social Sciences Federation of Canada,
using funds provided by the Social Sciences and Humanities
Research Council of Canada.

UBC Press gratefully acknowledges the ongoing support to
its publishing program from the Canada Council for the
Arts, the British Columbia Arts Council, and the Department of Canadian Heritage of the Government of Canada.

Printed and bound in Canada by Friesens
Cartographer: Anne Lynaugh
Copy editor: Camilla Jenkins
Designer: George Vaitkunas
Proofreader: Gail Copeland

UBC Press
University of British Columbia
6344 Memorial Road
Vancouver, BC V6T 1Z2
(604) 822-5959
Fax: 1-800-668-0821
E-mail: orders@ubcpress.ubc.ca
http://www.ubcpress.ubc.ca

For my grandmother, Elly Rothe-Hansen Porsild, and for Judith

Contents

Illustrations, Maps, and Tables

Preface

In the summer of 1935, deep in the Yukon's Sixtymile mining district, a young Danish immigrant unpacked the family belongings and set about creating a home out of a tiny mining cabin. Only a few weeks earlier, this woman had given birth in Whitehorse. While she, her four-year-old daughter, and the new baby rested for the coming trip, her husband and two mining partners had built a sixteen-foot canoe that would take them some 300 miles down the Yukon River to the Sixtymile district. When the party set out the baby was twelve days old. This little 'bush baby,' as they called my father, was diapered with old flannels and moss from the nearby creeks and put outside in a packing crate to prevent jaundice.

Over and over, I have asked my grandmother to tell me stories of her incredible journey from urban, middle-class Denmark to the poverty and hardships of northern Canadian bush life. The same woman who once played piano in the concert halls of Copenhagen relates each story with a shrug that indicates her travails were nothing special. 'We did what we had to do,' she says. Growing up with all the conveniences of North American life, I found it hard to imagine the conditions under which my grandparents lived, worked, and raised their children. Even though very little had changed in the operation of a small family mining claim in the Yukon since the Klondike gold rush forty years earlier, my grandmother does not look back on her years on the Sixtymile as a period of drudgery. She cared for her growing family as well as for her husband's two mining partners under what could only be described as very rudimentary conditions. During the long dark winters she performed the laborious tasks of cooking and washing by kerosene lamp and candle light. To wash children, clothing, and dishes, she hauled and melted endless buckets of ice and snow. Where the wind blew the snow in, she chinked and re-chinked the mud and moss between the logs in the cabin walls. Her years on the Sixtymile were some of the happiest in her marriage.

Together, my grandparents Bob and Elly Porsild built a future for themselves in the Yukon. Bob was also a Dane, and although a scientist by training, he trapped, fished, and prospected to support his growing family. Elly fed the men, looked after the household, and tended her children – she delivered two more girls while the couple lived on the Sixtymile. In this remote part of the dominion, Elly Rothe-Hansen Porsild learned to speak English, be a wife, a mother, and a Canadian. As their children reached school age, the family moved first to Dawson and then to Whitehorse. After the Second World War they established a roadhouse: the lodge at Johnson's Crossing in the southern Yukon. Like so many other Yukon pioneers, they never left. My grandfather now rests in the Yukon Order of Pioneers cemetery on Gray Mountain while my grand-mother, after nearly a century on this earth, keeps tabs on her large and far-flung family from her home in Whitehorse.[1]

Having heard the stories of my grandparents' experience in the 1930s, I wondered what the Yukon was like for the men and women of the Klondike gold rush of 1898. For if the Yukon is remote today, and it was certainly remote and isolated in the 1930s when my grandparents arrived, what was it like at the end of the nineteenth century? And how in the world did a community of nearly 30,000 people appear in this far distant wilderness? When thousands of people left kitchens, offices, farms, factories, and lumber camps to join the stampedes to the gold fields of the Klondike, what did they find when they arrived? What was it like to leave those distant homes and arrive in one of the most beautiful yet coldest, most isolated outposts of the British empire? To find the answers, I embarked on a journey of discovery that took me back to my grand-mother's kitchen in Whitehorse and then to archives and kitchens across North America.

Acknowledgments

BOOK MANUSCRIPTS are very rarely prepared by the author alone. In my case I relied on the support and assistance of many people in Canada, the United States, and Europe. My family and friends, scattered throughout the world, were my mainstay.

From Boulder to Cripple Creek, Colorado, and from Vancouver, BC, to Lincoln, Nebraska, my husband W. Clark Whitehorn read and re-read the manuscript, correcting my overly passive voice and catching many errors, large and small. Clark's humour – and insistence that a hike up a mountain could solve all things – saw us through some very difficult times over the course of the project. I know I tried his patience in many ways and I thank him for forgiving me my trespasses – not to mention my profanities.

On my many research trips to the Yukon, I frequently called upon my grandmother, Elly Porsild, and my cousins, Jordan and Norma Davignon, for meals and accommodation, and they always provided these and so much more. I am also grateful to Jo and John Brown, Ellen Davignon, and the rest of my large extended family in Whitehorse, who provided all the moose meat, cinnamon buns, beer, birthday cake, and conversation I could digest. Thanks also to the members of the Whitehorse Golden Age Society for welcoming me to their cribbage tournaments and for so generously sharing with me their stories and memories of earlier days in the Yukon.

My father, Aksel Porsild, instilled in me a love and respect for the northern landscape and an appreciation of the human and nonhuman history that transpired there. One of the great joys of this project has been sharing with him and his wife Lorene my enthusiasm for things both northern and historical. My mom, Joyce Bevington, as well as my siblings, their spouses, and children have all provided their own forms of support and kept me grounded in reality over the years. I am particularly grateful to my sisters, who both asked me to take time from scholarly pursuits to assist in the births of their first born. If I ever wondered what it was like for women to survive childbirth in the Klondike, I had only to recall those deliveries in the Hague and London. Those two family events are the proudest moments of my career. To my niece Amanda and my nephews Alan, Mark, Ryan, Matthew, and Jesse: thanks for reminding me of what is really important.

My friends have been my most faithful supporters over the years. Because of a friendship established long ago in Edmonton, Anne Lynagh of Yellowknife spent many hours for very little pay producing the maps you see here. In Ottawa, Lorna Maclean listened to many of my not-so-scholarly tirades over the years and calmly brought me back to the matters at hand, while Dianna Thompson accompanied me on numerous journeys – wilderness, professional, and musical. Bonnie Belchamber in Saskatchewan, and Lynn Hogan and Michel Tatlock in Quebec all offered me their unconditional and loyal friendship. I am touched and amazed by the love and kindness of all these people.

I am also grateful to the many archivists and librarians in Canada and the United States. In particular I would like to thank the staff of the Yukon Archives, who assisted me on so many occasions. I am also grateful to the staff at the Dawson City Museum, the Provincial Archives of Alberta and British Columbia, the National Archives of Canada, and the National Archives of the United States, who provided assistance at various stages in my quest. I very gratefully acknowledge financial support from the Social Sciences and Humanities Research Council, the Fulbright Program, Carleton University, and especially the Northern Scientific Research Training Program at the Department of Indian and Northern Affairs Canada. May all of these institutions and agencies continue to fund and assist young scholars' northern projects.

I must also acknowledge some deep debts to a number of scholars. Kerry Abel, my doctoral supervisor at Carleton University, was always supportive. She was a thoroughly professional and fair critic and an encouraging mentor. Bruce Hodgins, Marilyn Barber, John Taylor, and Mike Whittington, the members of my doctoral committee, provided insightful comments and suggestions that proved most helpful in revising the manuscript for publication. It was a long way from the University of Toronto, but after a trip to meet the donkeys of Cripple Creek, Sylvia Van Kirk volunteered herself as an irreplaceable role model and treasured friend. American poet and writer Gary Holthaus shared with me his deep understanding of and great love for the West, while Colorado historian Tom Noel cheerfully shared with me his wealth of knowledge about western mining communities. Laura Macleod at UBC Press was as encouraging and helpful an editor as any young scholar could hope to have. Thank you, every one.

Through it all, my friend Judith Anne Sellick never doubted, as I so often did, my ability to see this project through. Whenever I needed anything, Judith always rushed to provide it. Now, as she faces her own mountainous struggle, I strive to provide her a pitiful fraction of the same support. And finally, I owe more than words can convey to my grandmother, Elly Porsild. Her love for and dedication to the Yukon over more than half a century have been my inspiration; her warmth and encouragement are a joy and a comfort to me. To these two remarkable and courageous women, I dedicate this book.

Gamblers and Dreamers

CHAPTER 1

Gamblers of a Hundred Hells
and Dreamers from the Seven Seas

The discovery of gold-dust in Dawson
sent swarming through the waterways
of sub-Arctic Canada a heterogeneous
horde – gamblers of a hundred hells,
old-time miners from quiet firesides,
beardless boys from their books,
human parasites of two continents,
and dreamers from the Seven Seas.

AGNES DEAN CAMERON, *The New North*

O N 16 AUGUST 1896, a Tagish man named Keish, his Anglo-American brother-in-law George Washington Carmack, and his nephew Káa Goox discovered gold on a creek they called Bonanza. This creek was a tributary of the Klondike River, and the discovery claim was located a few miles from the junction of the Klondike and Yukon rivers. The moccasin telegraph (that informal bush network that carried news far and wide) and the international newspapers soon had the whole world talking, which in turn sparked a stampede of grand proportions. In Europe and Asia, Italy and Japan, San Francisco and Toronto, women and men from all walks of life dropped everything to participate in the 'last great gold rush' of the nineteenth century.

Explorers, fur traders, and prospectors first penetrated the Yukon's interior from Alaska in the 1840s. These men eked out limited earnings in a land that was at once rich in resources yet stingy in rewarding their efforts. Then in 1886 a group of Alaskan prospectors discovered large gold deposits in the Fortymile district. As information about the gold discoveries spread south through the coastal mining and logging camps of the Pacific Northwest, the handful of miners in the Yukon grew to several hundred. By the time Keish and his partners staked their claims on Bonanza Creek, about a thousand non-Native men and women were living in the unorganized region that would become the Yukon Territory.

As word of 'tons of gold' travelled across Canada and the United States, gold fever spread. Soon people were selling their farms in Manitoba, abandoning their factory jobs in Ontario, and packing up their general stores in Colorado to make the long trek north. And what a trek it was! The average gold stampeder could expect to travel 2,500 miles and had to choose from four major routes, each with its own rewards and perils. By far the fastest, easiest, and most expensive way to the Klondike was the 'all water' route. This brought argonauts north along the coast – steamers left from San Francisco, Seattle, Vancouver and Victoria – to northern Alaska, where they disembarked at St Michael, at the mouth of the Yukon River. At St Michael they transferred to a river steamer and journeyed upstream the remainder of the distance to Dawson.

Less well-heeled stampeders disembarked from their ocean steamers at Dyea and Skagway, on the southern coast of Alaska. Here they packed or hired others to pack their goods over the coastal mountain via either the Chilkoot or the White Pass to the headwaters of the Yukon River. Then, at lakes Lindeman and Bennett, they built or bought boats and floated with their goods downstream to Dawson. The less expensive, less popular – not to mention more arduous and difficult – routes were the two primary overland trails. The first headed north from Edmonton, over the Athabasca Landing Trail, travelling north to the shores of Great Slave Lake, along the Mackenzie River, and over the interior mountains into the Yukon. The second trail went overland from the coast and interior mining camps of British Columbia, up the Stikine River valley and through the Glenora District, joining the Yukon River at the mouth of the Teslin. Whatever route they chose, stampeders left home with a great sense of hope and adventure.

There was a second stampede in 1898, which few people wanted to acknowledge. That was the flow of failed stampeders searching for a route back out. Many stampeders remarked in their diaries and letters that during the voyage inward, they passed large numbers of disgruntled people coming back across the Chilkoot and White passes, having 'worn themselves out trying to get claims with gold.'[1] Oddly, such encounters seem to have had little impact on most who were on their way to Dawson, except

Because the Klondike adventure was both expensive and dangerous, many pooled their resources and set out in groups. These men left their homes in Nanaimo on Vancouver Island, pooling their money, goods, and labour in their quest for gold.

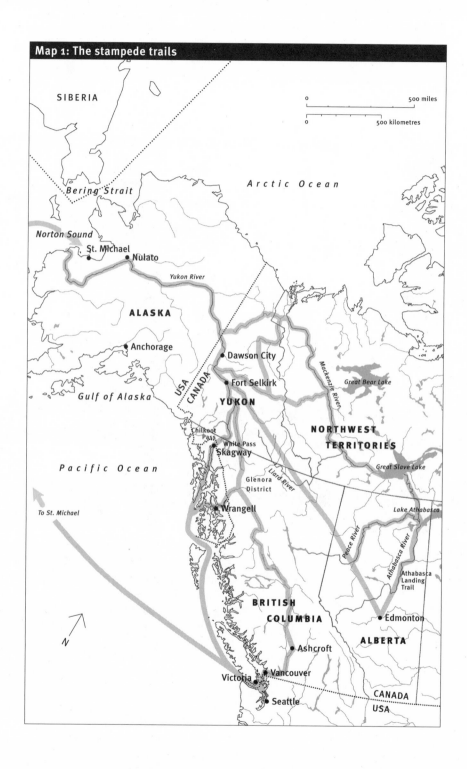

Map 1: The stampede trails

perhaps to stiffen their resolve. Still, others became disillusioned and turned back before ever reaching the gold fields. Worn down by the travails of the trail, they returned home never realizing the dream much less seeing the gold camp.[2] This was the case with the twenty-member Garner party, which left Fresno, California, in August 1897. Leaving late in the year, and heading overland through Edmonton, the party was forced to winter at the Métis settlement at Spirit River. Two members of the party contracted scurvy there, and by the following July, 'at a point estimated to be 110 miles to [the] summit of Sifton Pass,' the party turned back and returned to California.[3]

Many stampeders arrived in Dawson only to find all the promising gold claims staked. Many of these turned around and trudged back over the same trail they had travelled only a few weeks before.

An alarming number of stampeders died in the struggle to reach the fabled gold fields. Such was the fate of one man who left Sault Ste Marie for the Klondike via the Athabasca Landing Trail in the fall of 1897. His diary indicates that he froze his foot in December and since he could no longer walk, figured himself 'done for.' His partner went on ahead, taking with him most of the pair's provisions. Abandoned, this unfortunate man froze to death and was discovered almost a year later in a small tent, with a stove, a few sticks of wood, a small bag of flour, half a blanket overcoat, an axe, and a five-dollar bill.[4] The Sault man was not a unique case, for many others perished on the overland routes as the man who discovered the body tersely observed: 'Such are the gruesome tales of the Liard. Many of which never came to light.'[5] The Stikine route through northern British Columbia was also perilous, its dangers prompting one stampeder to blaze the following poem into a tree:

> And this is the grave the poor man fills
> After contracting fever and chills
> From tramping over the Stickeen hills
> Leaving his family to pay his bills.[6]

Queen City of the North

Whatever the travails of the trail, as many as 50,000 were successful in reaching the gold fields. When the earliest Klondike stampeders arrived at Dawson City in 1896 they found little more than a jumble of tents and shacks on a mud flat. Here, a handful of North West Mounted Police attempted to maintain 'law, order, and good government' in the face of a human tidal wave. Within two years, the gold stampeders transformed this mud-flat camp into a bustling town of 30,000 souls, complete with churches, hospitals, schools, and libraries. Although the city shrank substantially over the next few years – about 10,000 people called it home by the turn of the century – individuals and families alike stayed to work, play, and go to school. In short, the people of Dawson created a community that resembled, in most respects, a more southern Canadian city of similar size.

Two long-time traders and grubstakers, Joseph Ladue and Arthur Harper, moved their trading post to the mud flat soon after the Bonanza discovery in 1896. More importantly, they had the great foresight to apply for a permit to plot and sell town lots on the site. They called the new town Dawson City, after the Yukon surveyor and government geologist George M. Dawson, and during that first winter of 1896-7 it was home to approximately 500 people. Meanwhile, Ladue established himself as the proprietor of the town's first and most crucial businesses: a sawmill and a saloon.

By the summer of 1898, the clutter of canvas tents and log huts on the mud flat had been transformed by enterprising residents into a bustling town complete with banks, law offices, wood frame hotels, theatres, dance halls, churches, and even a hospital. Stampeders poured in from up and down the Yukon River joining the mad rush to stake mining claims and establish businesses to serve the growing population.

This book is a social history of a mining camp created in a few weeks which then developed into a permanent settlement and a complex society over the next few years. Dawson is only one community, to be sure, and therefore this work has the limitations of all case studies. But case studies make a valuable contribution to our understanding of historical problems. Because of Dawson City's unique time, place, and raison d'être, a careful examination of its formation can change the way we look at the formation of communities – especially mining communities. Concentrating on the experiences of the so-called 'anonymous citizens' helps us to understand who controls community development and how that development affects local residents. A careful study of the people who lived and worked in

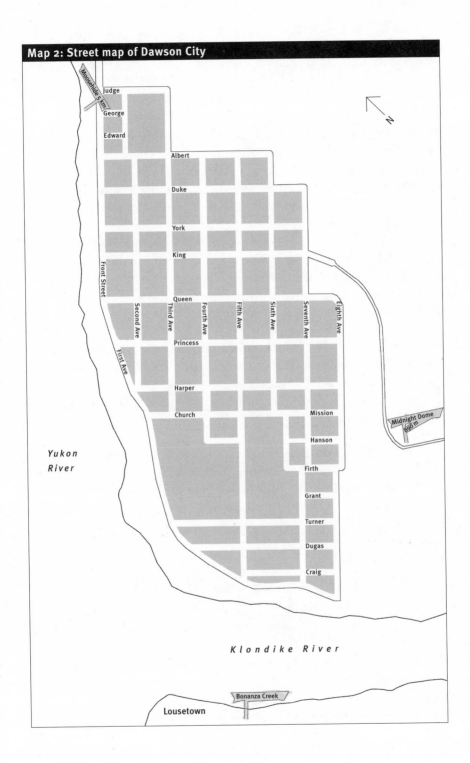

Map 2: Street map of Dawson City

Dawson demonstrates, for example, that they came from the four corners of the globe and that many of them remained in the area for a considerable length of time.

Social history has taught us that we cannot understand the past unless we study 'ordinary' people like my own grandparents. Furthermore, recent studies in environmental, gender, and ethnic history have shown that we cannot understand the historical experience of ordinary people unless we examine the world within which they lived and worked. Making a detailed study of an individual community and the people who made it their home both briefly and for extended periods is one way to understand this experience.

Was Dawson a town full of men, as I had always heard, or were there women like my grandmother quietly going about the business of establishing their families? If so, were these happy years, as they were for my grandmother, or years of pain, disappointment, and heartbreak? Did they grow rich, as they had dreamed they might? Did they leave or stay? Where did they go? What was it like to be a part of the great Klondike stampede? The sources I consulted clearly demonstrated that a great many women came to the Klondike as wives and mothers. For some the result was tragedy, for others great fortune. For most, the Klondike move was one of many strategies individuals and families undertook to try to better their fortunes. And even if they never 'struck it,' they would not have traded the experience for all the gold in Bonanza Creek.

In the pages that follow, I have attempted to reconstruct several key components of Dawson City between 1896 and 1905. Rather than concentrate on administrators, bureaucrats, and other celebrated figures of the period, as other Klondike historians have done, I have chosen to focus on the more anonymous men and women who lived and worked in Dawson in its earliest years. The experience of the ordinary Klondiker, then, is at the heart of this book. The results challenge pre-existing notions of an egalitarian, transitory, male mining camp and demonstrate that a heterogeneous and stratified community emerged early and remained long after the gold rush ended.

Dawson City began its long history as a necessary and pragmatic grouping of people, services, and supplies at a practical location, the confluence of the Yukon and Klondike rivers. Its citizens shared a universal purpose: the quest for wealth and opportunity. It grew into a complex urban supply centre that served a multitude of smaller mining camps in the surrounding Klondike and Yukon drainage basins. It also became

Dawson, June 21, 1899.

a permanent community, complete with families, senior citizens, schools, churches, and libraries.

Through a detailed examination of memoirs, diaries, and reminiscences of Klondikers, I have come to believe that the residents of Dawson were both aware of and valued a sense of community. Indeed, they demonstrate a surprising tendency to settle and remain for extended periods – a fact that challenges previous assumptions about the inherent transience of mining communities. Further, both the temporary and long-term residents of Dawson played an important role in the formation of their community. Indeed, as in most new cities, individuals initiated and supervised the founding of necessary services and institutions, and this participation fostered a high level of community involvement and commitment. When external forces – a distant federal government, for example – tried to restrict the nature and level of these services, local residents objected strenuously to the intrusion.

In Dawson City, a combination of forces created a community that was at once unique and familiar to its residents. The primary economic base of placer gold mining, while individualistic in theory, usually required partnership among miners. At the same time, distance from family and friends often required individuals to choose business partners from new social and economic networks. Miners and small business owners alike made these connections with others of similar religious and cultural backgrounds or with individuals who shared a common place of origin. Still, the Klondike brought together a wide array of individuals from a multitude of ethnic backgrounds. Interaction with other ethnic groups was a new and sometimes upsetting experience for many Klondikers and they established familiar institutions – churches, hospitals, school, ladies' aids, and fraternal societies – in order to provide some sense of stability and familiarity in their new locale.

By establishing these familiar institutions, Klondikers were trying to ease the anxiety that came with the economic instability of Dawson. The city's growth was severely hampered, for example, by its single resource base and the distance from its markets in Vancouver, San Francisco, and beyond. These factors restricted opportunities for the diversification of the labour market as well as for business. Mining remained the primary industry throughout Dawson's history, a situation rivalled in recent years only by tourism. Most of all, geographical distance from supply centres and a limited communications system demanded that familiar structures and institutions be adapted to suit local conditions.

The popular image of the Klondike is a frontier of white, male adventurers who overcame great physical and geographical obstacles in their quest for gold. Here, in the last great gold rush of the nineteenth century, we have been encouraged to believe that every man had an equal opportunity to make the big strike. These brave male adventurers of course needed to be wary of the multitude of undesirables ready to exploit their inexperience and good fortune. Native people were sneaky and opportunistic, eager to capitalize on any opportunity to soak newcomers with exorbitant freighting and boat-building rates. Women camp followers regularly and mercilessly preyed on miners as fast as they could head for town. To combat such evils a peerless detachment of Mounted Police arrived and set about maintaining dominion law and order by commanding fear and respect from a debauched American horde. It was a man's world made respectable only after the turn of the century with the arrival of white, middle class women who miraculously swept out the corners of dirt and vice and 'civilized' Dawson City.[7] Or so Klondike historians have suggested.

These images endure despite recent scholarly attempts to correct them. Canadians and Americans alike love to love the Mounties and this is nowhere better evidenced than by a recent television 'Heritage Moment' that portrays an oh-so-British Mounted Police Superintendent Sam Steele exercising Canadian sovereignty over the unwashed masses of American prospectors in the Klondike. This despite the fact that anthropologists and historians like Julie Cruikshank, Morris Zaslow, Ken Coates, and Bill Morrison have been attempting to redress some of these stereotypes for years. In Cruikshank's work, for example, we see First Nations people within the context of their own communities and hear First Nations women in their own voices. Zaslow, Coates, and Morrison for their part have quite rightly emphasized the Klondike gold rush as part of the more general historical development of the Yukon. Melanie Mayer and Frances Backhouse have demonstrated the importance of the role women played in the great Klondike adventure. These approaches have provided valuable context for other scholars and led the way for new historical investigations. Still, the myths and symbols have endured and historians have not undertaken a detailed examination of Dawson's population before now.

Dawson City began much like other mining towns in British Columbia, Alberta, and Ontario. The town started in 1896 as a supply base for prospectors and soon developed into a rudimentary camp community.

As the number of prospectors increased, the expanding supply businesses moved from their tents and lean-tos into more permanent wooden cabins and frame hotels. Because the resource held out well beyond the initial rush and because large companies moved in quickly to establish reliable communication and transportation networks, Dawson grew into a permanent community complete with social, political, and legal institutions. The only unique feature of Dawson's development, really, is that it displaced an existing community and in many ways evolved at the expense of that community. The flats at the junction of the Yukon and Klondike rivers had been the Han First Nation's summer fishing village. Gold stampeders, however, brushed aside the Han as they rushed to establish the new supply base. The Han were forced to relocate their village to a reserve three miles from the growing non-Native community.

Was this new community a male frontier of equal opportunity? Did Klondikers throw off Victorian standards of behaviour and class rigidity in their mad rush for gold in the 1890s? The answer is a resounding no. Many Klondikers remembered Dawson as a highly stratified society. Dr Barrett, for many years a physician at the local Catholic hospital, recalled that Dawson's original core of women and families was augmented by the arrival of many more in the fall of 1898 and spring of 1899. The growing community soon featured a social élite, which drew membership from the ranks of the professional and business class and almost completely excluded mining and labouring people. Barrett called them 'the nucleus of 400' among whom 'hospitality and good fellowship flourished to a degree unthought of in older Canadian communities.'[8] The highest ranks of the civil service and professional sector made up this nucleus for many years. The same core of people, diminished in number but equally strong in influence, were encountered by Pierre Berton's mother when she arrived in Dawson ten years later. Mrs Berton explained that Dawson at that time contained four social 'levels.' The first level included 'the commissioner and his wife, and worked its way down through the judges and offices of the police, the high civil servants, the heads of the large companies, the bishops and church people, the bankers and bank clerks, lawyers and nurses until it stopped with us teachers.' Teachers, then, were at the very bottom of Dawson's 'upper crust.' Berton referred to the second level as the 'downtown crowd' or business sector. The third level was reserved for the 'average' citizens: miners, labourers, police officers and tradespeople 'who were, in turn, several steps above the dance-hall girls and prostitutes of Klondike City.' These, of course, ranked only slightly above the bottom layer, which she described as 'half-breeds and Indians.'[9] Clearly, everyone fit somewhere within Dawson's hierarchy. Residents themselves were aware of these social distinctions, and they closely resembled those made at home in Ottawa, Montreal, Victoria, and San Francisco. These patterns of social distinction, established early in the formation of the community, became even more entrenched as the community matured.

Dawson City residents were members of a highly structured and cohesive community. The continuity I describe here indicates that many Klondikers who decided to come on a whim stayed to make Dawson their home for an extended period. The severe climate and geographical isolation of the Yukon also led to the development of an inside/outside dichotomy. The idea that everywhere beyond the Yukon's boundaries – the Mackenzie River to the east and the sixtieth parallel to the south – was 'outside,' acted as a binding agent for Yukoners. The concept of insiders and outsiders also separated 'cheechakos,' greenhorn newcomers, from 'sourdoughs,' relative oldtimers. The elevation of the 'sourdough' over the 'cheechako' gained expression in the establishment of the Yukon Order of Pioneers, a fraternity that originally limited its membership to men who had been residents of the territory before the Bonanza discovery. Boasting about the number of years they had resided in the region, in fact, was a favourite pastime of many pioneers. The Yukon pattern of identifying 'outsiders,' then, emerged early and fostered a sense of cohesiveness and community by identifying and holding in esteem those who demonstrated a commitment to the region – a feature of northern life that remains in full force today.

It is interesting to note that this pattern has parallel counterparts in other regions. It might be compared to the Maritime habit of identifying those who 'come from away' or to Ontarians who proudly boast that their familial origins lie in the Family Compact of Upper Canada. There is a natural and logical human need, it seems, to reward and hold in esteem those members of a community who have seen it through both good times and bad.

The esteem Klondikers placed in the sourdoughs, along with an emerging white collar government and professional bureaucracy, also lent a structure to the new community that was in many ways familiar to its residents. Indeed, far from being a democratic mining camp in which all citizens were of equal stature, social hierarchy was one of the first identifiable features in Dawson. The distance between labouring, business, and professional people was felt keenly by local residents, who frequently remarked upon it. Residents of the Han village of Moosehide and the red-light district called Lousetown, for example, were not invited to society functions in Dawson. Even in the less affluent parts of town, complex subgroups emerged that created their own social worlds, complete with pecking orders. In the red-light district, for example, women organized themselves into a distinct hierarchy based on popularity and notoriety, a phenomenon I have called the 'scarlet ladder.' Placer miners, as we shall see, organized themselves both ethnically as well as by the size and type of their mining operations. Social division and distinction were not limited to Dawson's upper crust.

Social structure aside, historians have typically assumed that frequent moves hindered the growth of northern communities, but in the Klondike stability was as strong a force as transience and mobility in the process of community formation. From the outset, Dawson residents moved within a set of social relations similar to those in much older Canadian settlements and this assisted them in feeling at home in the new town. They also created their own unique customs to foster a sense of belonging. When the ice went out of the river each year, symbolizing the end of winter and the start of navigation, Dawson residents abandoned their mines, offices, school lessons, and even church services to rush to the riverbank and celebrate. On this day cheechakos became sourdoughs: they had endured their first Yukon winter and their neighbours congratulated and rewarded them. Klondikers always came and went, to be sure, but a core of individuals and families remained, making a lasting commitment to the region and providing the sense of community they all shared.

Means and Methods

Perhaps the most obvious question that confronts historians of the Klondike gold rush is, 'Where did all these people come from?' Historians estimate that as many as 100,000 people set out for the Klondike gold fields between 1897 and 1899. Some of them ran out of money or courage (or both) before reaching their destination, while some stopped to take up other opportunities along the way. At least half of them reached their goal. They came, quite literally, from around the world and from all walks of life. Perhaps the most accurate assessment of their variety survives in the memoir of Agnes Dean Cameron, who described them as a mixture of 'gamblers of a hundred hells, old-time miners from quiet firesides, beardless boys from their books, human parasites of two continents, and dreamers from the Seven Seas.'[10] Despite the recent outpouring of literature on the

Klondike, we know little about the average women and men who left their kitchens, offices, factories, and farms to risk it all in the last great gold rush.

The international nature of the Klondike rush is striking. Accounts by travellers – which survive by the hundreds – refer to this fact frequently. Klondike stampeders regularly encountered 'outfits from everywhere, North America, Australia, England and France, all fired with gold fever.' Such people came by the thousands to the gold fields of the Klondike between 1896 and 1905. Interestingly enough, while historians have generally acknowledged that the Klondike contained representatives of almost every nation, they have also assumed incorrectly that it was 'a community largely composed of Americans and expressing American frontier ideology.' Morris Zaslow first made this statement in 1969 and twenty years later, when two of his students reprinted the article, his assumptions remained unchallenged.[11] Popular and academic historians alike have emphasized this American component of the Klondike, tacitly accepting the idea that the Klondike gold rush was really an American rush played out on Canadian soil.

The notion that the Yukon mining region was simply an extension of the American frontier has led to a lively debate over why the Klondike rush proceeded in a relatively ordered and nonviolent manner. Studies have generally concluded that while the participants in the rush were Americans accustomed to American frontier justice, British controls – Canadian laws enforced by the Mounted Police – prevailed to produce an orderly society in the Canadian wilderness.[12] The recent outpouring of popular literature and television documentaries highlighting the centennial of the gold rush has reinforced these stereotypes.

The assumption that the Klondike was an American community on Canadian soil can be, to some degree, explained. First, until recently there have been no reliable sources with which to verify earlier population estimates. Second, many Klondikers themselves perceived American dominance within the community as self-evident. One Dawson miner noted that it 'was well known that we Americans made up ninety percent of the Dawson-Klondike population.'[13] While this figure is wildly exaggerated, it illustrates that the *perception* of American predominance existed within the community itself. The Americans did, after all, establish and operate a consulate in Dawson City in 1898, and they dominated ownership of the largest transportation and mercantile companies throughout the period. Adding to the perception of American dominance, many of the earliest prospectors (and hence many of those who staked the first fabulous claims) were Americans. George Carmack, Clarence Berry, and George Snow, three of the most famous Klondikers, for example, were among them, and the news media of the day made much of this fact. Thus has the myth of the 'American Klondike' endured.

The Klondike, however, was more than just a gang of unruly American miners tamed by Mounties in red serge. By looking carefully at Klondikers' diaries and memoirs as well as newly available census material, we find a different portrait. We discover, for example, that the Klondike attracted people of more than forty nationalities, among them English and French Canadians, Americans, Britons, Danes, Swedes, Norwegians, Italians, Greeks, Chinese, Japanese, and Russians and Poles. By comparing three sets of quantitative data, I discovered that the majority of Klondikers were not Americans at all. They accounted for 40 percent, a high ratio to be sure but balanced by an equal proportion of Canadian and British Klondikers. The non-North American-born component of Dawson amounted to about 20 percent of the population. These people came – quite literally – from the seven seas (Table A1).

Close analysis of the statistical information presented in the tables in the Appendix allows us to discover many facts about the nature of Klondike society. First, we learn that people from over forty countries lived in Dawson during the gold rush period. This indicates that the community that emerged at the confluence of the Yukon and Klondike rivers really did resemble the 'heterogeneous horde' that Agnes Dean Cameron described. This is a significant finding for it is difficult to argue that Dawson was an American mining camp on Canadian soil when recent studies show that American mining camps looked very different. American boom towns like Grass Valley, Nevada, and Georgetown and Cripple Creek, Colorado, for example, boasted American-born populations of 80 percent or higher in the same period.[14] The population of Dawson City had a distinctly international flavour.

Like any other town, Dawson required a core of professionals, merchants, skilled tradespeople, labourers, and service personnel to sustain itself. In Dawson between 1896 and 1905, people reported ninety-four different occupations. Miners and manual labourers made up the largest occupational group, but they regularly came into contact with lawyers, teachers, nurses, and carpenters.

While the newspapers often referred to the Klondike as 'every man's gold rush,' the reality was that many people found their job opportunities limited. Women, Native people, and other minority groups all demonstrated a strong tendency to cluster in unskilled and low-paying occupations. The nature of this clustering suggests that few new opportunities presented themselves in the Klondike. Single women, for example, confined their participation in the labour market almost exclusively to unskilled service sector occupations. The exceptions to this rule were a few professional and entrepreneurial women. It is worth noting that contrary to popular myth, prostitution was not the primary occupation for Klondike women. The majority of women reported their occupations as 'wife.'

French Canadians and African Americans, as well as Japanese, Scandinavians, and Germans, also demonstrated a high degree of occupational clustering in the Yukon. African American men, for example, tended to work in the barber trade while women of the same ethnicity displayed a similar pattern in domestic service – particularly as laundry workers. Japanese men found employment almost exclusively in restaurants and domestic service. Scandinavians tended to gravitate toward skilled and semi-skilled trades such as carpentry and mining. French Canadians, the single largest non-English-speaking group, worked most often at mining and manual labour. While a number of French Canadians pursued careers in the civil service, few operated business or mercantile operations. The Jewish community also demonstrated a high degree of occupational clustering. All of the twenty-seven Russian and Polish Jews, for example, worked as tailors while in Dawson.

The commercial sector, while it contained smaller ethnic subgroups, was dominated by Anglo-Americans. This group was a powerful political and social force in Dawson and its visibility may also account for assumptions about an American majority. At the same time, Americans were largely absent from the professions in Dawson, a phenomenon due in part to Canadian licensing restrictions and the civil service patronage system. In both the small business and professional realms, women of all nationalities remained a small minority.

Families, of course, are an essential component of any community, and there were plenty of them in Dawson from its earliest inception. And although more than half of Dawson's adult female population reported 'wife' as their occupation, they supplemented the family income in a variety of ways that the census taker did not record. Many Klondike women kept their households afloat in hard times by taking in laundry and sewing or selling baked goods – services in great demand given the large single male population. Other women took in lodgers, sold wild blueberries and cranberries, or hired out their children to run errands and supply neighbours with chopped kindling. Klondike families employed numerous strategies to ensure their own survival.

Married and single women alike seized the Klondike as an opportunity to better their fortunes and many of them participated in full-time waged labour. Among those who worked for wages, the largest group reported service sector employment such as waitressing, doing laundry, and performing domestic service. Outside the service sector, traditionally female employment also predominated: ninety-three women worked at skilled trades such as needle work, sixty-eight operated small businesses – most often millinery shops, lunch counters, or lodging houses – and eighty-four worked as teachers, nurses, nuns, and other professionals.

The sex ratio of the Yukon was always the demographic figure most in flux. There are no reliable figures from the period before 1896, but several early residents commented that the number of women was very low in proportion to men.[15] At the time of the Mounted Police census in 1898, 1,195 females resided in the Territory, accounting for 8 percent of the population. Dawson City itself boasted the slightly higher figure of 12 percent. The female population rose steadily, reaching nearly 20 percent in Dawson by 1901 (see Table A8).

These demographic factors made Dawson look rather different from southern communities of similar size. Adult single women were the group in shortest supply and therefore in highest demand. In 1901, for example, there were 4,202 single people, and 3,899 of these were men. Within this pool of single adults, over 75 percent were in the marriageable range of twenty to thirty-nine years of age. There were thus almost thirteen single men for each of the 303 single women in town as late as 1901. The absence of 'respectable' places where both sexes could socialize and where courtship could take place further accentuated the social tensions caused by high male to female ratios.

Take place it did, however. Church and newspaper records indicate that at least one wedding took place each month in Dawson's early years and more than 1,000 married couples called Dawson home in 1901. The figures for the 'conjugal condition' of Klondikers reveals that while single people predominated, married people made up fully 32 percent of the population.[16] Close examination of married couples' census returns also reveals distinct patterns of family strategy. Rather than waiting for their husbands to establish themselves before joining them, most women travelled with their husbands and children to Dawson or followed with the children very shortly afterward.[17]

Despite the small number of single women and the few respectable places to court, weddings were frequent and celebrated with great enthusiasm.

Klondike families were just as ethnically diverse as Klondikers as a whole. French Canadians, Scandinavians, and Eastern European Jews demonstrated clear patterns of chain migration as well as social and geographical clustering. These groups tended to settle together in clusters of individual men and families, both in Dawson itself and along the gold-bearing creeks. Settling near one another created linguistic and cultural enclaves within which individuals could form and maintain social, religious, and business relationships. Such enclaves encouraged people to stay longer and to invite others 'back home' to join them.

Religion also fostered community commitment in Dawson. The religious sphere in Dawson was fiercely competitive. The Church of England, or Anglican church, was first on the scene in 1896. The Catholics arrived the following year and when the rush began in earnest in 1898, the mainstream churches and other social institutions quickly joined the effort. By 1901, nineteen religious congregations had established themselves in Dawson (see Table A10). Competition between Protestants and Catholics for dominance was an important factor in the establishment of the city's infrastructure, and the quick result was the construction of two hospitals – one for each group – several wooden church buildings, and a shelter for the poor.

The Church of England's stronghold on the Native community prevailed even after the rush began, and all the First Nation residents at Moosehide Village in 1901 reportedly professed the Anglican faith. The Roman Catholic church registers for many of the outlying Native communities, however, list a number of baptisms and marriages – the priest often performing both rites for an individual on the same day.[18] Most western religious denominations were well represented in Dawson, and there was a strong ethnic component to their congregations. Almost all Dawson's Scandinavians reported themselves Lutherans, for example, while all of the Russians professed Judaism. Similarly, the French, Irish, and French Canadians were overwhelmingly Catholic. These religious and ethnic affiliations provided an important forum for forging social and business networks.

Social and religious networks notwithstanding, historians have assumed that Klondikers were a highly transient population. Yet if people were constantly coming and going, how is it that Dawson City has continued to exist for more than a hundred years? The answer is that a core of people have remained in Dawson to 'see it through' the hard times, acting as a stabilizing force. Klondike miners, prostitutes, merchants, and white collar professionals all demonstrated a marked tendency to remain in the region for extended periods.[19] In fact, in 1901 two-thirds of Dawson's citizens – 5,000 individuals – had been residents of the Yukon for three years or longer. Taking into account that a mere 1,000 non-Natives had been residents of the area before 1896, this is a considerable figure in comparison to that for other settlements from this period. Michael Katz, for example, found a persistence rate of about 50 percent over a year and a half in his famous study of Hamilton, Ontario, while Ralph Mann found persistence of only 15 percent in ten years in Grass Valley, Nevada.[20] Thus, while it may be true that Klondikers continued to come and go – 16 percent of the population in 1901 had been resident in Dawson only a few months – thousands demonstrated an inclination to stay on (see Table A13). Unfortunately, until the National Archives of Canada releases the 1911 and 1921 manuscript census material, the only figures we have to measure this pattern end in 1901. Still, it will come as a surprise to most students of Canadian history to learn that residents of Dawson City, Yukon, tended to remain in their community longer than did the residents of Hamilton, Ontario. This indicates that residents of the new city of Dawson believed that it had the potential to become more than merely a flash-in-the-pan mining camp.

Dawson City from the earliest period of settlement had several distinct characteristics. First, the ethnic component was approximately evenly split between those of American and those of Canadian and British birth. While there is no doubt that Americans were prominent and numerous in Dawson City, they did not constitute a majority of the population. Second, the non-British and non-North American-born proportion was significant, accounting for about 20 percent of the population. Third, while adult males clearly predominated, women and children also participated in the gold rush from its inception. Fourth, stability, or persistence, was at least as strong a force as transience in this northern community. Finally, in the absence of established networks, ethnicity formed the basis for a number of occupational clusters, providing at the same time a business and social network for particular groups. There was also a strong propensity for ethnic and religious groupings to coincide and this reinforced informal networks for work and social life. It is the interaction between ethnicity, gender, and class that makes Dawson a splendid choice for a community study. Analyzing the complexities of this interaction allows us to see the human face of gold rush history.

CHAPTER 2

The Original Yukoners
and the Klondike Gold Rush

T HE NATIVE PEOPLE of the Yukon were severely and permanently affected by the gold rushes of the late nineteenth century. As the human flood to the Klondike intensified, the original Yukoners experienced direct and lasting contact with non-Natives, first on the Alaska coast and continuing along the Yukon River in both directions from its source to its mouth. When the dust settled, the largest mass of newcomers had settled in the territory of the Han, the people of the middle river, and it was they who held the dubious honour of having three major gold discoveries in their territory. The Han also accommodated the first permanent non-Native settlements in the Yukon. They continued, as did other Native groups, to be heavily involved in the fur trade while participating only tangentially in the new mining economy. This process of accommodation and adaptation is evident throughout this period.

There are seven distinct groups of aboriginal people in the Yukon: the Tlingit, Tagish, Kaska, Tutchone (Southern and Northern groups), Han, Gwich'in (also referred to as Kutchin or Loucheux), and Inuit. All but the Tlingit and Inuit are Athapaskan speakers, although all five Athapaskan groups speak distinct languages. Each of these groups was affected in turn by the waves of non-Native immigration experienced in the late nineteenth century.

In the pre-mining Yukon economy, there were two major lines of trade. From the southwest, the coastal Tlingit groups of the Chilkat, Chilkoot, and Taku travelled over the mountains to the interior to trade eulachon oil, shells, and cedar bark baskets for caribou hide, fur garments, and native copper. The bulk of this trade involved the Tagish and southern Tutchone people. In the northern Yukon, the Gwich'in dominated as intermediaries, trading goods obtained from other Gwich'in, Han, and Northern Tutchone for oil, bone, and tusks from the Alaskan Koyukon and Inuit people.[1]

Although they had been trading on the Alaskan coast for many years, it was not until 1834 that the Russians established a trading post and mission at St Michael, at the mouth of the Yukon River. For the next decade they set about exploring the lower Yukon River, expanding their trade inland from the coast. In 1839, the smallpox virus, brought in by the Russians, exterminated more than half of the Koyukon people in the St Michael area.[2]

In the same period, Russian Orthodox missionaries worked among the surviving people in the St Michael area. In 1845, another mission was built farther up the Yukon River in the interior. Here, at Russian Mission, Iakov Netsvetov built a church in 1851. By 1853, he boasted nearly 2,000 reported converts. Netsvetov, a priest born of Russian and Koyukon (an Alaskan Native group) parentage, set about vaccinating Natives against smallpox whenever they would assent.[3] Russian fur traders also visited the mission, using it as a post from which to penetrate the interior of the Alaska and Yukon territories.

At the southern border of the Yukon, Tlingit people controlled access to the interior through the mountain passes before Russian contact. Maintaining this control, they were able to ensure their monopoly on the interior trade. They established an extensive fur trade network, bringing furs from far up the Yukon River for trade first with Russian, and later with British, traders. By the time British traders arrived in the southern Yukon interior in the 1840s, the coastal Tlingit and the interior Athapaskans were operating a highly developed system of trade.

British traders and missionaries pushed into the Yukon first from the east, where they were already involved in the Mackenzie River basin. Direct

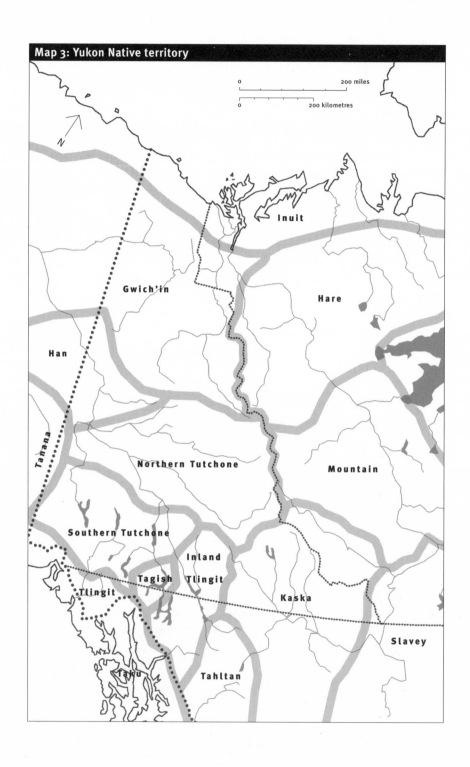

Map 3: Yukon Native territory

trade began with the establishment of LaPierre House in 1846 on the Bell River. The British conducted their trade from a series of posts established along the Yukon River between 1840 and 1890. For most of the inland people, this new trade system brought the first direct contact with Europeans. The trader Robert Campbell, for example, recorded that when he encountered a group of Northern Tutchone in 1843, they were taken 'completely by surprise, which almost amounted to awe, as they had never seen white men before.'[4]

The new group of traders also disrupted existing trade networks, at least temporarily. Campbell, for example, challenged the Tlingit trading dominance in the interior by establishing Fort Selkirk on the Yukon River in 1848. After seven uneasy years of competition, the Chilkat destroyed Campbell's fort in 1853. The Chilkat maintained control of the mountain passes from the coast as well as over the majority of inland trade for another thirty years.[5]

The first foray of Protestant churches into the region began in 1861, when the Anglican Church Missionary Society (CMS) arrived. The Reverend W.W. Kirkby arrived in that year to visit the people of the Yukon River valley. In 1862, he was joined by Robert McDonald, a Métis missionary from Red River recruited by Kirkby to work among the people of the subarctic forest. McDonald was well suited to northern missionary life, serving among the Gwich'in at Fort Yukon, LaPierre House, and Fort McPherson. Like many other CMS missionaries, McDonald made his permanent home among the people to whom he ministered, marrying one of his parishioners, translating parts of the Bible, and teaching the people to read in their own language.

Throughout the 1870s and 1880s, the CMS proselytized among the original Yukoners, establishing missions and counting converts. In many cases, it was the clergy who moderated and directed relations between Native people and the developing fur trading and mining society. The Reverend William Carpenter Bompas, arriving initially in the Mackenzie district in 1865, played a crucial role in this mediation, first at Fortymile and later at Dawson City and Carcross.[6]

In addition to bringing new goods and new religions, traders and missionaries brought diseases against which local communities had no defence. These spread in successive waves, from coastal epidemics of smallpox in 1838 and 1862, to influenza epidemics both on the coast and in the interior in the 1890s. None of the Native communities went untouched by European disease. The Reverend McDonald's journals, for

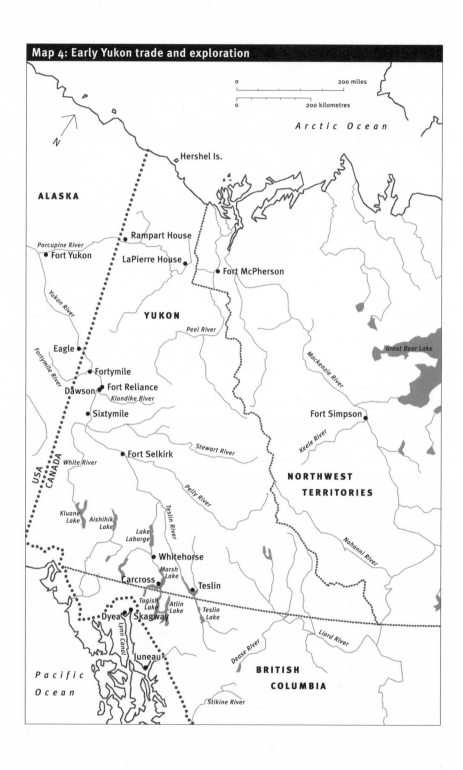

Map 4: Early Yukon trade and exploration

0   200 miles

0   200 kilometres

Arctic Ocean

ALASKA

Hershel Is.

Rampart House

Porcupine River
• Fort Yukon

LaPierre House •

• Fort McPherson

Yukon River

YUKON

Peel River

Eagle •

Mackenzie River

Great Bear Lake

Fortymile River

• Fortymile

Dawson •• Fort Reliance
Klondike River

• Sixtymile

Fort Simpson •

Keele River

• Fort Selkirk

Stewart River

White River

NORTHWEST

TERRITORIES

Pelly River

USA
CANADA

Kluane Lake *Aishihik Lake*

Lake Labarge

Teslin River

Nahanni River

• Whitehorse

Marsh Lake

Carcross • • Teslin

Tagish Lake *Atlin Lake*

Dyea • Skagway

Teslin Lake

Lynn Canal

Juneau •

Dease River

BRITISH

COLUMBIA

Pacific Ocean

Stikine River

Liard River

example, bear sad testament to the successive waves of smallpox, whooping cough, tuberculosis, polio, and influenza that devastated the Gwich'in people.[7]

Looking for the Yellow Rock:
The Coming of the Early Gold Prospectors
Private traders and prospectors began arriving in the interior Yukon in the mid-1870s. The first were two *coureurs du bois*, François and Moise Mercier, who established themselves as the Alaska Commercial Company representatives at St Michael and Fort Yukon respectively. Three Americans soon joined this group. Leroy McQuesten, an American miner and trader, was a veteran of the California and British Columbia gold fields. Arthur Harper, also a veteran prospector, was an Irish-born American who had followed the Rocky Mountains northward from the gold fields of British Columbia. Alfred Mayo was a former circus performer and prospector originally from Kentucky. These men arrived in 1873 and by the following year had set up a post called Fort Reliance on the Yukon River, a few miles downstream from the mouth of the Klondike. Ironically, this soon-to-be-abandoned post was almost on top of what twenty years later became the townsite for Dawson City. Harper and Mayo stayed here, while McQuesten moved farther downstream to Fort Yukon. Here, in Han territory, they found promising prospects and a lucrative fur trade. Harper, Mayo, and Ladue became not only fur traders, suppliers, and prospectors but grubstakers as well. It was largely through these men's encouragement that other prospectors soon followed. The supply base thus established, private traders could now support the prospecting ventures of others.[8]

The arrival of these private traders further upset the Native system of trade and social relationships. Under the new system, traders advanced food and goods to Native trappers in anticipation of their fur production. Unfortunately, the Native trappers often used up the supplies before the pelts were ever brought in. This system also placed greater stress on animal populations, for more than ever the trapper was bound to the demands of a single trader and his market. Often, of course, this meant travelling farther distances to trap animals that were no longer abundant in the usual hunting grounds.[9]

George Snow noted some of the negative effects of the new contact between the Native communities and the growing number of trappers and prospectors in the late 1880s. Snow remembered that the Tagish people of the Upper Yukon suffered starvation as a direct result of this contact during the winter of 1888-9. In the autumn of 1888, the Tagish people brought in most of their dried meat and fish along with their furs and traded them for tobacco, tea, sugar, blankets, and cloth. Having traded nearly all of their summer harvest, the people experienced severe hardship and deprivation during the following winter, when game was scarce.[10]

The Tagish people's cousins, the coastal Tlingit, had controlled the mountain passes leading from the southern Alaska coast to the headwaters of the Yukon River, which were the major transportation route for the region. Until 1880 they prevented non-Tlingit and -Tagish people from gaining access to the interior Yukon via this route, determinedly maintaining control through the first forty years of European trading and proselytizing even as prospectors sent word out that they had found gold in the riverbeds of the interior. This frustrated many early explorers and prospectors since all agreed that the Tlingit controlled the shortest and easiest route to a large fur-bearing and possibly gold-bearing region. As well, gold and silver mines discovered near Juneau brought a growing number of non-Native prospectors to the area just south of the Lynn Canal Tlingit communities in the late 1870s. Conflict was brewing both between factions within the Tlingit community and between the Tlingit and the miners. As Captain Lester Beardslee, US Navy commander at Sitka, later remembered, 'The [Yukon] country was reported to be rich in minerals, and the miners were very desirous of penetrating it, and it seemed more than likely that sooner or later, bodies of them would undertake to force their way in which case serious trouble would probably have occurred.'[11]

Pressure from the newcomers caused friction within the coastal Tlingit communities. Younger Tlingit, who wanted to resist pressure from outsiders to exploit their land and resources, opposed the older and more moderate members, who favoured compromise. When Kohklux, headman of the Chilkat, attempted to negotiate peace between the clans in September 1879, violence erupted and he was seriously injured. As both sides prepared for war, Kohklux was approached by Beardslee, who offered military support and supplies in return for rights for miners to travel through Tlingit country into the Yukon. Although Kohklux faced a good deal of local opposition, he and the other regional Tlingit chiefs negotiated an agreement with the Americans in February 1880. The blockade of the mountain passes would be lifted on the following three conditions: prospectors would be accompanied by Tlingit guides to ensure no trading took place, they would hire Tlingit slaves as packers, and they would use the less important route, the Chilkoot, rather than the Chilkat.[12]

After forty years of fiercely protecting their territory, the coastal Tlingit allowed a party of nineteen prospectors to climb the Chilkoot Pass, arriving at the headwaters of the Yukon River in June of 1880. The result was that the interior of the Yukon was now accessible from all directions: upstream from the mouth of the Yukon at St Michael, downstream from its headwaters at Lake Lindeman, and from the Mackenzie basin to the east. The floodgates were open.

'Indian No Want Him, White Man No Want Him':
Social and Cultural Interaction in the Yukon
The mixed blood people of the Yukon have a long history, although very few historians have written about them. Koyukon women on the Alaskan coast, for example, entered into sexual relationships with Russian traders at St Michael from the earliest contact. Creoles, as the children from these unions were locally known, played an important role as guides and interpreters in the early exploration period. From the 1830s, Creole men were instrumental in the exploration of the Yukon River from St Michael to Fort Reliance. Creole women often married Russian traders or Creole men, further enlarging the subcommunity of people of mixed blood. Two of the better known Creoles were Semen Lukin and Andrei Glazunov. Glazunov had been educated by Russians in Alaska and was fluent in a number of languages, including Russian and 'Kodiak Eskimo.' These two and others acted as interpreters and guides for Russian traders and explorers and made a good living for themselves. Subsequently, many of the so-called 'Russian' traders were actually Creole men, themselves products of the trade relationships between Russian traders and Native Alaska women.[13]

The trader at Nulato in 1867, for example was Ivan Pavaloff, son of a Koyukon woman and a Russian trader. Pavaloff married a Nulato Koyukon woman named Mlanka and together they had nine children, several of whom became well-known Creole guides and traders. By 1880, five Creole guides were living at St Michael, five at Russian Mission, and three at Nulato. These probably included Ivan Korgenikoff, John Minook, Pitka Pavaloff, and Sergi Cherosky. It was a close-knit community, and Cherosky later married Pavaloff's daughter Erinia.[14]

Other traders and explorers, including William Dall, Moise and François Mercier, and Arthur Harper also employed Creole guides and interpreters. Dall, Mike Lebarge, and a Creole guide named Ivan Lukin, for example, travelled from Nulato to Fort Yukon and back in 1860. Cherosky, Pavaloff's son-in-law, acted as interpreter for François Mercier and Harper at Belle Isle. Cherosky caught gold fever while he was in the interior, and it was he and Pitka Pavaloff who discovered gold at Birch Creek in 1892. Other Creole men found a calling beyond guiding, trading, and mining and entered the religious life with the Russian church. Iakov Netsvetov established Russian Mission, and Zachary Belkhov served the Native villages of the lower Yukon River from 1868 to 1896 as a lay priest.[15]

The Russians were not the only Europeans to establish families in Alaska and the Yukon. Within the Hudson's Bay Company (HBC), marriage *à la façon du pays* was also common. The records from HBC post at Rampart House, for example, show that between 1890 and 1892 alone, six children lived with their Native mothers and HBC fathers.[16] Although the written record does not always reflect this, such unions also occurred among Canadian and American missionaries, private traders, and prospectors. They benefited both parties. The husband gained companionship, domestic services, an interpreter, guide, and access to his wife's family and community for social and economic purposes. The benefits for the woman were often not as great, for she frequently found herself in an unfamiliar pattern of living, at some distance from her family. Still, she usually gained access to a wider range of European goods and could derive increased status as the wife of the local trader or missionary. Fort McPherson's first missionary, Robert McDonald, himself a Métis from Red River, married Julia Kutug, a Gwich'in woman, and together they had at least two children. Later, the Church of England's Bishop Bompas somewhat reluctantly arranged for the marriage of the Reverend Benjamin Totty and a Native woman. Bompas on the whole was not in favour of such matches, but he admitted that Native wives often encouraged missionaries to remain in the North for longer periods, while non-Native wives generally encouraged the opposite.[17] Ironically then, while interracial relationships were frowned upon, they often strengthened the position of both the cleric and the Church in the region. With or without Bompas's blessings, relationships between Native women and local traders, prospectors, and missionaries were common enough that the CMS was forced to establish a school for children of 'mixed blood' at Fortymile in 1892.

Unlike the Creoles of Alaska and the Métis of the Canadian prairies, no identifiable 'mixed blood' group emerged in the interior Yukon. Historian Ken Coates argues that this was because Yukoners of mixed heritage, barred from the non-Native community, remained within Native society. While this appears to be true after 1896, the evidence indicates that in the earlier period it was not always the case. In the early 1890s,

Tlingit and Tagish women and men worked as packers to carry Klondikers' goods over the Chilkoot Pass.

there were eleven Métis children living in the mission house at Fortymile. One of the Han trappers explained that Métis children lived with the missionary because the community considered them neither Han nor white: 'Indian boy, Indian want him, white boy, white man want him. Half breed no Indian, no white man. Indian no want him, white man no want him.' This is a telling comment on the state of race relations in the early Yukon.[18]

Both communities eventually absorbed the children of these alliances as adults, yet little is really known about most of the Métis of the Yukon. When interviewed in 1963, Charlie Isaac of the Moosehide band remembered that his grandfather had had four wives, one of whom was of mixed blood. Other Métis women married non-Native men and spent their lives on the family mining claims. At least a few reportedly found their niche in the ever-present pool of mining camp followers: 'Half a dozen half-breed women, with more or less of the blood of Russian fur traders in their veins, composed the demi-monde of either camp [Circle City and Fortymile]. Full-blooded squaws performed the household duties in some cabins for a civilized lord and master. But the "squaw man" was the exception. In no part of the world where isolated white men live among aborigines was the man who had a native mistress held in greater disrespect than here.'[19]

However unrespectable, sexual relationships between Native and non-Native people existed. And while the extent of the 'disrespect' is unclear, negative attitudes about such relationships seemed to have escalated after the arrival of the non-Native wives of the missionaries and Mounted Police officers in the mid-1890s, for statements like that above do not occur earlier. Clearly it is no accident that intermarriage seems to have decreased at the same time that improved communication and transportation networks increased the number of non-Native women and made reliance on Native linguistic and geographical skills unnecessary. Native and Métis women became, in modern terms, redundant. Ken Coates and William Morrison have concluded from this that by the 1890s 'short-term affairs were defensible, if not entirely laudable, but those few white men, like George Carmack, ... who lived with the Indians, had moved beyond the pale. They were "squaw men," an epithet of particular virulence which signalled the intense distaste in the white community for their social preferences.'[20] It seems, then, that the period when a Métis group could have emerged to become quite important was eclipsed by the deluge of non-Native stampeders.

The emergence of a distinct group of Métis aside, 'country marriages' were extremely important to Native people, traders, miners, and missionaries until after the turn of the century. Closer examination of some of the so-called 'squaw men' indicates that white perceptions of such relationships were only a small part of a much more complicated portrait. An informal network of cross-cultural connections operated in the Yukon from the earliest period. As we have seen, traders and missionaries in the years before 1896 made strong and lasting alliances with Native groups and often their marriages – as well as nonsexual friendships between men – reinforced and extended these associations.[21] Traders and prospectors, too, made such alliances with reciprocal benefits. George Carmack is the most often cited example of the prospecting 'squaw men.' He is also a good example of extended alliances.

Carmack was an American prospector who spent much time among the Tagish people of the upper Yukon hunting, prospecting, and trapping. In the late 1880s, Carmack became the constant companion of Keish, a young Tagish man known later as Skookum Jim Mason. Soon after he became Keish's partner, Carmack married one of his sisters. When this woman died, Carmack followed local custom and married another sister, Shaaw Tlàa, whom he always called Kate. Carmack's relationship with the family of Kate and Jim continued for many years. The men packed supplies for other miners, hunted, fished, and prospected together, and Kate and George had a child together. Kate performed the multitude of never-ending tasks known to bush wives: gathering and

Shaaw Tlàa, also known as Kate Carmack, was married to George Carmack, who struck it rich at Bonanza Creek.

chopping wood, tending fires, melting snow and ice for water, gathering and preparing food, caring for their child, and dressing skins to make the family's clothing.[22]

Carmack and Keish, along with Keish's nephew Káa Goox – non-Natives called him Dawson Charley – together claimed the discovery that started the Klondike stampede. All three men staked claims on the creek later called Bonanza. At the same time, other non-Natives, notably Robert Henderson, were deliberately excluded from hearing of the find. The story goes that Carmack, in a breach of miners' etiquette, did not directly inform Henderson of the Bonanza strike. It seems that Henderson had offended Carmack by behaving rudely toward Carmack's Tagish wife and brother-in-law.[23] Here then, was a strong and reciprocal relationship based on friendship and family ties – a relationship that tolerated no racial slights from the likes of Henderson.

The American and British traders also recognized that Native wives could be very important to their success. Kitty Smith, a Tlingit-Tagish elder interviewed by Julie Cruikshank, summed up the indispensable contribution of women's labours in these mixed marriages by stating, 'She does everything, that Indian woman, you know.' It is no accident that Arthur Harper, Joe Ladue, and Leroy McQuesten, the most successful and long-lasting of the Yukon traders, all had Native wives. McQuesten went to Dawson too late to stake but acquired a claim, built a new warehouse for the Alaska Commercial Company, and prospered. Retiring to California, he built himself 'a luxurious house ... and live[d] out his days with his Indian wife in well-earned comfort under warm southern sunshine.' Historian Alan Wright noted that Harper left the Yukon in 1897, sick with the tuberculosis that killed him the following year. The fate of Harper's Yukon Native wife is unknown, although the couple's son Henry Harper was living at Moosehide in the 1930s. Ladue, another early trader and the man who plotted Dawson's original townsite, also married a Native woman. He, like his friend and partner Harper, died from tuberculosis shortly after the Klondike gold rush. Although the written record is almost completely silent on the subject of the other Native wives of the traders as partners, lovers, and interpreters, these women formed a valuable bridge between the trader and the people who brought him their furs.[24]

The Deluge Begins: The Beginning of Non-Native Settlement
The coastal Tlingit had been in direct contact with non-Native traders and seafarers from at least the eighteenth century. Yet nothing could have prepared them for the commotion caused by the Klondike gold rush. The Tlingit had jealously guarded the mountain passes until 1880, when they allowed non-Natives to use the Chilkoot Pass for the first time. The agreement between the Tlingit and the prospectors that year initiated the Tlingit's lucrative packing trade. After large gold deposits were discovered at Fortymile in 1886, there was a regular stream of prospectors through

The Klondike gold rush began when long-time friends Keish/Skookum Jim (standing second from right) and George Carmack (seated far left) discovered gold on Bonanza Creek.

the passes, culminating in the Klondike stampede of 1898. Between 1885 and 1900, then, tens of thousands of people passed through the Tlingit villages of Dyea at the foot of the Chilkoot Pass and Skagway at the foot of the White Pass before crossing the mountains to the northeast. The result was a sustained period of dramatic and important change for the coastal communities of the Lynn Canal.[25]

The diaries and memoirs of the stampeders are liberally sprinkled with commentaries on the Aboriginal people they encountered. William Elliott, for example, began his diary at Dyea and kept it throughout his journey to Dawson, chronicling his perceptions of at least nine Native villages along the way. For most of the men and women of the Klondike stampede, the journey to Dawson constituted their first encounter with Native people, which probably accounts for their detailed and voluminous recorded observations on the subject. Of all the Native people Klondike travellers met, the coastal Tlingit are most often described, presumably because they were the first group that the majority of newcomers encountered.[26]

The mountain passes separating the interior of the Yukon from the Alaska coast were long and steep. Travellers, each with a necessarily large amount of supplies, faced a formidable task in hauling these over the passes on foot. The shortest route, the treacherous Chilkoot Pass, was too steep and narrow for dogs or other pack animals, so goods had to be carried in numerous relays. Here, for more than a decade, the Tlingit carried out a lucrative packing business, collecting steep fees for hauling the supplies of prospectors and other travellers. The Tlingit, of course, had negotiated a monopoly on this business as one of the conditions of opening the route to prospectors in the first place, a fact that many later came to resent. Yukon pioneer George Snow and Dominion Surveyor William Ogilvie both hired Tlingit and Tagish packers in 1887 and 1888, and both men commented on the sophistication of Native business acumen.[27] Tlingit participation in the transportation trade continued until the completion of the White Pass railway in 1899.

In the first few years of the Klondike gold rush, all prospectors with sufficient means hired Native packers to carry their goods to the summit of the passes. For the Tlingit, who had foreseen just such a situation, the revenue from the packing trade helped offset new competition from non-Native fur traders in the interior. When the Klondike stampede began, the system had been operating for nearly twenty years. When the four young men in John McGregor's party set out to traverse the Chilkoot in 1897, for example, they hired all the Chilkat packers available to move 'at least

*A Klondike couple on the Chilkoot Pass.
Like many others, this couple probably
hired packers to carry the mandatory
1,000 pounds of supplies.*

half of our outfit to the summit.'[28] This trade provided employment for many young Tlingit men and women. The Tlingit's Tagish relatives also found opportunities in this trade, most notably Keish and his brother, both of whom were married to Tlingit women. Three of Keish's sisters married Tlingit men who probably also engaged in the packing business. Packing for wages offered supplemental income to the local trapping, hunting, and fishing economy.

One of the most striking images of the Tlingit packing business was captured by Klondike photographer Frank LaRoche. In Dyea in the summer of 1897, he photographed 'Don-a-Wok, Old Chilkoot Chief and Chief Isaac' in front of a wooden building with a sign reading 'Isaac Chief of Chilkoot Packing and Specialty.' Don-a-Wok, he reported, was eighty years old and ruler of 'all the Chilkoots.' Isaac was described as the 'active' chief and general contractor for the packing trade.[29] The photo shows the two men posing with a young boy, all three the very essence of dignity and prosperity.

And prosperous the business was, although reports vary over the rates charged. The Englishman Robert Kirk stated that the Chilkat were charging forty cents per pound to carry supplies to the summit during the summer of 1897. John Secretan, a man less impressed than most by the Klondike generally and Native people in particular, was also at Dyea in 1897. He reported that the people he referred to as 'beasts of burden' charged ten cents per pound to 'stagger over mountain passes' with the heaviest of loads. Robert Oglesby claimed that he paid his packers fourteen cents per pound during the same summer.[30] It is quite likely, of course, that the Chilkat and Tagish packers adjusted their prices to reflect weather conditions, the number of packers available, and the size of individual loads.

Of the people themselves and their village, there was also a wealth of reports. Robert Kirk wrote that the people of Dyea were 'smaller in size than the average white, but they are strong and are able to carry surprisingly heavy packs across the mountains to Lake Lindeman, a distance of twenty-seven miles.' The weight of the packs varied, according to the reports, but seem to have ranged from sixty to 100 pounds. Other stampeders recorded, with some shock, that young girls also engaged in the packing business, working alongside their brothers and fathers. Native wives and mothers caused comment as well, for their efforts both as packers and for their ceaseless efforts in the village drying salmon and preparing hides.[31]

Another flourishing industry, of course, was the whisky trade, and this could apparently interrupt the packing business. One stampeder recorded that while he was in Dyea in 1896, the steamer *Katie* arrived and the captain did a brisk trade in whisky with the Tlingit. The villagers then went on a spree that frightened most of the non-Natives in port. This stampeder was stranded for almost a week afterward as he failed to engage any of the people in packing, for he reported that they were still recovering from a 'spree.'[32] The whisky trade was one of the negative side effects of the new economy on the coast.

When Native men were busy with the fall hunt or when the whole village was preoccupied with marriage or other celebrations work could effectively cease. Before 1897, then, they could and did negotiate their own terms of work. This could even lead to a strike, much to the inconvenience and annoyance of their clients. When Josiah Spurr's party discovered that the Chilkoot trail past Sheep Camp was too rocky and steep for their pack horses, for example, they attempted to engage a group of Chilkat packers to carry their freight. Spurr's group offered to pay six cents per pound. Knowing full well that with the freight half way up the mountainside Spurr's party was helpless without them, the Chilkat demanded nine cents. The stalemate held for a week, when another party came along offering to pay a higher wage gladly. Grudgingly, Spurr negotiated the Chilkats' terms, and the goods were packed to the summit. Wrote Spurr, 'It was a genuine strike – the revolt of organized labor against helpless capital.'[33] Organized labour or not, this was clearly a business, and the Tlingit had plenty of experience in business negotiations, as they so ably demonstrated.

Yukon and Alaska Native people had an intimate knowledge of their territory, its dangers and secrets. They maintained a close relationship with and respect for their environment. Just two hours before an avalanche killed dozens of Klondike stampeders in April of 1898, for example, the 'old Indian chief went up and drove all his people down the trail on a run.'[34] They also assisted many of the early prospectors and traders who explored and charted the country and its rivers. George Snow, an early prospector, remembered that on his 1888 trip down the Yukon, his party shot the rapids at Miles Canyon because they had not known they were approaching. After a good scare, they sat on the bank and consulted the map 'drawn with a pencil on a piece of wrapping paper by Billy Dickenson, a half-breed Chilkat'[35] and proceeded through the next set of rapids without mishap.

The coastal Tlingit, then, were the first Native group encountered by the great Chilkoot stampede. Inland, the Tagish people were the next group to receive the wave of prospectors. The Tagish had a long history of trade and intermarriage with the coastal Tlingit, and although the opening of the mountain passes in the 1880s severed the Tlingit monopoly on inland trade, the customary pattern of marriage between the coastal and interior people continued. As we have seen, some Tagish people also participated in the packing business over the trails, although the extent of this participation is not known. Certainly Káa Goox̱, Keish, and his brother, Tlálkwshaan, all worked as packers at Dyea in the late 1880s. The Tagish people also engaged in business with the prospectors at Lake Bennett and Tagish Lake, the men selling timber and building boats, the women making and selling moccasins, mittens, and other garments.[36]

Many stampeders remarked on the people they met around these two lakes. At Tagish Lake, the people's longhouse was cause for much comment by the stampeders who passed it. In 1893, Frederick Funston's party was as fascinated by the longhouse near their camp as they were amused by the curious children of the Tagish families fishing nearby. Later, the North West Mounted Police established Tagish Post in 1898 to register the boats proceeding downstream to Dawson, adding yet another unaccustomed presence in the area.[37]

The successive waves of non-Natives throughout their territory had mixed results for the Tagish people. Like other inland Yukoners, the Tagish had participated in the new fur trade relationships of the 1870s and 1880s, but until the opening of the mountain passes, few had any direct contact with more than one or two non-Natives at a time. When the trickle of prospectors became a stream and the stream became a flood, their communities suffered at times. The combination of disease and new economic activities proved particularly dislocating. Skookum Jim's (Keish) family provides a clear example of this pattern. Of his seven siblings who survived childhood, three (a brother and two sisters) died in the influenza epidemics of the early 1890s. Keish survived as the only male sibling. Of his remaining four sisters, one perished on the Chilkoot and two married white prospectors and left the community. Only one sister married a Tlingit man in the customary alliance and settled at Carcross.[38]

From Lake Bennett and Tagish Lake, the golden highway led the stampeders north out of Tagish country and through the Southern Tutchone, or Stick Indian, territory. Veazie Wilson, who passed the Tutchone village at Lake Labarge in 1894 on his way to Fortymile, noted with some surprise that they had adopted European dress. He photographed the scene of trade, the Stick people receiving 'tobacco, whisky, guns and ammunition' for their furs and dried meat.[39] The Tutchone also

STR. W. S. STRATTON WRECKED IN ICE JAMS ON THE YUKON OCT. 24, 1899.

*Almost all people, supplies, and gold
came in and out of the Klondike on the
Yukon River on paddle wheelers like
this one. When freeze-up came it often
caught the last boat of the season in
dangerous ice jams.*

found a lucrative trade in piloting the stampeders through some of the Yukon's most difficult waters. While these pilots saved many boat loads of people and supplies from disaster, not all the stampeders were grateful for the availability of a Native pilot. John Secretan, notable for his bigoted remarks about the people of the coast, was even more virulent than usual about Natives he encountered on the river: 'The emaciated Indian pilot ... is one of the most contemptible creatures imaginable. Presuming upon his superior knowledge, he looks proudly down from his elevated pilot house position and despises his white employer, for whom he has a thorough contempt. White pilots being unobtainable, this aboriginal abomination is ... almost unendurable.'[40]

Such remarks illustrate the unwillingness of many Klondikers to accept Native authority over matters geographical. Aboriginal knowledge was ignored only at one's peril, however, for the river was treacherous in many places. Racism aside, the Southern Tutchone found lucrative work supplying wood to the passing steamers and navigating the Yukon River as pilots.

The Northern Tutchone, most notably those of the Pelly River, were next to receive the wave as the stampeders worked their way down the Yukon River. At the confluence of the Yukon and Pelly rivers was the Fort Selkirk trading post, and here many travellers stopped over. Thus many of them had a chance to record their impressions. In 1894, the post included a Tutchone village, the non-Native trader's store and cabin, and the Anglican church. The people of the Pelly River, reported one observer, were heavily involved in the fur trade both as producers and as intermediaries and were doing very well. Klondike stampeders often reported that Fort Selkirk was 'deserted' when they passed through for the Tutchones' trading and trapping activities frequently took them away from their village, a pattern that the gold rush did not change.[41] The Northern Tutchone also found a lucrative trade, selling meat to the prospectors who came down the river each year. Robert Kirk's party, for example, purchased moose meat from the Tutchone camped at the mouth of the Big and Little Salmon rivers in September of 1897. As at Tagish Lake, the women at Fort Selkirk made 'moccasins, fur caps and mittens to sell to the travellers.'[42]

'The People of the River': Gold Discoveries in Han Territory

Of all the aboriginal groups in the Yukon, it was the Han who were most deeply and permanently affected by the swelling tide of humanity that moved from the coast toward the junction of the Klondike and Yukon rivers. At the time of contact in the 1840s, the Han, who called themselves the

'People of the River,' were semi-nomadic hunters and fishers who maintained three large summer villages along the Yukon River. This relatively large population was supported by abundant fish and game. The three villages all became close neighbours of the mining communities of Fortymile, Dawson, and Eagle.[43] European contact, late though it came, delivered its usual devastating blows, and by the time of the gold rush in the late 1890s epidemics had reduced the number of Han to a few hundred.

The 1886 gold strike at Fortymile is important for two reasons. It marked the first of three major gold strikes in Han territory and also the beginning of large, permanent communities in the Yukon. The nature of the gold discovered at Fortymile also led to the development of year-round, sedentary operations. The result was a concentration of mining activity in the district drained by the Fortymile River and also that drained by the Klondike – Han territory.[44]

For the Han people along the Yukon River, this new pattern of mining meant prolonged contact with miners. Before the Fortymile strike, prospectors had traversed the region in small groups or in pairs, working the rivers and creeks as they went. Traders established posts that did double duty in furs and supplies with the Indians, as well as grubstaking and supplying the prospectors. The non-Native population remained transient; no settlements apart from the missions developed prior to 1886.

The gold find at Fortymile changed everything. First, it had the immediate result of concentrating a large number of prospectors in a small part of Han territory. Second, it demanded innovations in placer mining techniques. The 'yellow rock' so eagerly sought by the prospectors who came to the Yukon's interior was alluvial, or placer, gold. Unlike the hard rock gold of the Colorado Rockies, which had to be blasted out, crushed, and processed, Yukon placer gold occurred as flakes and nuggets in the soil and gravel along creeks and riverbeds. And while it was not quite as easy to collect as gathering up nuggets in potato sacks, as so many stampeders of '98 hoped, it could be extracted by a relatively inexpensive process. At Fortymile, new mining technologies were adapted by prospectors that allowed them access to the coarse gold found in the soil of the river banks and creek gulches as well as along the river's sand and gravel bars. More important, these innovations (described in detail in Chapter 3) allowed miners to work their claims all year round. A supply and service community could now be established, as there soon developed a semi-permanent market. Unlike the highly individualistic and nomadic prospecting that miners had engaged in during the preceding decades, the nature of the Fortymile discovery fostered the establishment of a longer term community.

The Han people were severely and permanently affected by these changes. For just as mining activity was now concentrated year round in a limited area, so was non-Native hunting. Game depletion soon followed, disrupting the people's hunting and trapping patterns in the Fortymile district. An almost immediate shift to a cash economy occurred as the Han relied less on salmon and devoted more time to supplying meat and furs to the non-Natives. Availability of alcohol and a stronger reliance on non-Native food sources accompanied these changes. This cycle was repeated on a much larger scale in the Dawson area ten years later, and shortly afterward at Eagle as well. In addition, the Han communities were weakened by epidemic disease, particularly diphtheria but also smallpox, influenza, and typhoid.[45]

Fortymile gained the distinction of being the first semi-permanent mining community. Abandoning Fort Reliance to follow the miners next spring, traders Leroy McQuesten and Arthur Harper quickly set up a post at Fortymile in 1887. The sudden and unexpected change in trading policy created by the closing of both the post at Fort Reliance and the one at Belle Isle, which François Mercier abandoned the same year, was a serious blow to the Han. The people later known as the Dawson or Moosehide band, who lived near Fort Reliance, by this date depended on European trade and now faced long and often dangerous journeys to the Fortymile post. The dangers came in the spring and fall, when the river either broke up or froze. Getting caught in either could mean weeks of walking to or from the post. When the Reverend Richard Bowen visited Nuklako – the community near Fort Reliance that was to become Dawson City in 1895 – there were no non-Natives in the neighbourhood even though the Han people were heavily dependent on the fur trade. In fact, the nearest trader upstream was Joe Ladue at the Sixtymile post, while Fortymile mining camp was fifty-three miles downstream.[46]

By 1893, two adjacent communities were well established at Fortymile, the Han remaining segregated from the miners. Here about 200 miners and 100 Han spent the winter of 1892-3. This pattern of segregation had developed around the posts in the rest of the Yukon, and it continued at Dawson City. In Han territory, this was in part due to the efforts of the Reverend William Carpenter Bompas of the Church Missionary Society, who arrived to minister to the Native people of Charlie Village in 1892 and who insisted on the separation of the two communities.

Four unidentified women from the Han village of Moosehide pose in a Dawson photographer's studio, 1898.

Bompas believed very strongly that the miners were having a negative effect on the Han community of Charlie Village. In 1893, he wrote twice to Ottawa asking for the regulation of liquor traffic at Fortymile for the sake of Native-white relations. When the government acquiesced and sent a contingent of Mounted Police, however, it was for sovereignty and security rather than for Native welfare. While the North West Mounted Police immediately imposed an interdiction on Native drinking and especially on the sale of alcohol to Natives, their attitude was less than sympathetic toward the 'People of the River.' Commanding Officer Charles Constantine regarded the Han as a nuisance, calling them 'a lazy, shiftless lot [who] are content to hang around the mining camps. They suffer much from chest trouble and die young.' He proceeded to ignore them as far as possible. These were, for all intents and purposes, Constantine's instructions from Ottawa, as he acknowledged: 'When I came to this country [my instructions were] that the Indians were not to be recognized in any way which would lead them to believe that the Government would do any thing for them as Indians.'[47]

The Mounted Police did, of course, exert control over the sale of liquor to Natives soon after arriving at Fortymile. Ironically, as Ken Coates has pointed out, this effectively concentrated alcohol consumption in the Native villages and in the miners' cabins.[48] Further, Constantine soon found that when the people could not buy commercial liquor, they consumed a homebrew made from molasses, sugar, and dried fruit. For all his efforts to keep contact between the two groups to a minimum, Bompas reported his dismay upon learning that the 'Indians have learned from them to make whisky for themselves, but there has been much drunkenness of whites and Indians together with much danger of the use of fire arms.' Constantine too, noted that the liquor alternately intoxicated the Natives, made them violent, and poisoned them.[49]

Alcohol abuse was not the only negative outcome of the new and prolonged contact between the Han and the miners. When the Reverend Bowen returned to Fortymile from Fort Reliance in December 1895, he found the Han all sick with typhoid. Their numbers steadily diminished from this and other diseases. As well, Bishop Bompas's efforts notwithstanding, the two groups interacted both socially and sexually, for eleven Métis children were residing at the mission house in Fortymile by 1895.[50]

In the hope of establishing good relations between the aboriginal residents and the newly arrived Mounted Police, Bishop Bompas organized a meeting of Han people near Fortymile with Commander Constantine.

This first meeting set the tone for further relations between the two groups. When the Han expressed their discontent with the miners selling their people whisky and shooting their dogs, Constantine merely directed them to tie up their dogs and avoid whisky. This did not set the stage for good relations between the non-Natives and the Han or between the Bishop and Constantine.

The pattern of cultural segregation that Native and non-Native residents established at Fortymile continued at Dawson. Just as the Han of Charlie Village remained separate from the miners in the Fortymile camp, Bompas ensured that the people at Nuklako were also isolated from the new town after 1896. Here, however, the Han had to be removed, for their original summer village was incorporated into the new townsite of Dawson. The issue of where they were to be relocated was complicated by the fact that Bompas first moved them to the government reserve – the land on which Constantine planned to build the Mounted Police barracks. Constantine claimed that the Bishop did so deliberately to annoy him and to get his claims addressed. Wrote Constantine, 'I don't propose to be bluffed ... by an arrogant Bishop who thinks the only people worth considering are a few dirty Indians too lazy to work, and who prefer starvation.'[51]

At the request of Bompas, and over the objections of Commander Constantine and William Ogilvie, the Department of Indian Affairs reserved a parcel of 160 acres of land for the Han, situated safely three miles downstream from their previous village; the site of the new city of Dawson. More than thirty Han families were removed to a plot of land precisely the same size as a single homestead offered to prospective farmers on the Canadian prairies at this time, an irony that seemed lost on government officials. The Department also required the Han simultaneously to 'relinquish any claim, so far as the Department is concerned, to the site of the old Indian village at Klondak [Nuklako].'[52] The new reserve became the village of Moosehide.

By relocating the Han, the Canadian authorities saw their responsibilities toward them fulfilled. For although the people of Moosehide repeatedly requested an extension of this reserve land, they were unsuccessful. Commissioner Ogilvie, in fact, advised the Department of the Interior that the extension should not be granted until they were sure that all the gold had been taken out of the area. Thus, when non-Native prospectors discovered gold on Moosehide Creek and adjacent gulches in 1900, the ground became immediately available for staking. This became the pattern of dealing with the question of land and treaty rights throughout the period, the government reluctant to grant Native people any land title for fear that gold would be discovered on their land.[53]

Relations between the Han and the developing mining community were thus characterized by segregation more than by accommodation. By removing to a site several miles downstream, the Han community originally at Dawson remained separate from the developing city throughout the boom period. Meanwhile, like their friends and relatives at Charlie Village near Fortymile, the Moosehide band adapted their customary hunting and fishing practices to encompass the ready cash market for meat and dressed skins. And while the Han seemed willing and able to accommodate the mining centre that sprang up on their old fish camp, the developing new community ignored their presence as far as possible.

Cornelius Osgood, the anthropologist who first studied the Han, estimated that at the time of contact in the late 1840s, there were approximately 1,000 'People of the River' living in three bands of roughly equal size. In Dawson by 1901, there were eighty-one Native people living at Moosehide: eighteen families and one household that contained six single men and two women, all in their teens or early twenties. All of these people were members of the Han First Nation with the possible exception of the latter household, which seems to have been made up of Peel River Gwich'in. When Josiah Spurr visited Fort Reliance in the spring of 1896, about 200 Indians were living in a village of cabins at the mouth of the Klondike, salmon fishing. This indicates that the Moosehide band was diminished by at least one-half and perhaps by more than two-thirds in the initial years of contact. Disease brought by the massive influx of non-Natives and a contaminated water supply – the village of Moosehide was relocated *downstream* from the new metropolis – was presumably the largest factor. Although Dawson's public health ordinance of 1899 forbade its largely non-Native residents from using the downstream water supply, the new village of Moosehide was located within the downstream flow area identified as contaminated. Epidemics of typhoid, smallpox, and diphtheria ravaged the community in this period.[54]

Both before and after the arrivals of the hordes of gold stampeders, the Han First Nation participated in the mining economy in a seasonal and peripheral manner, adapting their activities as best they could to meet the many changes taking place around them. Hunting, trapping, and fishing remained the central and permanent male occupations. Indeed, in 1901 all thirty adult men in the Moosehide band reported their main occupations as hunting and fishing. Supplying meat was an important

Moosehide Village, the Han community originally located at the site of present-day Dawson, was located two miles downstream from the new northern boomtown.

industry for the people of the river, and the miners relied on the Han and other groups such as the Gwich'in to provide a fresh supply during the long winter months. John McDougal's company, for example, employed at least two mixed blood men who kept the camp supplied with fresh moose meat during the winter of 1899-1900. That this was a common occurrence is confirmed by Dawson's first American consul, James McCook, who noted the previous spring that there was oversupply of meat due to moose and caribou that had been 'brought in by the Indians in large quantities.' The depletion of game that accompanied the miners and competition from non-Native hunters soon forced Native people to participate at least occasionally in a host of other economic activities.[55]

In the early days at Fortymile, most of the Native miners were Creoles and other mixed blood men. At Dawson, the few Native miners we know anything about were Tagish, not Han. The men who became known as Skookum Jim, Dawson Charley, Patsy Henderson, and Caribou John, for example, were all members of the Carcross-Tagish First Nation. Native women were not represented in mining in any formal way in the records. Of course Native women, as we have already seen, continued to play an important albeit almost invisible role as general labourers, wives, companions, mothers, and camp cooks in both Native and non-Native households, but Native women do not appear to have recorded any claims themselves.

That the Han did not join their Tagish colleagues in locating and operating their own claims is due to several interrelated factors. The first was the influence of Bishop Bompas. Bompas spent much time at the beginning of the rush discouraging contact between the miners and the Han for moral reasons. As well, the Bishop's animosity toward all 'whites,' including the Mounted Police, discouraged non-Natives from attempting to recruit a Native labour supply. Second, if other non-Natives shared Constantine's opinion that the Moosehide people were lazy and unwilling to work, this probably also inhibited recruitment. Third, the physical segregation of the Native village discouraged direct interaction between the two communities.

Finally, the most important factor was that the seasonal economic pattern of the Han simply did not fit very well with that of mining. They engaged in wage employment but in a way that suited their existing seasonal cycle. When the gold rush began in earnest, the Han were still heavily engaged in the fur trade. During the winter when the miners were thawing and digging on their claims, the Han were either preparing for or engaged in the winter hunt, an endeavour that took many of the men

*After Dawson's first typhoid epidemic, the
Arctic Water Co. did a brisk business
as local residents were forced to purchase
water hauled from well upstream of the
growing community.*

away from the village for extended periods. The miners' busiest period, spring clean-up, also occurred at the same time that the Han at Nuklako and later Moosehide were busy preparing their nets for the salmon run. In spring and summer, the Han harvested and preserved the running salmon. Thus, when men from the village did participate in mining ventures it was most often done only on a casual basis.

Much work remains to be done on the issue of sexual interaction between Han women and the miners at both Fortymile and Dawson City. The sources suggest that Native prostitution occurred occasionally at Fortymile but did not develop at all in Dawson. They also indicate that intermarriage between Natives and non-Natives was uncommon in greater Dawson City by 1901. Indeed, I found that no Native women participated in prostitution in Dawson and only three mixed marriages were in evidence in Dawson and Moosehide at the time of the 1901 census. The only non-Native person living at Moosehide in 1901 was the Reverend Totty, who resided with his Native wife and their children. From all evidence garnered here, it appears likely that many couples of mixed marriage made their homes on the creeks and in the bush.[56]

Julius Price noted in 1898 that Dawson City's red-light district, known as Klondike City or Lousetown, was 'a dirty little place, half mining camp and half Indian village, either half dirtier than the whole.' In fact few Native people lived in Lousetown; by the time of the 1901 census there were only two Métis families in town, the Buteaux and the Drugals, and a Native miner named Steve Mattler. If few Native and Métis people lived in Lousetown, even fewer called Dawson City proper their home. One of these was Jennie Sicke, a twenty-nine-year-old Tagish woman who resided in South Dawson in 1901. Sharing the same address were John Charles, a carpenter from Sweden, Thomas Graham, an Irish miner, and Fred Styker, an American carpenter. While it is possible that Jennie was a prostitute or that she was employed to tend house for these men, it is more likely that she was cohabiting with one of them for her occupation is listed as 'beadwork' rather than the usual 'housekeeper' reported by so many others in similar situations. Sicke reported no real estate or mining claims, but she held personal property (including three dogs) valued at $275.[57]

Ken Coates posits two possible reasons for the low rate of mixed marriages between Natives and non-Natives in the Klondike. First, the social stigma placed on men who consorted with Native women – the so-called 'squaw-men' – discouraged intercultural sexual relations. Second, the relative availability of non-Native women within a few years of the gold discoveries prevented the miners from having Native wives and mistresses.[58] While these explanations seem to have some application, they are not sufficient. Social stigma, for example, has rarely prevented men from entering into at least casual sexual encounters with women, Native or otherwise. A number of the traders and prospectors from the period before 1896, for example, lived with Native women for extended periods, and these unions were important for personal, social, and economic reasons. George Carmack, as we have seen, refused to apologize for his Tagish wife and partners, even though some of his mining colleagues disapproved. Miners and businessmen who remained in such relationships may be underrepresented in Dawson because they preferred to live in the bush and on the creeks. That is to say, perhaps the so-called 'squaw men' were less disposed to settle in or near the new metropolis of Dawson and are thus less visible. This possibility certainly warrants further research, and an in-depth study of the creek settlements outlying Dawson might shed new light on this issue.

The most logical explanation for the limited sexual interaction between Han women and non-Native men is that the Han themselves played a large role in determining the extent and the nature of the contact with the newcomers. Sex ratios within the non-Native population did not approach equilibrium in the Yukon until well into the twentieth century, and the simple presence of non-Native women therefore does not explain the apparent low incidence of sexual relations between the two cultures. Rather, additional social pressure to minimize sexual contact between the Han and the mining communities probably came from within the Han community itself. In August 1895, for example, the Reverend Bowen reported that the Chief of Charlie Village near Fortymile had prevented a 'massacre of the white prospectors, who had been thoughtless enough to lure the Indian squaws into their homes and into the dance hall.'[59] While the miners showed themselves undaunted by any social stigma attached to these women, they also displayed a blatant disregard to the objections of the women's families. The men of Charlie Village, however, became violent over the mistreatment or perhaps abduction of their wives and daughters. Here again, the influence of Bishop Bompas must be taken into account, for he was very influential. At Dawson and Moosehide, certainly, contact between Natives and non-Natives was kept to a minimum, probably through a combination of the above factors.

Although the Han participated little in the mining economy other than as primary producers of meat, furs, and fish, other Yukon Natives participated to a greater extent. As noted earlier, the Tlingit, Tagish, and Southern Tutchone all worked in the fields of transportation, navigation, and communication. Men from all parts of the river found employment as pilots and navigators on the steamers, and others worked as guides and packers for miners and non-Native hunters. Mounted Police Commander Charles Constantine noted in 1896 that the Alaska Commercial Company was paying an Indian $500 to take the mail out, presumably over the Chilkoot Pass. Even a young and disfigured Native could find employment on the river, for Robert Oglesby hired 'a hunch-backed Indian boy' as his pilot when he went to Circle City in late August, 1897. River steamers regularly employed Native pilots in order to navigate the treacherous Yukon River. As one pioneer remembered, 'Indians had a lot to do with traffic on the river in the early days. Stern wheel steamboats in the late '80s and early '90s would always pick up an Indian at different camps to pilot with the Captain. The Indians knew the channel and they would stand at the wheel and advise the Captain ... They always knew the water in their district.' Native men found employment also on river steamers as deck hands, wood suppliers, and stevedores.[60]

From his interviews with Gwich'in elders of the Peel River band, anthropologist Richard Slobodin discovered that a number of community members had taken part in the gold rush economy at Dawson City. Although Slobodin refers to them as the 'Dawson Boys,' it is clear that this group also included women. Slobodin learned from the Peel River people that they had engaged in at least fourteen major summer occupations, including deck hand, scow pilot, carpenter, motorboat mechanic, pool-hall handyman, licensed trader, laundry worker, and mining camp cook. The people thus altered their seasonal hunting and fishing patterns to accommodate new forms of waged labour and small business. These findings correspond to the commentary of non-Native Yukoners, who frequently recorded in their diaries and memoirs that they had encountered Yukon Native people engaged in similar occupations.[61] It is worth noting that while the data employed here and the results of Slobodin's study both indicate that a number of occupations were open to Natives, these are not reflected in the 1901 Census for Moosehide, which records all residents' occupation as 'hunter and trapper.' It seems clear that hunting and trapping were simply the major economic pursuit in this period.

The informal policy of segregation, begun for the benefit of the Han, seems to have continued throughout the period. In addition to residents of the village of Moosehide, only six Natives resided in Lousetown and four in Dawson City proper at the time of the 1901 census. Of the four adult men, two reported employment as trappers, one as a miner, and one as a steamer pilot. Of three adult women, one was employed at 'laundry,' one at 'beadwork,' and one as 'wife.'[62] The remaining three were children. The low number of Native residents in Dawson suggests that both informal and formal processes were at work to discourage integrated settlement.

Of course, Natives did not always engage in legal activities. Henry Easton Phillips, a Chilkat Tlingit from Alaska, was arrested in Dawson in July 1901 for selling liquor to Indians. His liquor business was doing well, however, for he quickly paid his fifty-dollar fine rather than serving a one-month jail term.[63] Other Native people may also have participated in the liquor trade, although this has not been documented.

There are several possible explanations for the relatively low participation rate of Native people in the Dawson economy by the turn of the century. First, perhaps as the rush waned greater competition in the labour market diminished the opportunities for Natives. Certainly by 1901 there was a good deal of seasonal unemployment in Dawson. Second, racism as exemplified in the numerous references to 'lazy and dirty Indians' surely limited opportunities for Native workers. Third, Native wage labour was probably underreported, since it is highly likely that the census taker simply assumed that no one at Moosehide participated in the wage labour economy rather than asking individuals to state their occupation. Fourth, the seasonal patterns of hunting and fishing, along with previous Native experience of non-Natives and the encouragement of missionaries, probably combined to discourage large scale wage labour participation. Finally, it is certainly possible that the People of the River were simply uninterested in gold rush activity and *preferred* life on the land.

Unlike the Han, the Peel River people reoriented their seasonal pattern of activity with the advent of the gold rush. Although they continued to hunt and trap during the winters, they made frequent trips to Dawson to sell meat at inflated prices. By 1901, the majority of the Peel River band was trading in Dawson and spending part of the summer at Moosehide engaged in casual wage labour:

> When we came we didn't stay right here [Moosehide]. We come, go back, and stay at the head of the Blackstone, other side from here a hundred miles. We come to Dawson in winter to sell meat. We'd come with our dog teams and we were very busy selling meat. We were trapping, got some little fur, too. We camped sometimes eastward

toward the Bonnet Plume Flats. Summertime, though, everybody come down here. Even the old people. They got Communion right here. We would stay in June and July, sometimes only one month, sometimes half a month. They we go back again, using dog packs all the time.[64]

The Peel River presence could actually explain why one of the households in Moosehide contained only one generation at the time of the census. Later on, as the fur trade diminished, some of the Peel River people moved to Moosehide permanently, as in the case of Richard Martin, a Gwich'in man from Peel River and an Anglican minister.[65]

Because the Han did not integrate themselves into the mining economy during the boom period, it might be expected that they escaped the effects of the inevitable bust. This was not the case. By 1900, the effects of instant and mass contact had taken their toll on the people at Moosehide, and they suffered both disease and famine. With the corruption of the water supply and increased contact with large numbers of non-Natives, dysentery, diarrhoea, and tuberculosis had severely harmed the people of Moosehide. At the same time, they were increasingly unable to sustain themselves as the gold rush waned. In part this was because competition for the severely depleted game had increased. In fact by September of 1901 there were reported 'fully a thousand men ... engaged in hunting and trapping, exclusive of the Indians.' The Han also experienced competition in the salmon fishery, their main food source. In addition, forest fires destroyed hundreds of acres of game habitat in the summer of 1898, the result of gold stampeders' carelessness. These factors produced difficulty for the Han not only in the cash economy but also in their very subsistence. The North West Mounted Police, as representatives of the government, were eventually forced to step out of their passive role and disburse food at Moosehide in 1904. They did so to avert a potentially severe famine, although they usually required Natives and non-Natives alike to exchange labour for such relief.[66]

Conclusions

The search for gold proceeded in waves from the middle of the nineteenth century in the Yukon, culminating in the stampede of 1898. Successive waves of missionaries, traders, and prospectors moved from the Alaskan coast to the interior, leaving, quite literally, no stone unturned in their search for the yellow metal. First to be affected were the coastal groups, the Koyukon at St Michael and the Tlingit at Dyea and Skagway. These people took advantage of the early rush, providing a ready labour force of packers (Tlingit) and river pilots (Koyukon). As the prospectors moved east, the interior people built boats, acted as guides and pilots, and provided meat, skins, clothing, and wood. In return, their land burned under raging forest fires, their game was overhunted, their drinking water was contaminated, and by 1914 huge tailing piles lay where creeks had always run.

In 1847, the Han were one of the last North American Native groups to experience European contact. Fifty years later their territory was host to the 'largest city north of Winnipeg.' The Han people participated in a limited way in the economy of Dawson but remained separate from it. Unfortunately, this strategy did not prevent their community from being stricken by disease, their land and resources from being ruthlessly pillaged, or the people from feeling the effects of racism.

CHAPTER 3

The Thrill of the Chase:
Miners and Other Labouring People in Dawson

N REACHING DAWSON CITY three main tasks faced each of the thousands of stampeders. First, they had to secure housing. Most spent the first few weeks in their tents on or near the river banks while they looked for cabins to rent or purchase, or lots on which to build. Second, they had to acquaint themselves with local systems of commerce and communications. This included learning to use gold dust as currency, standing in the long line at the post office to receive a letter that might have preceded them to Dawson, going to public meetings to hear southern newspapers read aloud, and mailing letters back home to inform friends and family of their safe arrival. Finally, they had to secure a means of earning a living.

The economy of the Klondike depended on the fortunes and labours of working men and women. From laundry worker to miner, from stevedore to wife, semi-skilled and unskilled workers made up 65 percent of Dawson's workforce.[1] In the early years of Dawson City, manual labour and service sector employment were almost always available, although the market was very unstable. Workers were often able to draw high wages, but in this resource-based community work was rarely steady and job turnover was very high. Workers also faced an extremely high cost of living, which offset many of the benefits of high wages. For those who laboured as miners the situation was slightly different, as individuals often sank the profits from one endeavour into the next or used them to pay off debts from previous ventures.

Slightly more than half of the 4,600 semi-skilled and unskilled workers in Dawson were miners (see Table A4). Whether they owned and operated their own claim or worked for wages on another, mining was open to all Klondikers for this was 'everyone's gold rush' after all. Doctors, lawyers, loggers, farmers, accountants, and waitresses who could afford the ten-dollar mining licence became miners overnight. They came from all over the world to seek their fortunes in the Klondike. Those who stayed beyond a few weeks were usually willing to put their hand to anything if their mining ventures failed, and these would-be miners could just as easily be found working on the docks, cleaning house, chopping wood, or tending bar. If you asked them, they might well have answered that these occupations were just temporary; they were sure to make their big strike on the new creek they were going to stake.

Yet mining was not the only occupation of Klondikers; it took all kinds of labour and all kinds of labourers to build a prosperous wilderness community, and if Klondikers shared a single characteristic it was versatility. The vast majority tried their hand at various forms of labour and commerce in the Klondike. One of the earliest forms of wage labour in the Yukon was found in the packing trade. Since all goods and supplies coming into the Yukon by land had to be carried over steep mountain passes, from 1885 on prospectors and traders who could afford to do so hired packers to carry their supplies. Although the Tlingit and Tagish people held a monopoly on packing and demanded steep wages, especially before 1898, a few non-Native men and women also performed this work in the later period.[2]

Not only non-Native men but also women laboured in the packing trade. One of these, a woman who called herself Texas Bill, worked during the summer and fall of 1897 on the Chilkoot Pass. Undaunted by Victorian notions of womanhood, she was one of the most reliable packers on the trail and 'carried goods over the pass the same as men.' A young civil servant from Ontario critically observed that Bill's skirts were 'of the bifurcated pattern,' and that she walked with a most unbecoming 'wild western swagger.'[3] While Bill may not have felt constrained by contemporary constructions of femininity then, her colleagues on the trail were not all as open-minded.

Harriet Pullen also made her living in the Klondike packing trade. Pullen arrived in Skagway in 1897 on her own and was soon joined by her three children. At first she managed to support her family by selling bread and pies. Having saved enough money to pay the freight on a team of horses, she began a successful packing operation between Skagway and Lake Bennett over the White Pass.[4] The White Pass was longer and less steep than the treacherous Chilkoot, and therefore it could accommodate pack animals. Native and non-Native packing companies alike almost instantly dissolved in 1899, however, when the newly completed White Pass Railway made its first run from Skagway to Carcross. The Tlingit returned to trapping, trading, and fishing for their livelihood, while Mrs Pullen opened an inn near the railway terminal at Skagway. One contemporary remembered that she was still running her hotel in Skagway in 1910, and she 'went through hardships aplenty, but was never daunted. If a stableboy got drunk and failed to show up, she would hitch up the horses and take the bus to the train or boat to get the passengers.'[5] Texas Bill disappeared from the record, but like many others, she had probably seen the writing on the wall when the railway construction crews arrived and moved on to greener pastures.

Many early Klondike diarists noted that anyone with a strong back and willing disposition could have all the work he or she wanted in the Yukon.[6] Along the routes inward, men who set up whipsawing pits to saw lumber for sale or who built boats on commission quickly earned wages far exceeding rates in the South. Similarly, many enterprising women set up cook tents along the trail and on the creeks where their beans, bread, pies, and doughnuts (this was Canada, after all) brought high returns from hungry travellers.

Once the stampeders reached Dawson the same held true, for there was no shortage of work to be done in building a supply and service centre that would meet the needs of the tens of thousands of stampeders flocking toward it. Men were needed to build hotels, saloons, warehouses, and cabins, replacing the city of tents and lean-tos. Jobs as woodcutters, sawyers, and carpenters were readily available in the early years, especially in the summer when so many were prospecting on the creeks. Even after the rush had slowed to a trickle, numerous fires kept Dawson carpenters and builders in high demand. Work, at least in the busiest summer

Gold dust was both the primary product and the currency of the Klondike. Almost all business transactions were negotiated in it.

months, was plentiful and the demand for services was high. In Dawson and the nearby creek communities, the demand for cafés, lunch counters, saloons, and laundries ensured that the service sector offered both employment and business opportunities. The woman who operated Mary's Coffee House on Bonanza Creek, for example, reportedly left the Klondike after seven years with $50,000.[7]

As one of Canada's busiest inland ports in the period, Dawson provided many men with work on the docks. The many boats that arrived daily in the summer months had to be loaded and unloaded, warehouses had to be stocked, and fuel for the steamers had to be supplied. Workers who had left similar back-breaking jobs in Montreal, Vancouver, and San Francisco found themselves working here when their dreams of making the big stake dwindled. Frank Mortimer was one of these. Mortimer arrived with his family in 1900. Arriving as the rush faded, Frank and his wife Grace had no luck in their mining ventures and Frank went to work on the Aurora Company's docks. Though employment on the docks brought reasonably high wages it was seasonal work, and Mortimer found it difficult to support his wife and their two-year-old son on his salary. After their second summer in Dawson, the family had little to show for their efforts, having managed to acquire assets totalling $50.[8]

While the Mortimers struggled to make ends meet, others reported that stevedores could earn excellent wages as long as navigation was open, bringing in seventy-five cents per hour and commanding long hours. Other waterfront employment such as running a hoisting engine could bring $6 per day and command a seven-day work week. This was an excellent wage, rivalling as it did wages for labourers on the creeks which hovered around $6 to $7 per day throughout the period.[9] Like mining though, longshoring was a summertime occupation, and the beginning of freeze-up signalled work stoppage. For the Yukon River was the lifeline of the Klondike; all goods, provisions, and people came in over at least some portion of it. Once the river froze over in the fall – usually in early October – almost no goods or people came in or out until the spring thaw. During the winter months, when food and fuel costs rose, labourers had a very difficult time finding gainful employment.

The disproportionate number of single men – thirteen single men to one single woman in 1898 and three to one by 1901 – created a huge demand for services. Not surprisingly, restaurants, laundries, saloons, and dance halls thrived. This sector also required a large number of men and women as bartenders, waiting staff, dancers, musicians, and cleaning staff.

These jobs paid much better in Dawson than they did in the South, although employers found that staff members were easily drawn to the gold fields at a moment's notice.

At its peak Dawson offered its 30,000 residents scores of restaurants and cafés, all requiring cooks, waiting staff, and cleaning crews. As late as 1901, when the population of Dawson had shrunk to about 10,000, almost 400 people were employed in this industry. Restaurant work did not bring wages as high as other unskilled work such as longshoring, for example, but it could net an employee $25 per week plus meals, or a little over $4 per day. Certainly these wages were higher than some Klondikers had ever earned before. The young Joe Tanner, for example, boasted in a letter home to his mother, 'This is the best country to work for wages. I was wise when I left Boston for the West, the East is no place to make money.' Joe was working in a restaurant when he wrote this letter, but he had previously worked at several forms of manual labour. Like many other young men who went to the Yukon to help support their families back home, Joe Tanner enclosed $40 for his mother in this letter.[10]

Like restaurants, commercial laundries found a steady market for their services in the mostly male Klondike community, and they employed nearly 100 people as late as 1901. Just as in the South, laundry was often an ethnic occupation. Dawson had at least three Asian laundries in the early period, and a number of African American women were also employed in the trade. One laundry, operated by three Japanese men, demonstrated that the chain migration patterns so common elsewhere in North America were also at work in the Klondike. George Omura was twenty-five when he arrived in the Yukon from Japan in 1899. Establishing a laundry there, he took on Yetara Ishikaro and Takeyero Kaku as partners when they arrived the following year. Two Chinese men also operated laundries in Dawson in 1901 although little information exists about their lives.[11]

While the Chinese and Japanese launderers tended to be single men, all six African American laundry workers were women. These women represented about 10 percent of all Dawson's African American population in 1901. They all appear to have run their laundry businesses out of their homes, indicating that these were very small operations, yet they maintained them for considerable lengths of time. Josephine Arnold, Millie Brown, Josephine Hanly, and Molly Brown all arrived to set up their businesses at the height of the rush in 1898, while Mrs Agu had arrived in 1897 and Martha Daniels in 1899.[12] It is difficult to determine whether these women tended to stay in Dawson longer than the average Klondiker out of a conscious choice or because they were too poor to finance a relocation. Arnold and Millie Brown certainly had a difficult time making ends meet as there is strong evidence to indicate that they subsidized their laundry business by occasionally working as prostitutes. Information about the social and economic status of the other women was unavailable.

Women from a variety of other ethnic backgrounds also worked in the laundry business in Dawson. Josephine Phillides was a Belgian-born woman who had arrived with her Greek husband, Anthony, in 1898. (They were both naturalized Canadians by 1901.) Together they ran Dawson's French Laundry, a business that Josephine reported was 'doing well' in 1901. That their dream of fabulous wealth had not been realized is evidenced by the fact that like many other couples, the Phillideses subsidized their living costs in 1901 by taking in a lodger, a forty-five-year-old waitress named Elizabeth Daly.[13]

More women took in laundry on a piece-work basis than set up commercial operations in Dawson. This is probably because the piece system required little capital investment and could be combined with other domestic responsibilities such as child care. While taking in laundry could provide women with an important source of income, it was heavy and tiresome work; wood and water had to be hauled, and soap, starch, and even washboards were scarce and therefore very dear. Before 1899, however, when demand far exceeded services, laundresses 'wrote their own ticket,' and more than one miner found that getting his shirts cleaned depended entirely on the 'inclination' of a laundress to accept his orders.[14]

Although there was no shortage of work, few women grew rich in the laundry business, despite newspaper reports to the contrary. There were a few celebrated cases, of course, like the 'coloured' woman who was reported to have made $5,000 as a laundress during the winter of 1897-8.[15] Another enterprising woman set up a bath tent on Dawson's river front in 1897. Charging a dollar for a hot bath in one of Dawson's only full-size tin tubs, she also provided a laundry service to her clients. Within two years she was reported to have made $10,000.[16] Laundering though, like mining, was a back-breaking and tedious way to make a living, and after the first year of the rush few laundry operations appear to have been more than moderately successful.

Domestic servants were hard to find in Dawson from the earliest period and, it seems, even harder to keep. With the high ratio of men to women, single female servants constantly received 'better offers.' Take, for example, the young Irish woman who came to the Klondike region in 1895 as

The high proportion of single men to women made the restaurant business a lucrative one for enterprising women. These two women are likely the proprietors of the Arcade Restaurant. For many families, the Klondike was one of a string of gold rushes in which they participated, seeking their fortunes and willing to sacrifice a great deal of comfort in the process.

a servant 'in the family of a storekeeper at Fortymile.' She held her position for a very short time and soon left to marry a miner 'who afterward
struck it rich.' This was apparently a common phenomenon, and a fierce
competition between men evolved whenever a young single woman arrived
in the vicinity. Even women well past the usual marriageable age reported
receiving proposals of marriage throughout their Klondike residency.[17]

In part due to the relative scarcity of women, and of women servants
in particular, the wage for domestic servants was roughly double the going
wage in the South. According to one Dawson resident, 'it is not possible
to get an ordinary servant for less than seventy-five dollars per month and
usually the wage is one-hundred dollars. Mr Girouard's servant was
brought in by Mrs Girouard from Quebec under contract [at $50 per
month], and this accounts for the low sum paid her.' This servant was
Marie Lemieux, who had arrived with Madame Girouard in 1901.[18] It is
difficult to discern whether domestic service contracts were common in
Dawson, for this is the only such reference. Certainly some female 'housekeepers' and sexual companions were employed on a contractual basis by
men who could afford them. About the 'respectable' servants, we know little. It is likely, however, that if one government official engaged a servant
this way, some of his colleagues probably did likewise. None of these
employers seems to have undertaken legal action for breach of such a contract, though, indicating either that contractual servants willingly accepted
their much lower pay or that the Girouard household was highly unusual.
Certainly Lemieux seems to have been satisfied to remain under contract
in Dawson for at least three years.

The majority of Klondike women apparently found domestic service
an unattractive option. Elizabeth Jones came to Dawson in 1900, when she
was twenty-three years old, and worked for a year as a household servant.
Finding the work just as tedious in Dawson as it had been in her home
town in Ontario, she soon traded domestic service for a position in a local
saloon. The lively atmosphere of the saloon seems to have suited Jones
much better, for she lavished high praise on her new employer in letters
to a friend. Still, like most women who worked in the saloons and dance
halls, Jones was under no illusions about her position within Dawson's
social hierarchy. Indeed, when Jones and a friend attended mass on New
Year's Eve, she reported her surprise at not being 'struck dumb either for
being such heathens.'[19]

Before 1899, when women were particularly scarce in the Klondike,
service sector work – those positions we have come to know as 'pink collar'

occupations – brought considerable wages. Anna DeGraf, a widow who went north looking for her son in 1894, put her hand to numerous jobs over the next fifteen years in the Yukon, all of them in the service sector. In 1894 in Circle City, a group of miners asked Mrs DeGraf to care for a 'sick girl.' In exchange for three weeks of light nursing care, Mrs DeGraf received $300. These are staggering wages when compared with the $40 per week mine labourers earned and perhaps reflect not only the value of nursing skills but the value the men placed on the young sick woman (presumably as prostitute) as well. Mrs DeGraf did not find her son, and she soon she returned to her home in the United States. She journeyed again to the region in 1898 and found herself stranded in Skagway without supplies when the steamer company failed to deliver her cargo. For two weeks the sixty-year-old DeGraf worked at a lunch counter in exchange for board and lodging until her provisions arrived. She eventually made her way to Dawson, where she set up shop as a seamstress and dressmaker. Although older than most of her contemporaries, Mrs DeGraf is a fairly typical example of a working class woman who laboured in traditionally female occupations throughout her life in the Yukon.[20]

Service sector work, whatever the wage, was not always steady, and many Klondikers found themselves repeatedly out of work. Georgia White discovered this firsthand. White was a young mother who ventured to the Klondike to escape a bad marriage and to earn some extra money. Leaving her children in the care of others in San Francisco in February 1898, she worked her way to Dawson at whatever jobs she could find – hotels and restaurant jobs and whenever possible as a private duty nurse. Between the lack of steady work, distress at being separated from her children, and contracting typhoid, White spent a very difficult four months in the Klondike. Despite her travails though, between March and June of 1898 White managed to send a total of $80 home in support of her children before taking sick. Ill and disillusioned, Georgia White left Dawson on one of the last boats out before freeze-up in September of the same year.[21]

Georgia White was typical of the many Klondike stampeders whose Klondike sojourn lasted a single season and who never put their hand to mining. Tappan Adney, one of the most famous chroniclers of the gold rush, remarked that the vast majority of Klondikers never actually mined but worked at manual labour or in the service sector in town.[22] Many of them, like White, returned home with little to show for their Klondike adventure save the knowledge that they had followed their dreams and participated in the world-famous event.

Klondikers who arrived to find the creeks completely staked often turned their hands to manual labour. The long and severe winters required every Yukon household to keep a large supply of cord wood for heating and cooking. It is not surprising, then, that one of the most commonly reported occupations of male labourers in Dawson was 'wood chopper' – nearly 100 in 1901 alone. So great was the need for an ample supply of fuel that the North West Mounted Police used the judge's sentence of 'hard labour' to keep the government woodpile well stocked. At least one local official reported that this had the desired effect, since the 'terror of sawing wood for the Government' was an effective deterrent against crime in Dawson. The Salvation Army initially offered its tenants shelter in exchange for chopping wood. The result was that during the winter of 1898-9, Dawson had a surplus of cord wood in town, for there was an oversupply of unemployed would-be miners.[23]

'People of Chance': Placer Miners in the Klondike

In the placer mines of the Klondike, doctors, lawyers, loggers, farmers, homemakers, grocers, and bartenders all rubbed shoulders. Mining was a hard way to make a living and one at which the chance of success was not always high. As a rule, only those who arrived in the Klondike gold fields very early managed to stake prosperous claims. When most of the gold stampeders arrived in Dawson in the summer of 1898, they found little ground available for staking.

Disappointed and in debt, thousands of disheartened stampeders turned around and went back out over the same trail. Henry Dow Banks, for example, left with nine other men from his home state of Massachusetts, along with six from California, four from Vermont, six from Connecticut, and several others in March 1898. Banks reminisced that the going got very rough as the party penetrated farther into the north country, and they sold all but their most necessary goods. Men like these rarely lasted more than a year in the Yukon, for when they arrived in Dawson and discovered that all the claims had been staked, a combination of depleted resources, severe climate, and acute disillusionment forced many to leave. As with the Banks party, most Klondike stampeders 'never did get any gold.'[24]

Of course, while thousands of Klondikers came and went rather quickly, thousands more stayed to make Dawson their home for years. Of those who stayed miners constituted the single largest occupational group, and they also formed a rather representative cross-section of Klondikers. Miners had almost identical ethnic backgrounds to the general Klondike population. Thirty percent were Canadians, an equal portion were American born, 15 percent were British, 6 percent were Scandinavians, 8 percent were continental Europeans, and others of foreign birth made up 11 percent. Over half were under forty years of age, and the vast majority – over 75 percent – were unmarried. Within the general population, 56 percent reported themselves married. The mining population was even more overwhelmingly male than the general population – 99 percent compared to 85 percent overall.[25]

Married and single miners alike came from all walks of life. Many were career prospectors and veterans of the gold camps that abounded in western North America. Nevertheless, on the creeks and in Dawson itself a veteran prospector was likely to have a greenhorn as a neighbour in the next cabin. The hundreds of accountants, clerks, and farmers who abandoned their southern livelihoods to join in the mad rush for gold in the Yukon hurried in to mine next to sourdoughs who had devoted years to the search. The irony of the Klondike was that these greenhorns, or 'cheechakos' as they were referred to by other Klondikers, were as likely to strike it rich as the oldtimers. The great gamble of the Klondike was that an average-producing claim might overnight turn into an Eldorado of huge proportions, and no one knew who was going to be next.

The first placer miners of the Yukon River valley had restricted their efforts to mining sand and gravel bars along the rivers and creeks. Their proximity to water allowed the bars to thaw seasonally, while the river banks were permanently frozen. Although it escaped the problems of permafrost, bar mining was often a risky venture as bars were easily flooded or washed away. Gulches on the other hand – ravines or trenches for run-off, or small tributary creek beds – contained small amounts of water that could be easily diverted in order to get access to pay dirt. At Fortymile, new techniques were adapted to allow better access to the coarse gold found in the frozen soil of the river banks and creek gulches. During the summer months, miners could mine the top two feet of gravel with relative ease. Once they reached permafrost, they built fires to thaw the subsoil, scraped that layer off, and built a new fire, going deeper and deeper in the belief that the richest deposits would occur just above the bedrock. Using fires for thawing, the miners could work all through the winter months. Hauling it up with windlasses, they piled the thawed soil beside the mine shaft until spring run-off provided the water necessary to wash or sluice the gold from the dirt. Placer mining on banks and in gulches could thus be carried out year round.[26]

The gold that Keish, Káa Goox, and Carmack discovered on Bonanza Creek was similar to the Fortymile deposits, and the stampeders from Fortymile simply transferred their operations when news of the latest strike reached them. In most of the Klondike mining district, the richest dirt tended to be forty to sixty feet below the surface. Miners located this pay dirt by sinking a number of prospect holes in different parts of the claim to determine the extent and thickness of the 'pay streak.' Miners then lifted out the soil and gravel which they then 'rocked,' or sifted, separating the heavier ore from the gravel, and then sluiced it with water to remove the remaining silt and soil.[27] Soon, every available saw, axe, and hatchet were in use for taking the timber adjacent to the claims to build the flumes, sluices, and rockers needed to get the new diggings operational. Experienced miners with entrepreneurial leanings also applied to the federal government for timber leases in order to earn extra money. They then sold timber to neighbouring miners for fuel for the winter diggings.

The life of a Yukon placer miner was a difficult one. It was a hard, dangerous, and often heartbreaking way of life that only occasionally yielded great results. The miners worked furiously during the long days of summer when the creeks were running and there was plenty of water for sluicing. Through the long, dark days of winter they toiled over the smoke-filled mine shafts, operating windlasses in forty-below temperatures, and ate poor provisions that often gave them scurvy. Still, as one mining wife put it, while the 'fortune ever eluded us ... the chase was far more interesting and exciting.'[28] And a chase it was, for many of them had followed the gold camps through California, Australia, Colorado, and British Columbia before coming to the Yukon. Speculation followed by hard work was the only way to see if a claim would pay, and bitter disappointment was often the only tangible reward for months, sometimes even years, of hard labour.

Because the Klondike district was suitable primarily for placer mining in the boom period, it was everyone's gold rush in a real sense – at least in the beginning. Indeed, part of the appeal of the Klondike rush was the low capital investment required in the actual mining. After stampeders had paid the costs of the journey and secured a claim, little capital was necessary to set up a mining operation. A gold pan, axe, pick, and shovel cost a few dollars and these, along with adequate provisions, were sufficient to get started.

Every Yukon miner was required to purchase a free miner's licence before he could stake a claim or perform mining work in the Klondike.[29]

*The Klondike was a family affair for
hundreds who found no shortage of work
in operating a mining claim.*

Then he could prospect as he pleased. When he found a spot he wished to mine, he marked its parameters by driving in four stakes and then journeyed to the nearest mining office to record his claim. In return for his recording fee, the miner received a one-year lease on the claim. The mining licence cost $10 and the usual recording fee was $15. This system did not always operate smoothly and there were numerous allegations of corruption in the Office of the Gold Commissioner in the early period.[30] Also, because miners often travelled great distances from their mines to the recording office, discrepancies resulted and the office sometimes had to send surveyors out to verify claims. Sometimes miners were forced to re-stake entire creeks. Thomas Wilson's party fell victim to these circumstances in 1898 when they attempted to record Discovery and six other claims on Barlow Creek. After mistakenly hearing that no one else had recorded there, they arrived at Stewart River to find that although the Discovery claim had not been registered with the mining recorder there, it had been recorded in Dawson City almost a month earlier. The official at Stewart also informed them that two of their most promising claims were on crown property and therefore not available for staking.[31] Disappointed, the party was forced to return to Barlow Creek to re-stake all of their claims.

Miners encountered other problems, among them not having the required recording fee. Various strategies could be employed to get around this problem. Rather than record all the new claims, Wilson's party decided to record and work only the most promising until they had taken out enough gold to be able to record the others. This system also required watching over the unrecorded claims to ensure that no one else seized the opportunity to record or 'jump' them. The first United States consul in Dawson noted that he spent most of his time the first year 'listening to grievances in regards to persons who stake claims and afterwards cannot get them recorded.'[32]

Wage labour formed a large portion of mining work because miners had to keep their property 'worked' or 'represented' for a portion of each year in order to maintain their placer claims. Miners who owned several claims or who were otherwise absent from their mines paid labourers to perform the representation work. Labour on a placer mine included cutting, hauling, and sawing wood for miners to build cabins, sluices, rockers, and a host of other mining works. Once the construction projects were complete, a miner had to dig prospect holes, then remove, sift, and sort the resulting gravel. During the winter months, miners had the

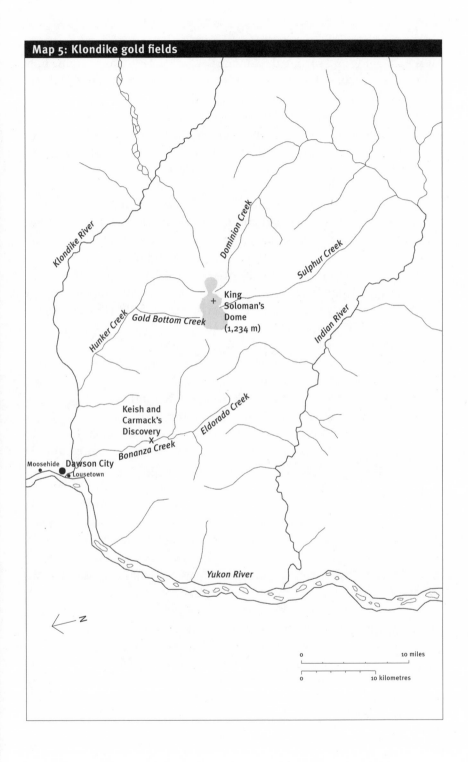

Klondike River

Dominion Creek

Sulphur Creek

Hunker Creek

Gold Bottom Creek

King
Soloman's
Dome
(1,234 m)

Indian River

Keish and
Carmack's
Discovery
X

Eldorado Creek

Bonanza Creek

Moosehide

Dawson City

Lousetown

Yukon River

N

| 0 | | 10 miles |
| 0 | | 10 kilometres |

laborious job of tending fires in an effort to melt the frozen earth in order to keep digging and sorting the 'dumps' of gravel. Here then was the bulk of the Yukon demand for workers, for all of this required manual labour. Work was thus readily available and the wages usually high, although this varied with the labour supply. In fact, labourers' wages tended to be higher on the creeks than in town, where there was a larger labour supply.[33]

Yukon placer mining, while individualistic in theory, often required more labour than a single miner could perform, and most miners operated their claims in partnership with other miners or by hiring casual labour. Due to a shortage of labour on the creeks claims, mine owners often worked out complicated contracts with employees. Etta Endl, for example, hired former Dawson stableman Ed Morrison to represent her mining claims while she went to work as a cook for another outfit. For a period of just over three months, Morrison billed Endl $250. It is not clear how much work had been done for this fee, but at approximately $75 per month – the same wage he had been making previously as a stableman – he was probably working nearly full time.[34]

Like so many other Klondikers, however, Morrison soon discovered that getting paid was a bigger problem than finding work and resorted to legal action in order to receive his wages. Endl for her part was not in a position to pay Morrison, for she herself was waiting for the Treadgold Company to pay her wages.[35] Others, like Elbridge Bartlett, entered into contracts in which their wages were 'payable at wash-up,' when wages could be more or less extracted from the gravel itself.[36] If a mine did not pay, however, very often neither could the mine's owner.

The creeks, then, provided a large number of jobs for manual labourers. Many of these labourers came, like John Grace, from the lumber camps of the lower west coast. As had so many others, Grace travelled from one part of the United States to another before finally finding work in a lumber camp near Tacoma, Washington, in the 1890s. When news of the Klondike strike reached him, Grace and two other woodsmen laid down their axes, bought supplies in Seattle, and started for Dawson, where they were too late to stake but found plenty of labouring work.[37]

While some miners found casual wage work on the creeks, others obtained a 'lay' instead. Working a lay meant working a claim for an absentee owner and receiving a percentage of the gold removed. Marie Richer, a Dawson woman with mining interests, hired George Rice to work her lay in 1901. Rice was a young American-born miner who had come to Dawson during the great stampede of 1898. Rice failed to make his fortune immediately as he had planned, for he arrived in Dawson only to find all the most promising mining claims staked out. Determined to 'make a go of it' he turned his hand to labouring on other people's claims. Under the terms of his agreement with Richer, Rice leased her claim on Moose Creek for a dollar per year. He performed all representation and mining work in exchange for giving Richer 25 percent of the 'whole of the gold or gold dust extracted from the said claim.' While the opportunity here was grand, the claim was not a good one, and neither Rice nor Richer got rich from it.[38]

Though not every Klondike miner made his or her fortune, some of course did, and their stories are as varied as the four corners of the world from which they came. Some miners invested their fortunes wisely and lived out their lives in comfort. Others spent their entire fortunes on the proverbial wine, women, and song. Still others made the big strike only to lose it again in the next mining venture or a bad real estate investment.

Many who arrived very early or who were already prospecting in the region claimed ground that yielded thousands of dollars in gold. This was the case for three young men, Andrew Anderson and the brothers Robert and Charles Karlson. All three were born in Norway and had migrated while in their teens to the logging camps of Santa Cruz, California, in the early 1890s. Together the trio went north in 1894, first to Juneau and later up the Yukon River. Dreaming of making their fortunes, the trio alternately prospected and worked as woodcutters to earn money for mining supplies and provisions. In the fall of 1896 Robert Karlson was one of the first to stake on Bonanza Creek after Keish and Carmack discovered gold there. Robert quickly sent for his brother and Anderson. The following spring, after taking out over $7,000, the Karlson-Anderson partnership sold their claims to 'Big Alex' McDonald for $50,000.[39] Planning to take their fortune home to Norway, the Karlson brothers headed for Dawson to celebrate the end of their years of poverty. They left Anderson in charge of the claim. Sadly, their spree in town left them both ill with typhoid fever and they died shortly afterward.

Bad luck continued to plague the Karlsons even after their deaths, for like so many miners, they had never drawn up legal papers documenting their partnership with Anderson. Thus, before the estate could be settled, affidavits had to be obtained to determine Anderson's share of the estate. While the estate was being settled, the Department of the Interior deposited the money in trust. Unfortunately, the trust company went bankrupt before the estate was settled and the money was never recovered. Not only did the Karlson boys perish before enjoying their windfall, but neither their partner and friend of many years nor their family ever received any profit from the 'big strike' that had cost these two young men their lives.[40]

While the Karlson story is an extreme case, many Klondikers risked and lost everything in the stampede for gold. Mortgaging their homes and farms, quitting their steady but boring southern jobs, thousands of young men and women like the Karlson brothers gambled it all in the Klondike rush. All of them were prepared for some level of risk, lending weight to sociologist John Findlay's argument that miners and gamblers in many ways share a single profession. They were *all* 'people of chance.'[41]

Big Alex McDonald was another of these Klondike gamblers. Known in the early part of the rush as the King of the Klondike, McDonald went from rags to riches and finally back to rags. A born speculator, he prospected and did well in the Yukon but made most of his fortune by buying up promising claims – including the Karlsons' – in the early years. Like so many other miners, McDonald was always generous with a windfall, and he donated the bulk of the amount needed to reconstruct the Catholic church after it suffered a fire in 1898. Ten years later, the boom had bust and so had Big Alex's fortune. He died in the winter of 1909 on one of his creek claims. The sum of his properties amounted to about $30,000, but when his estate was finally settled it did not cover all of Big Alex's debts.[42] Buried with his confrères in the Dawson cemetery, the grave of the man who was once King of the Klondike remains today marked only by a simple and dilapidated wooden marker.

While many Klondikers never realized their dreams of becoming millionaires, King of the Klondike Alex McDonald did. Such fortune was fleeting, however, and he died penniless in Dawson in 1909.

Robert Service spoke for McDonald and many of his prospector friends when he wrote: 'Yet it isn't the gold that I'm wanting / So much as just finding the gold.' These lines from 'The Spell of the Yukon' succinctly indicate that for the men of chance, it was never too late to make good. The hope of discovering a new strike or even the fabled 'mother lode' kept sourdoughs prospecting for years. And there was just enough luck among them to encourage their efforts. Well after the boom for example, a Finnish miner washed up over $70,000 worth of gold on a hillside claim that 'had been prospected for many years and given up as almost worthless.'[43] It was exactly this chance that brought them to the Yukon and it was the same chance that kept them there for many years.

Many who 'struck it,' like Clarence Berry and his family, soon returned to their places of origin with their fortunes. The Berrys are perhaps the most famous Klondike family, possibly because they embodied the dream and the romance so many others sought. A former small businessman from California, Clarence Berry had joined the small stampede to Fortymile in 1894. A year later he returned to California, where he married his childhood sweetheart, Ethel Bush. Together the couple returned over the Chilkoot, down the river, and back to Fortymile. When Clarence's claims yielded few returns, he took a job as a bartender. So it was that he happened to be in the saloon that August afternoon in 1896 when George Carmack arrived with news of his Klondike discovery. Clarence was among the first to rush to Bonanza Creek, where he staked the soon-famous claim number 'Forty Above' and later also two claims on Eldorado Creek. Here, just like the women who laboured on less prosperous mining claims, Ethel cooked, cleaned, and laundered for the miners in a primitive cabin, while her husband cleaned up over $100,000.[44]

Clarence and Ethel made the journey south to purchase supplies and visit family once more in 1897. When they returned, they brought Ethel's sister Edna Bush as well. It appears that Edna accompanied the Berrys back to the Yukon to provide company and assistance for Ethel on the mining claim. This was a common enough pattern, for many families encouraged brothers, sons, or sisters to join them and help on their claims or in their businesses. Indeed, Henry Berry had already joined his brother and was working on the original Bonanza Creek claim when Edna arrived in 1898. Edna had the luxury of being kin to one of the Klondike Kings, and while she was expected to help Ethel with domestic chores both along the trail and on the claim, her Klondike experience was made easier by the fact that the family had already 'struck it.' She also fell in love with and soon married Ethel's brother-in-law Henry Berry, thereby keeping the fortune within the family. The Berrys remained in the Yukon until 1900, when they followed the gold rush to Fairbanks and later invested their wealth in the developing oil industry in California.[45]

Though many people took their fortunes south, many others stayed and made Dawson their home, putting down roots even though the big strike continued to elude them. The size of their fortunes seems to have had little to do with this decision. Long after the rush was over, for example, Adolph Dominy continued to prospect the creeks and gulches of the Klondike. Dominy was an Austrian-born miner who first called Dawson his home in 1898. In the summer of 1915 his body was found up the Hootalinqua River, where he had been continuing his quest. One of the many who never made his fortune, at the time of his death Dominy's estate totalled $4.50.[46]

For many sourdoughs, the Klondike rush was one of a long series of gambles in which they invested. John Finlayson was a Scottish-born explorer and prospector who had come to the Fraser River country in 1858. One of the first to prospect in the Stikine and Cassiar districts, he also joined the rush to the Yukon, although he was by then nearly eighty years old. Finlayson, 'while he never made a big stake, ... always had plenty of money for his immediate needs until a short time before his death.'[47] Like so many of his comrades, Finlayson died a pauper, dreaming yet of making his big strike.

Like Dominy and Finlayson, Frank Breau was a career prospector convinced that his fortune lay buried somewhere in the creek beds of the Yukon. Breau, like so many other French Canadians, had come to the Yukon in 1897 as a miner and never left. He died in 1912 still dreaming of finding the mother lode. After a lifetime of prospecting, at the age of sixty, Breau left his heirs a grand total of $24.15.[48] Although the Klondike gold rush had ended almost a decade earlier, many sourdoughs never gave up the quest. The spell of the Yukon held Dominy, Finalyson, Breau, and many others firmly in its grip.

A large number of French Canadians came to the Klondike, and the majority were miners and labourers. Many of them did very well in the Yukon. One oldtimer, Joseph Dubé, remembered that a man named Mercier from Ste Anne des Plaines had staked a very good claim and that several others, including a Monsieur Picotte and his three brothers, had also made their fortunes in the Klondike. In addition to their reputation for being hard workers and lucky prospectors, French Canadians were noted for a propensity to settle in small enclaves: 'We call the two places where they are thickest, "Little Paris" and "Little Quebec,"' remembered oldtimer Ed Lung. In Dawson alone in 1901, there were over 400 French Canadian residents.

Klondikers came from the four corners of the globe, and many homesick miners named their cabins and mining claims in honour of their distant homes. French Canadians formed the largest non-English-speaking group in the Klondike.

Among this group a network developed, centring on the Ottawa Hotel on Third Avenue, owned by French Canadian businessman Joseph Cadieux. Pierre Treufe, Charles Renaud, Cyrus Sicotte, Pete Sutherland (francophone despite his name), and Jean Daumay resided there. These men, all in their early forties, were doing moderately well. Treufe and Sicotte each owned claims worth $5,000 and real estate worth $2,000 after four years in Dawson. The rest claimed assets of about $2,000 each.[49] Early in Dawson's history, French Canadians tended to meet informally in the hotel's saloon, where they shared information and established friendships and business connections. The Roman Catholic church also offered a place within which French Canadian men and their families could meet and interact socially. St Jean Baptiste Day in June was a large and widely celebrated annual event in Dawson, further indicating the important presence of this group.

The ethnic clustering of French Canadians was even more noticeable on the creeks, and this phenomenon continued well into the early years of the new century. The village of Paris, for example, was almost completely French Canadian, convincing the local anglophone blacksmith to leave in 1905 because he was 'tired of baching and living among the Frenchmen.' That the community of 'Frenchmen' also included women and children is evidenced by the fact that six French-speaking children from Paris attended the nearby school at Caribou Creek the same year.[50] On Glacier and Miller creeks, too, French Canadians established small enclaves. Like other Klondike men of chance, these miners were reluctant to relinquish their quest, and as late as 1907 miners such as LaFortune, Lesperance, Demaray, Chantelois, Lemieux, Paradis, Bourdelais, and Paquin continued to work their claims, being rewarded with a moderately successful annual output of $16,000 altogether.[51]

The French Canadians looked after one another by sharing information about mining prospects, acting as translators, teaching each other English, and assisting each other in finding work. The musician Gédéon Pépin, for example, acted as a translator and employment agent for several young French Canadian men he met on his trip to Dawson.[52] For friendless new arrivals, Cadieux's saloon offered an informal place to gain information about mining claims, lodgings, and employment. Very often French Canadians found their first Klondike jobs in the employ of other Quebeckers. Alfred Leblanc and Michel Poliquin, for example, both went to work representing a claim belonging to Monsieur Mercier for $50 per month when they arrived in 1898.[53] Cultural identity, then, offered a basis of forming business and social networks.

While Dawson's international population annually celebrated both Queen Victoria's Birthday and the Fourth of July, the large community of French Canadians also held an annual celebration on St Jean Baptiste Day, 24 June.

Although most Klondike placer miners were men a few women also worked in this sector. Nellie Cashman was an old hand at mining, coming to the Yukon in 1897 from the gold mining districts of Arizona. The Irish-born Cashman was a lifelong prospector and veteran of the Cassiar, Tombstone, and South African gold rushes. At nearly fifty years old, she could not resist the call of the Klondike. Like so many others, Cashman arrived too late to stake on the rich ground, but managed to purchase both a 'fraction' and a regular claim. A fraction was a sliver of ground or a partial claim. A fraction was created when the Dominion Land Survey measured a group of claims and found one to have been staked on the wrong dimensions, thus throwing off all the other claims. Rather than re-staking all the other claims – and stirring up controversy – the surveyor usually marked off the 'fraction,' reported it to the mining recorder, and opened it for staking. Cashman mined her own claims side by side with her male colleagues, and like them she had no regrets: 'I took out over one hundred thousand dollars from that claim ... and I spent every red cent of it buying other claims and prospecting the country. I went out with my dog team or on snow shoes all over that district looking for rich claims.'[54] To support her mining habit during her seven-year residence in Dawson, Cashman operated first the Delmonico short order restaurant and later a grocery store.

As a veteran miner Cashman was the exception, for only 1 percent of Yukon miners in this period were women, and references to women miners are few and far between in the sources. The local newspaper, for example, reported that Mrs Butt's claim on Gold Run Creek was earning a dollar per pan in 1899, although the account does not specify whether Mrs Butt was doing her own work on the claim. Jane Clifford arrived in the Yukon when she was thirty-one years old in 1898. Her hard work seems to have paid off moderately well, for after three years she had accumulated personal property valued at $1,000, including a dog. She had not managed to purchase any real estate in three years, and she left a blank in the column for 'value of claims,' indicating either that she was working for wages or that her own claims were nothing worth recording.[55]

Life as a miner, and especially as a single woman miner, was not easy, and few followed Cashman and Clifford's lead. A significant number, however, owned mining property. In fact, nearly 700 mining claims – 3 percent of all Klondike claims – registered in the period were located by 527 women, indicating that many women located several claims. A few like Nellie Cashman worked their own mines but they seem to have been the

exception. Although evidence is sparse, the largest group of women probably staked claims in order to increase the family's mine holdings. Since
individual miners could record only one claim per creek, a wife's claim
doubled a couple's prospects. Even if they lived on their own mining property though, these women rarely performed the day-to-day business of
mining, there being little time left after food preparation, child care, and
laundry. Women such as Ethel Berry, Mrs Anderson, and Kate Carmack all
took in laundry and mending or sold bread, beans, and pies to the neighbouring miners. Some were the sole support for the family when the mining claim failed. Such was the case of Ella Shand, who accompanied her
husband and friends on a prospecting trip up the White River so that she
could stake a copper claim near her husband's, thereby doubling his claim
size. Mrs Shand herself had little interest in mining. She ran a roadhouse
that formed the mainstay of the family's existence, providing a relatively
steady income to support her husband's constantly failing mining ventures.[56]

Other women confined their mining interests to investing, or grubstaking, and many of these were admired by their peers. Gédéon Pépin
remembered several 'mature women with a sharp eye for business' who
participated in mining speculation, including Carrie Lowe and Margaret
Mitchell. Martha Black was one of these, although the miners she grub-
staked never seemed to do very well. Mae Melbourne did much better.
Melbourne invested $5,000 in claims on several creeks in the Dawson area
in 1899 and soon the local newspaper was describing her as the 'richest
woman in Dawson.' The *Klondike Nugget* estimated her worth to be in the
neighbourhood of $100,000. More common was the situation of Violenia
Evans, a widow who was the sole owner of number of claims and held a
one-third interest in a claim on Quartz Creek. Evans's partners on the
Quartz Creek claim retained 'all gold taken out' on it in exchange for representation work done on her other claims. A similar agreement was
reached by Margaret Mitchell, who paid Duncan McPhail fifty cents per
cubic yard of gravel taken out of her Hunker Creek claims. Other busi-
nesswomen, such as Annie May Enright, bought and sold numerous claims,
speculating and prospering throughout the boom years. For the majority
of women claim owners, hiring someone – usually a man – to represent
or work the mine was preferable to performing the work themselves.[57]

The nature of Klondike placer mining and the labour associated
with it changed after the turn of the century. By 1901, placer miners had
extracted the bulk of the gold along the creeks, and large companies
bought up claims in blocks, using dredges to extract the rest. As a result,

Enterprising women operated their own
businesses, like this unidentified African
American woman who sold lunches,
bread, cakes, and pies to hungry miners
on the creeks.

a fiercely competitive market developed for the sale and resale of claims as groups consolidated mines for hydraulic dredging operations. Commissioner Ross explained that the heyday of placer mining was over: 'There are no more Bonanzas or Eldorados and it is down to a business proposition – low grade ground and only by the assistance of machinery are they able to make it pay.'[58] The result was a series of concessions. These government grants allowed private interests to acquire large groups of existing and unrepresented claims, as well as the water and timber rights to those claims. By 1904, forty-four of these had been granted, the largest being the Treadgold Concession. Under the terms of this concession, the British-born A.N.C. Treadgold obtained a virtual monopoly over water resources, huge amounts of land, tax exemptions, and other privileges for a period of thirty years. Local residents and those with smaller operations were outraged, a feeling they expressed directly to Minister of the Interior Clifford Sifton, to no avail.[59] More and more, mining work came to mean waged labour in the employ of a few large operators. In the Klondike River valley in 1914, for example, the Canadian Klondyke Company alone operated four dredges, each dredge employing about 300 men for most of the year. Smaller hydraulic operations employed four to five men each but could work only in the summer, when water was available. The small operations usually worked from May to October. During the winter, men and teams of horses and dogs were employed to haul wood for the steam dredges. By 1914, it was clear that individual operators had become archaic, and their holdings were increasingly merged with the larger companies.[60] The days of the small individual- or family-owned mining claim were over.

Whither Thou Goest: Domestic and Family Life in the Klondike

Miners worked long hours, very often for low returns, but their wives and partners toiled equally hard. Kate Carmack and other Native wives of miners were perhaps best equipped to survive the harsh conditions and isolation of the mining life. Native women were accustomed to summer trips for the salmon runs and worked long hours preserving fish and fruit for the winter's supply of food and preparing skins for the family's clothing. Still, it was a hard life and one usually lived far from the women's own family and friendship networks. Non-Native women also recalled a lonely, difficult life on the creeks, endlessly doing laundry, repairing clothing, splitting wood, and preparing makeshift meals with few provisions. Joining in their husbands' quests, these women repeatedly packed up and moved from one creek to another. Separated from family and friends, often separated for months even from other miners, making a home for their families was a very difficult task. Additionally, mining wives were limited in their contact with other women by issues of race and class.

Although the dominant images of the Klondike portray the population as a fraternity of equals, close examination reveals that Yukon mining society maintained a number of race and class divisions. The fact should not surprise us, for this was the Victorian era, after all, and Klondikers carried with them values and ideas formed in the larger North American society from which they came. Thus while many miners lived with their Native wives and families on the creeks, there is no evidence of social or friendly interaction between Native and non-Native mining wives. Rather, as Frederick Palmer noticed during his visits to the creeks, couples of mixed heritage tended to socialize only with one another. Joe Powers, for example, had a claim near George Carmack's and 'as both had squaw wives there was a bond of union between them, and they visited back and forth a great deal.'[61] Palmer implies that these two families' common racial heritage was the basis for friendship and that they were shunned by the white miners and their wives in the area.

There is also evidence that non-Native women did not easily associate with either Native women or women of dubious sexual morals. One tired and lonely-looking mining wife, for example, told a visitor in 1898 that it had been three years since she had seen another white woman, and although she had heard of one only a few miles away on a neighbouring creek, she would not visit her because she was a 'bad woman.'[62] Isolation and loneliness were not sufficient reasons to abandon prevailing class and racial prejudices in the Klondike.

This situation carried over into Dawson itself, and it may explain why so few couples of mixed heritage made their homes in town. Sadie Stringer, the bishop's wife, for example, found out that Dawson society had a set of rules that did not easily accommodate ethnic differences. Mrs Stringer was one of the few Dawson 'ladies' who had Native women friends. Worrying that her Native friend might feel shy and uncomfortable among strangers, Mrs Stringer placed Mrs Kendi, 'an Indian woman from Mayo' in the place of honour at her side at a church tea, an action that offended and upset the other ladies present.[63] Racial divisions among women were thus present both along the creeks and in town, among both the mining wives and the social élite. We can only guess that this made an already difficult life even more so for the women who were the objects of these attitudes, for the record is silent on the subject of their reactions.

For many families, the Klondike was one of a string of gold rushes in which they participated, seeking their fortunes and willing to sacrifice a great deal of comfort in the process.

Mining wives of all ethnicities had a difficult time with domestic chores, especially in winter. Families kept their food in an outdoor cache, where it was always frozen solid. Although this preserved food well, it also necessitated a great deal of labour in separating and thawing it. As well, cabins were cold and draughty and wood stoves demanded a large and constant supply of kindling and chopped wood. Thawing ice and snow for cooking and washing was time-consuming and tiresome work, and like all chores during the long, dark winter months it had to be performed by candle and lamplight. During lean times, mining wives often had to 'make do' with what was available, however foreign the source. During the scarce winter of 1898 on the family mining claim, for example, Ethel Anderson Becker remembered her mother serving 'rabbits, rabbits rabbits ... We lived well, but mama never ate rabbit after we left the Klondike.'[64]

During the long days of summer, women and children often subsidized family mining revenues with other activities. Berry picking, for example, brought in food both for the family and for sale. For those willing to brave the sun and the bugs, cranberries could bring in $5 to $10 for a long day's work.[65] Other women baked bread and doughnuts – but only after they managed to master the intricacies of the Yukon stove and nonyeast raising – and sold these with baked beans to neighbouring miners.

For some Klondike families, the gamble paid off with returns few had ever dared imagine. This was true especially in 1896, the summer of the big discoveries. The Berry family took out $140,000 in one year, while George Carmack, his Tagish partners, and their families each took out similar amounts. John Miller, a neighbouring miner, took out $40,000 after expenses, and many others took out between $15,000 and $20,000 the first year.[66] By the summer of 1898, the region was almost completely staked and output was steady.

Most families probably made a living at mining, although few became wealthy. Isabel and John Crawford were perhaps more typical. This American couple, both in their early twenties, arrived at the height of the rush in 1898. Three years later, having tried their hand at a variety of mining enterprises, they had yet to make their fortune. Still the couple seem to have achieved a comfortable life, having accumulated over $500 in personal property and $1,800 worth of real estate.[67]

Most of the popular Klondike literature notes that the usual family strategy of Klondikers was for male stampeders to travel to the Klondike and get themselves established in the Dawson area before sending for their wives and families. This idea seems to have been based on impressions,

Many women were worn down by the primitive conditions and severe climate of the Yukon. Often living long distances from medical help, Klondike families made do with supplies at hand, even when the baby had to be fed from a whisky bottle, like this one, identified only as 'the First Baby on the Stewart River.'

and until the release of the 1901 census there was no way to verify the pattern. Data from the census do not bear it out; the most common strategy was for families to migrate together. Over 500 families completed census returns in 1901, and almost half of the wives and children reported arriving in the same year as the male head of household. Less than a quarter arrived a year later, and the remainder arrived two or more years after the male head of household.[68]

Other patterns also emerge from close analysis of the census material. One of the first things we notice is that despite the many employment opportunities, the largest number of women (over 700) reported their occupation to be 'wife.' This category is rather misleading of course, for no single term can encompass the myriad jobs Klondike wives performed. Mabel Moore was one of hundreds of women who joined her husband in his prospecting ventures. Moore and her husband had been mining at Douglas Island, Alaska, when word of the Klondike strike reached them. Her husband went up river to Dawson in the fall of November 1897 and she followed by dogsled in January. Prospecting on the streams of the Klondike watershed, a strict sexual division of labour developed: Mabel nursed, cooked, and repaired clothing for the members of the group, while 'Jim my husband, Arthur his brother, and Jack a friend of his would hunt, fish and prospect.'[69] This type of familial travel and prospecting arrangement was quite common among Klondikers, for it allowed a small party to pool resources and labour.

Many veteran prospecting wives would not have considered being left behind and they put their considerable experience to good use. In 1897, Della Murray Banks accompanied her prospector husband on yet another leg of the 'perennial search for fortune in which my husband never lost faith, though my faith grew small.' Mrs Banks negotiated a contract for herself with her husband's party at $50 per month. She justified this by stating that she knew full well that once on the trail the task of cooking would fall to her as a matter of course and so she thought she might as well be paid for her labour. A veteran of bush and camp life, Banks was the very personification of self-confidence and perseverance: 'We made camp in the rain at the head of the delta, having gone about seven miles [through salt-water marshes all day]. I got supper in the rain, by the light of a candle. Kneeling on the ground, I mixed biscuits – ninety of them, baked fifteen at a time in the sheet-iron stove. Thompson watched, saying that if he had to get supper that night there wouldn't be any. Well, I had walked as far as he had.'[70]

After freeze-up, Klondikers travelled over the frozen river surfaces by dogsled. Note the appearance of Gandolfo's store in the background. Gandolfo was a well-known and highly successful fruit and candy merchant.

Mrs Banks leaves little doubt in this quotation that she is disgusted at the double work day expected of women on the trail, and thus it is little wonder that she had insisted on being paid for her additional labours. Once established on the claim, too, women like Mrs Banks worked long hours assisting whenever and wherever necessary in the mining work in addition to performing all of the necessary domestic chores for their husbands and their mining partners.

George Snow, one of the original sourdough miners, also brought his family to the Klondike. Snow first prospected in the Yukon in 1888 and again in 1892. In 1894, he returned for a third time, this time combining prospecting with his profession as an actor. His 'Company of Players' included his wife, Anna, their two children, and his brother, Joseph. All family members participated in the theatre in the gold camp of Fortymile before relocating to Dawson after the new strike in 1896.[71] Snow was committed both to his family and to the long-term development and stability of Yukon mining society, for he was one of the organizers and founders of the Yukon Order of Pioneers, a fraternal society aimed at providing support for old-time miners.[72]

Another example of family migration is the case of Mae and Arthur Field. This couple came to the Klondike as newlyweds in 1898. Arthur staked a lucrative claim on Bear Creek, and the couple made their home there. In the first year the claim yielded $100,000. After the claim was worked out, Arthur lost the fortune in a series of bad business ventures and then deserted Mae. Destitute, she turned to the Flora Dora dance hall for employment. Talented and attractive, Mae Field was soon one of the most popular and famous performers in Dawson.[73] A mining family that got rich together did not always 'stick' together, and many families found that fortunes that appeared overnight often disappeared almost as quickly.

The pattern in which the male wage earner preceded his dependants to the Klondike also existed. Such was the case of the young Eugene Forget, who came to Dawson in 1899 to help support his family. A year later he was joined by his widowed mother and two sisters. Eugene's income of $150 per month seems to have been insufficient to maintain the family, however, and the women also went to work in Dawson. Madame Forget found work as a cook for $100 per month, while Delia worked as a sales clerk and Georgene as a waitress. The total family income amounted to $400 per month and even this proved little enough, for the 'value of personal property' for the whole family amounted to a mere $145 by 1901.[74]

SHRINERS BANQUET   'ST JOHNS DAY,
DAWSON JUN. 24 - 99.

*There were dozens of male fraternal
societies in the Klondike, among them
the Shriners, pictured here at their
annual banquet in 1899.*

To place such wages in a larger context, we can compare them to those reported by Michael Piva in his study of Toronto workers between 1900 and 1921. According to Piva's calculations, the average wage of a blue collar worker in Toronto in 1901 was just over $30 per month, compared to Madame Forget's $100 per month or the roughly $200 per month earned by Dawson's dance hall performers and bartenders. Piva also calculated that the cost of food, shelter, light, and fuel for an average Toronto household of five was about $38 per month, while in Dawson the monthly rent alone might be $125.[75] That the Forget family was barely making ends meet on a combined income of $400 per month indicates the extremely high cost of living in Dawson.

Another French Canadian family to arrive in stages was the Forrest family. Joseph Forrest was supporting his wife and four children as foreman of a small gold mine in Grass Valley, California, when news of the Klondike reached him in 1897. Sending the rest of the family home to Trois Rivières, Quebec, he went to Dawson. Joseph spent the winter of 1898-9 in Quebec with his family and then returned to Dawson with his eldest son Paul in the spring of 1899. In 1901, his wife and remaining children joined them.[76] Here the family remained until the First World War.

While some families intentionally undertook the Klondike adventure together or in stages, others attempted to 'make do' in separation. Mrs P.B. Anderson, who originally agreed to stay behind, arrived completely unannounced at her husband's mining claim on Eldorado Creek with their three young children in tow late in the summer of 1898. Mrs Anderson had boarded a steamer in Seattle and spent the following days continually seasick, then taken the new tram from Skagway to Whitehorse before boarding another steamer for Dawson. Having accomplished her goal and reunited her family, Mrs Anderson set about selling bread to the miners on the creek to supplement the family income.[77]

While Mr Anderson appeared pleased at the unexpected arrival of his wife and children, other women found their husbands less than pleasantly surprised when they reached Dawson. Minnie Wilkensen, for example, came to the Klondike in search of her husband, who had stopped sending support some time previously. She found him in Dawson, where he was earning $300 a month and living with another woman. Her fate after this discovery is unknown, but the author of the letter reporting the affair indicated that Mrs Wilkensen's case was all too familiar and that this 'is the case with a good many married men here, who have nice families on the outside and who ought to have more respect for their children and themselves if not for their wife.'[78] Perhaps it should not surprise us to find that the Klondike appears to have been an escape route for more than a few reluctant husbands. Sarah Patchell, a young bride from Nova Scotia, had a similar experience to Mrs Wilkensen when she arrived in Dawson unexpectedly, although Patchell's husband seems to have abandoned her for gold lust rather than for another woman.[79]

Other family members anxiously sought news of loved ones in the Yukon. Anna DeGraf spent more than twenty years searching to no avail in Alaska and the Klondike for news of her son, who disappeared in the early years of the Fortymile strike. Poor communication and mail service likewise resulted in a great deal of worry for many families around the globe. Josephine Phillides, for example, lost contact with her family after arriving in Dawson to establish the French Laundry. Desperate for news, Phillides's mother finally wrote to the American consulate in Dawson, asking for news of her daughter. The local newspapers also regularly published notices from all over the world seeking the whereabouts of family and friends.[80]

Conclusions

The vast majority Klondikers made a living through some form or combination of forms of semi- or unskilled labour. While labour was scarce and wages generally high throughout the period, these factors were offset by the high cost of living and repeated periods of seasonal unemployment. Not surprisingly, the largest number of labourers in the Klondike worked as miners, and almost all of these were men. Contrary to prevailing stereotypes about the Klondike, however, a great number of men worked for wages rather than operating claims of their own. Often this allowed them to save funds to stake their own claim or to purchase a promising claim already in production. In this way Klondike placer mining resembled prairie homesteading, as larger operators employed casual and seasonal help and used the profits to consolidate or increase their holdings. Casual labourers, for their part, moved from one employer to the next, negotiating terms of contract and gaining the skills and capital necessary to start up their own operations.

Crucial information about new discoveries and available labour spread through a network of miners. In the absence of long-time neighbours and kin, Klondikers created new networks based on combinations of place of origin, race, and ethnicity. Thus, a prosperous French Canadian might employ a number of francophone labourers to represent his claim, or a Coloradan might hire men he had known previously in Aspen.

Other social patterns emerged that make Dawson look much like southern Canadian cities of a similar size. Working class men and women found the labour market uncertain and experienced frequent periods of unemployment. Ethnic groups showed a propensity for certain occupations, such as French Canadians for mining and manual labour and Asians for laundry and food service. Women remained concentrated in what we might describe as conventional female or 'pink collar' occupations: domestic and food service, the sex trade, laundry work, and wife- and motherhood. While the stereotyped Klondike dance hall performer did exist – complete with feather boa and fishnet stockings – she was vastly outnumbered by the women who worked day to day in much more mundane pursuits.

Far from being a community of single workers, Dawson boasted a large number of families by the turn of the century. These families often migrated together as a unit and made Dawson their home for extended periods. Few of the thousands of migrant workers and their families got rich in the Yukon. Rather, they were typical of most working class families in North America and used a combination of strategies to sustain themselves and to build a future for their children.

CHAPTER 4

The Scarlet Ladder:
Work and Social Life in Dawson's Underworld

D AWSON'S UNDERWORLD was established as quickly as the city itself; between the summer of 1896 and 1905, Dawson City became home to hundreds of women and men involved in the entertainment and sex trades. These individuals tended to be young, poor, and from a wide variety of ethnic backgrounds. Their experiences illustrate that there was often a vast distance between life in the respectable and unrespectable worlds of Klondike society.

The Mounted Police early noted that 'fast women' and the 'sporting fraternity' accompanying them arrived within a few weeks of the Bonanza discovery. An early stampeder to Dawson, William Haskell, also noted that shortly after the strike, one of the dance halls from Circle City relocated to the new town, threw up a building, and set up 'about a dozen' women and a piano. As noted in the previous chapter, prospector and actor George Snow was one of these, relocating his Company of Players from Fortymile to Dawson in the summer of 1896. Vaudeville performers and camp followers from the adjacent mining districts were soon joined by their colleagues from the cities of the Pacific northwestern seaboard and beyond.[1]

In Dawson, there were two red-light districts to choose from in the early years. The first was known as Lousetown, or Klondike City, located across the Klondike River from Dawson. The second was a small district of brothels and back alley street walkers within the city itself. When Haskell arrived in the summer of 1897, he estimated that the population of Lousetown was about 300 people. By the following summer, the dance halls, theatres, brothels, saloons, and gambling arenas provided employment for somewhere between 500 and 1,000 people. Many of these operations were technically illegal, but local officials attempted to maintain order by regulating rather than suppressing their activities.[2]

Prostitutes were a visible and important component of this northern mining community, and the overwhelmingly male population proved a receptive market. Early trade in sex, like most other commerce in Dawson, was conducted first in tents and small cabins. Here, as elsewhere in town, gold dust was accepted as currency. In the earliest days of the rush, the Mounted Police turned a blind eye and allowed prostitutes to walk the streets and frequent saloons to solicit clientele. In fact, the Mounties made no arrests for prostitution-related offences until the spring of 1898. As the community evolved from a mining camp to a city, however, the police felt increasing pressure from a distant federal government, as well as from the local community, to control the sex industry. As a result, sexual commerce moved out of the public eye. As the city gained legal and social structures, the demi-monde was removed from public view – first off the streets, then into formalized districts, and finally out of the limits of the city itself.[3] In the process, the attitude of local authorities to sexual commerce within the community moved from a system of almost outright licensing to almost complete suppression. This had severe ramifications for both the women who worked in this sector and their clientele.

Crime and Morality in Dawson
For the most part, Yukon officials enjoyed a large degree of autonomy over the administration of the territory, and this allowed them to make decisions based on what they perceived to be in the community's best interests. Living and working within the community provided the Mounted Police in particular with an understanding of what was and was not appropriate. Striking a balance between community standards of behaviour and their duty to enforce Canadian laws, however, occasionally produced tensions and conflict.

Dawson's red-light district contained a strict hierarchy, the 'scarlet ladder.' Here, a local bartender poses significantly atop a ladder of local prostitutes.

The crux of the matter was prostitution. In the fall of 1899, after an outbreak of venereal disease in Dawson, the Yukon Council ordered 'that all harlots should be examined by a physician every month and should exhibit in their rooms certificates of health.' This order not only acknowledged the local presence and practice of prostitution in the Yukon, it effectively legitimized it. When information reached Ottawa that the police surgeon and health officer had been licensing prostitutes, Minister of the Interior Clifford Sifton was incensed and immediately demanded an explanation from the commissioner of the Yukon. William Ogilvie was unapologetic about the situation, which, he explained, had been in effect throughout the winter. There had been a great deal of 'sickness' the previous autumn, and while he confessed that the council understood that issuing certificates of health to the women was illegal and gave them a 'certain lawful standing,' he also stated that the action was taken because 'it was deemed in the best interests of the community to do so.' Fully cognizant that they could not ban prostitution completely from a mining camp, it was the council's view that a system of medical inspections was the best way to control the spread of infectious disease. Thus, the head of the council admitted that where the health and safety of the community were concerned, the law could and would be adapted. It was a means of working out the best solution under the worst of conditions.[4] Naturally, most local prostitutes proved willing to incur the expense of the medical examinations in return for being allowed to ply their trade unmolested.

In this initial skirmish over prostitution, Dawson City authorities moved quickly to appease the federal government. Upon receipt of Sifton's telegram in January 1900, the Yukon Council rescinded the order for medical exams. Unfortunately for relations between Sifton and Ogilvie, the prostitutes themselves found the practice of posting medical certificates – which quite literally amounted to clean bills of health – to be very good for business, and they maintained the practice long after the order was withdrawn, a situation the authorities were fairly helpless to stop.[5]

As much as the community acknowledged the inevitable presence and continuation of the sex trade, it was not without its own sense of propriety and morals. The sex trade was freely plied in the brothels, saloons, and even dance halls of Dawson and its neighbouring camps and the NWMP turned a blind eye to it as long as it was conducted in a more or less orderly fashion. After receiving a number of complaints about the entertainments at a local brothel, however, the Mounties arrested three

imose Of the last Public Game At Dawson. 12 PM. March 16th.1901. Dominion Saloon. 55

Although gambling was technically illegal in all of Canada, the Mounted Police allowed public gaming in Dawson saloons until the federal government forced them to reverse this policy in 1901. Depicted here is the last night of public gaming allowed in the Dominion Saloon.

French prostitutes, whom they later sentenced to prison with hard labour for participating in what the arresting officer described as 'exhibitions of a grossly indecent nature.'[6]

The process of tolerance and accommodation that developed in Dawson can also be seen in negotiations over the physical location of the red-light district. Originally, saloons, dance halls, and brothels operated shoulder to shoulder with greengrocers, banks, and assay offices. In February 1899, however, a fire in one of the hotels on Front Street destroyed much of the business and commercial district of Dawson and the source of the fire was traced to a prostitute's hotel room. While authorities acknowledged that the red-light district was a necessary and integral part of the community, they seized the opportunity to insist that it move farther away from the business portion of town.[7] Relocating to Fourth and Fifth avenues, the sex trade was soon doing a brisk business once more, albeit segregated from the more respectable commercial operations of Dawson. Again, the Mounted Police and local council proved willing to tolerate their operations as long as the denizens of the scarlet life were willing to abide by certain restrictions.

As the community stabilized and became more permanent after the turn of the century, local opposition to moral offences grew. In 1900, when the new school board decided to build Dawson's first public school on Third Avenue, agitation began for the removal of the prostitutes from the adjacent area. Since this area had been set aside specifically *for* the prostitutes only a year earlier, the NWMP and the council found themselves in a difficult position. In fact, the NWMP conducted an inquiry into how the new district was faring shortly after its relocation. After interviewing several of the forty-three women residents between Fourth and Fifth avenues who were working as prostitutes, the officer in charge concluded that the policy of segregation was working well. Responding to growing pressure, however, the Mounties undertook a policy of discouragement in the district, issuing a ban on 'all music, singing and noise' after midnight and prohibiting women from appearing publicly without 'proper attire.' Under increasing pressure from the community, the Mounted Police and the council eventually decided to remove them altogether, banning them from operating within the city limits from 1 May 1901.[8]

Of course, local opposition hoped that the so-called 'scarlet' women and their cohorts would find this second disruption sufficient encouragement to leave the territory altogether. But the authorities never went so far as actually to run them out of town or to suppress their activities in any rigorous way. (The NWMP were famous for issuing unwelcome foreigners with a 'blue ticket,' an order to leave on the next boat.) The women concerned were simply given notice to remove from Fourth and Fifth avenues. This last move actually put them outside the city limits altogether, further concentrating the red-light district across the river in Klondike City, or Lousetown.[9] The prostitutes, pimps, and their associates complied with the order and the authorities continued to tolerate their presence by prosecuting them infrequently. And while the new district was outside the legal limits of the city, it was in very close proximity.

Of course, just as the NWMP had predicted, outlawing prostitution within city limits only moved it underground and soon there were complaints that prostitutes were back in Dawson, operating brothels disguised as cigar stores and laundries. When only a few of these were prosecuted others moved back from Lousetown, and business continued as usual until complaints forced another flamboyant show of enforcement. This had the effect of temporarily quieting the moral opposition, but it seemed to do little to discourage the operators or their clientele.[10]

The Mounties took the same approach with public drunkenness, vagrancy, and dishonest gaming. Even though it was well known that gambling was illegal in Canada, most of Dawson's larger saloons freely operated gaming tables and wheels. In a community where wealth was easily gained and easily disposed of, gambling was simply accepted as a fact of life.[11] The NWMP were reluctant to ban open gambling, in fact, for fear of driving it underground. Superintendent Constantine's position was that the community was best served not only by allowing the gambling to continue but by allowing it to do so in the open, where it was more likely to be run honestly: 'All of the gambling in Dawson is done in the gambling halls, openly and subject to the observation of anyone and everyone; consequently what the miners call a square game is generally played. It was felt that if open gambling was suppressed, the gamblers would resort to secret methods.'[12] This graduated system of accommodation and control worked well in a community in constant flux, especially when the local authorities were willing to tolerate vice within certain limits. Conflict between local authorities and the demi-monde was minimized in this way, and the best interests of the community remained at the centre of law enforcement policy.

It was dissent from the South over the operation of the dance halls and gambling houses that shattered the system, undermining both local authority and the mutual respect achieved over time. The Laurier government in Ottawa came increasingly under fire in 1900, in southern Canada at least, for allowing an immoral and profligate atmosphere to prevail in the Yukon.[13] At Laurier's request, Clifford Sifton wrote again to the commissioner of the Yukon, stating that he had received a number of complaints about prostitutes frequenting and or being employed by saloons, in direct contravention of Canadian liquor laws. He then ordered the commissioner to 'summarily suppress' this practice, along with open gambling.[14]

Sifton and Laurier rested comfortably in the assumption that this would mark the end of gambling, vice, and immoral conduct in the Yukon, but they were soon disappointed. Commissioner Ogilvie responded with a direct refusal to implement the order: 'After much attention and consideration, ... it was deemed best to allow [gambling and the operation of dance halls] to go on as it was; and I may say that the members of Council are still of that opinion.'[15] It was obvious to the commissioner and the Mounted Police, who had to live in the community, that enforcing such an order from the authorities in Ottawa was not in the community's best interests, and further, that attempting to implement such an order would have disastrous results. The community had created its own balance between the 'red-light' activities and the more respectable everyday business and social life. Since it was generally accepted that prostitution and gambling were part of Klondike life, local sentiment deemed it preferable to regulate and control their open operation than to drive them underground. This was Ogilvie's position and he attempted to outline it to Sifton: 'Dance halls are an evil, which no one attempts to gainsay; but at the same time they are like many other evils, considered absolutely necessary under certain conditions. To abolish [dance halls] would be to throw a lot of women into a more vicious life, as many of these women would not resort to ordinary prostitution.'[16] Ogilvie implies here that his authorities were aware that some organized prostitution was occurring within the dance halls, but he clearly believed that this offered the female employees some degree of protection from abuses. Besides, he added, the council had often discussed what to do about prostitution in the dance halls but had failed to come up with any practicable solution.

It soon became clear that Ottawa was going to brook no argument on this issue. Sifton was furious over the refusal to implement a direct order and unsympathetic to Ogilvie's arguments. Sifton's Deputy Minister, James Smart, wrote to Ogilvie: 'I do not see that the ground taken by you is one that could be fairly advanced for the continuance of this evil.' That the suppression of these evils would drive the activity underground, 'could hardly, in this enlightened age, be such an argument as would appeal to the people of this country.' In Sifton's view there was no argument that 'would have any weight in justifying the violation of a law so well known and rigidly enforced in Canada.'[17] Local conditions in Dawson took a far back seat to the political heat Laurier and Sifton were feeling in Ottawa.

Ogilvie and Major Wood of the NWMP continued to defy Sifton's order, however, maintaining their position and claiming the support of both the Yukon Council and the community itself. They consented eventually to a system of tighter control, but stopped well short of the Laurier government's aim of complete closure of gambling and dance halls. Wood's compromise was to enforce new rules gradually, dragging his feet all the way, arresting and fining gamblers and ordering dance hall women and prostitutes out of the rooms over theatres and saloons. In this way, he argued, 'the immoral and gambling element'[18] might be encouraged to leave of their own accord. Mutual accommodation was still Wood's goal.

Of course dance halls, theatres, and casinos generated a great deal of revenue for many Dawson businesses. Once they realized that Ogilvie and Wood would be compelled to enforce the law, the operators of these establishments proved willing to adapt, and they moved from outright opposition to a plea for more time to make adjustments. Two dance hall proprietors complained, for example, that they had large amounts of local capital invested in their businesses and contracts with many of their performers for the duration of the winter of 1900-1. They asked to be allowed to stay open in order to meet their commitments over salary contracts, building leases, and paid-up liquor licences, conceding that if they could continue to operate they would more strictly control their female employees to prevent illicit activities.[19] Another letter in the same vein, this one from the manager of the Standard Theater added that enforcement of the law would force him to default on his liquor and dry goods contracts, harming other local businesses. He also stated that

> if the order preventing the sale of liquors by females is rigorously enforced ... a large number of people will be thrown out [of] employment at a season of the year when it is impossible for them to gain a livelihood in other lines; that a large volume of money will be taken out of circulation; that we will be compelled to meet our contract, leaving us penniless and in debt and that all branches of business in the city of Dawson and in particular dry goods and grocery houses will suffer severe losses.[20]

The proposed closure of dance halls and theatres prompted a vigorous response from Dawson's mercantile and business sector. The position of the dance hall operators was supported by a letter of petition by approximately a hundred other business people and merchants in Dawson in November 1900. The petition was accompanied by a letter from one of the local butchers, who stated that Dawson's entire commercial sector would be adversely affected by the proposed changes. He reiterated that a large number of people would be thrown out of work, harming the entire community.[21] And so the debate raged. In February of 1901 the Dawson Board of Trade again wrote to Sifton, supporting Major Wood and stating that it would be injurious to enforce the rule before the opening of navigation, for the large number of people who would face unemployment would have no way of leaving the country. They requested that the order be held in abeyance until 1 June 1901.[22]

It was clear as the winter progressed that the community was not willing to tolerate a ban on their only source of entertainment, and while the activities that continued nightly in the gambling and dance halls were illegal, the capital of the most respectable people in town was invested therein. Still, as much as the NWMP attempted to drag their feet on the enforcement issue, Wood and Ogilvie could not defy Ottawa's direct orders forever. When a telegram from the Department of the Interior arrived in January 1901, they had no choice. Wood commenced implementing the closure of the gambling and dance halls. Two days later he received notice that the Department had relented, 'in view of the representations' of the business community of Dawson. Executing a complete about-face, the Department announced that the dance halls and gambling houses would be allowed to re-open and continue to operate as requested until 1 June 1901.[23]

With some embarrassment, the Mounted Police had no choice but to allow the businesses to open up again. Understandably, as Ogilvie put it, the two back-to-back orders 'incensed a good many people' in town.[24] Local opposition to the dance halls, previously content in the knowledge that the establishments were gradually being regulated, became suddenly vociferous. Having had the theatres and gambling halls closed down for two days, they were irate when they were allowed to re-open.[25] For their part, the proprietors of the establishments and their patrons were angry at the disruption and lack of decisiveness on the part of authorities. The NWMP and Yukon Council were in a very difficult position, their authority having been completely undermined by a remote and autocratic federal government.

Performing on the Standard Theater Stage, 1901.

On the surface, the fight was all but over. On 1 June 1901 open gambling was outlawed, and in March of the following year the Yukon Council passed an ordinance prohibiting public dancing on all liquor-licensed premises. As time went on, however, the system of tolerance and accommodation was reinstated. Although gambling was strictly prohibited (and thus relegated to the 'back room' of cigar stores and saloons), the Mounties remained lenient regarding the operation of the dance halls. Until at least 1907, people still complained about the operation of the music halls and the dancing and drinking associated with them. The Orpheum Music Hall and the M & N Saloon, for example, were attached to each other and the female employees had private rooms that were also attached. Here, drinking, dancing, and prostitution continued, monitored but undisturbed, in the usual manner.[26]

When Robert Borden's Conservative government replaced Laurier's Liberals in 1911, the federal government renewed its insistence on enforcing liquor and anti-prostitution legislation. The new commissioner of the Yukon received his instructions in no uncertain terms: 'Use all the authority vested in you to secure such amendment to the liquor licence ordinance of the Yukon Territory and such other ordinances as bear upon the subject as to prevent the serving of liquor in any place of public entertainment or otherwise than over the bar according to the ordinary custom ... and to secure the prohibition of the serving of liquor or the attendance in the ordering of liquor by women.'[27]

When asked to investigate, the NWMP reported that the men they spoke to generally acknowledged that prostitution was still being carried on in the dance halls. They found about twenty women employed in each of the two remaining dance halls, many of them prostitutes who had previously worked in Lousetown or on the creeks.[28] The community itself, however, did not seem overly concerned about the situation. A new petition, signed by about forty merchants and other local business people, protested that the dance halls were operating under the provisions of the liquor ordinance, and posed 'no harmful influence upon any portion of the community.'[29] Legal, extra-legal, or otherwise, the community had little objection.

Local protestations to the contrary, the federal government wanted the issue resolved once and for all, and they ordered local authorities to revoke the liquor licences from the dance halls for the very last time. By December 1907, strict enforcement of the liquor ordinance had forced the M & N Saloon out of business, and the Flora Dora was conducting a

Many of the early cigar stores of Dawson were really small brothels in disguise, and it was difficult to distinguish between legitimate and exotic establishments.

much diminished trade, employing about fifteen women without a liquor licence.[30] By 1907, the system of mutual accommodation had given way to strict enforcement, especially where morality was concerned. With the closure of the dance halls and the rigorous monitoring of the liquor ordinances, the few people who remained employed in the sex and entertainment trades were forced to keep a low profile. If this profile was maintained, however, the NWMP turned a blind eye once more. As the superintendent of police informed the commissioner, there were still some women in town who, 'under the guise of dress-makers and keepers of cigar stores are said to be carrying on prostitution, but they are quiet, make no display on the streets, and except by reputation no one knows to what class they belong.'[31] No longer would the working women of Dawson paint their names on their doors or stand at a bar to solicit trade, but as long as they were discreet, the Mounted Police did not harass them.

Dawson's Scarlet Ladder: Social Hierarchy in the Demi-Monde
Throughout the debate over the control and regulation of prostitution in Dawson, the voices of the women who were most directly affected are absent from the record. The rules and regulations that determined the conditions of their work and daily lives changed without their input or consent. Yet hundreds of women worked in the sex and entertainment industry in Dawson, although until recently we knew very little about any of them. A look beneath the legal surface of the demi-monde reveals a highly structured and complicated social world.

There was a definite hierarchy among the women of Dawson. From their earliest arrival, non-Native women maintained a strict separation between those they described as 'respectable' and 'unrespectable.' Perhaps the clearest description of how women themselves perceived these distinctions is found in Martha Black's autobiography. There were three classes of Klondike women, according to Black: 'members of the oldest profession in the world, who ever follow armies and gold rushes; dance hall and variety girls, whose business was to entertain and be dancing partners; and a few others, wives with unbounded faith in and love for their mates, or the odd person like myself on a special mission.'[32] Respectable working women had a few, limited options, which included marriage and motherhood, teaching, nursing, and to a certain extent, small business. While several authors have recently attempted to debunk the myth that all Klondike women were prostitutes and dance hall performers, we still know very little about those involved in the sex and entertainment trades or indeed about the interaction of women of different racial and socio-economic backgrounds in Dawson.[33] Yet the life of red lights existed and a good number of women worked within it during the Klondike gold rush.

Dawson's scarlet world was complex and status within it depended on race, ethnicity, and sexual and social skills, among other things. Each woman found her place on the ladder, and each rung contained its own advantages and restrictions. The venues from which women carried out sexual commerce and other entertainments reflect this stratification. Kate Rockwell, a notorious dance hall performer of the period, commented at length on the strict hierarchy within the scarlet world of Dawson City. From her testimony it seems clear that for 'unrespectable' women, the hierarchy started with the dance halls and worked its way down. The top rung was reserved for the headline performers. Beneath these were what might be termed the middle class of the unrespectable women: the chorus performers, singers and dancers of lesser talent and renown, and the private mistresses of the local élite. Next came the working women from the more expensive brothels and the independents who often ran what they called 'cigar stores.' Farther down the ladder were the women who worked in the cheaper brothels and hurdy-gurdy houses. Finally, at the bottom of their own social scale were the women who lived and worked in the cribs of Paradise Alley. Here in the scarlet world of Dawson, social divisions were clear. This may very well be a common feature in mining camps, for Mary Murphy has found evidence of an almost identical stratification among prostitutes in Butte, Montana, in the same period.[34]

The highly paid, top-billed actresses, performers, and courtesans of Dawson enjoyed a prominent position in both the demi-monde and the larger community. Headliners like Rockwell and Cad Wilson were salaried employees of the dance halls, often with long-term contracts, who enjoyed a more stable and comfortable standard of living than chorus line women. They were given the choice numbers in the performances, were provided with accommodation by the theatre company, and had the lucrative job of entertaining men privately in 'boxes' between shows. Male box patrons paid a fee for being so privately entertained and were encouraged to purchase exorbitantly priced drinks, on which the women received a commission.

These women became legendary for sporting thousand-dollar Paris gowns in their performances and for decadent habits like bathing in champagne. Yet many of the dance hall queens also acted as hostesses in the dance halls after the shows, often wearing full-length black skirts and white shirtwaists rather than the feather boas and fishnet stockings we have come to associate with them. The more modest costume gave the illusion of middle-class respectability to the establishment, presumably to encourage a higher class of clientele and present a more attractive image. Due to their position, headliners enjoyed a degree of selectivity and had the option of becoming intimate with their admirers, but they did not normally engage in sexual intercourse for money. Government officials were well aware of this ambiguity, as the commissioner himself explained to the minister of the interior when advising him against shutting down the dance halls, noting that to do so would force many performers into prostitution as a last resort.[35]

Next down the ladder from the headline performers were the chorus line dancers. These were the women who 'worked the floor' after the stage show, dancing with the miners and encouraging them to buy drinks. The dancers, like the headline acts, were also paid employees and likewise received a percentage for drinks sold. Chorus performers sometimes – although not always – held contracts and thus enjoyed some job security. Like the headliners, chorus line women might or might not be prostitutes, for as Rockwell herself noted, the line between performers and prostitutes was a fine one and 'sometimes a girl blended.' This 'blending' is clear in the Mounted Police records, which show that they occasionally arrested dance hall performers on charges of prostitution.[36]

Dance hall women, however glamorous they may have appeared to their customers, worked gruelling hours: six nights per week, often in twelve-hour shifts, ending at seven or eight in the morning. (The dance halls were closed only on Sundays.) According to one of their clients, the women's usual duties consisted of performing on stage, then 'rustling the boxes,' which he described as entertaining a miner in a private box and encouraging him to order drinks. After the show, around midnight, women employees were expected to mingle with the crowd on the floor, partnering dances for a dollar each and selling more drinks. Remarked a sympathetic young man from Ottawa, 'These poor devils keep this up night after night, all year round, drunk every night as they cannot help it if they want to do business.' For the long hours, the regular employees earned between $150 to $200 per month plus commissions – more than double the salary of a male clerk in the Office of the Gold Commissioner.[37] It was hard work, however, and the life was extremely expensive. Rockwell remembered that the performers all had to purchase their own costumes and to change both their routines and costumes frequently in order to maintain their top rung positions.

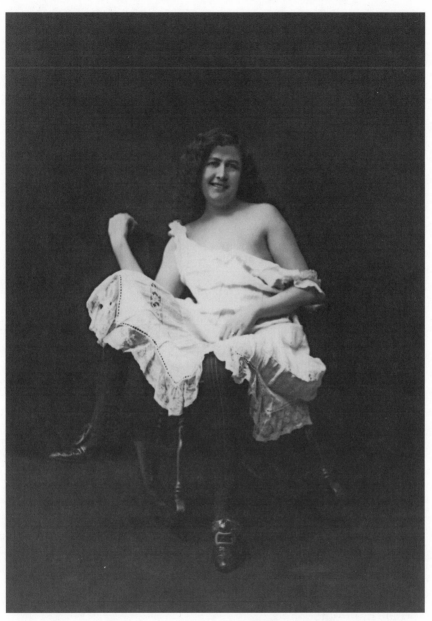

The dance hall performer known as the Belgian Queen poses for the camera in a local studio.

Of course some of the performing women were prostitutes as well as vaudeville performers, but it is impossible to state with any certainty what proportion practised both trades. Certainly several women inmates of the Dawson jail were both dance hall employees and common prostitutes. Kitty Henry was one of these. In 1901 Henry reported herself as an actress and dance hall employee. A year later she found herself charged with being drunk and disorderly when the Mounted Police arrested her along with her pimp, Felix Duplan. Kitty Henry – alias Katherine Howard – was described by the arresting officer as a camp follower, most lately of Cripple Creek, Colorado. The Mounted Police recorded her occupation as 'soubrette [housemaid] and prostitute.' Meanwhile, her Paris-born pimp, Felix Duplan was arrested for living 'off the avails.' In an all-too-common series of events, the judge convicted Kitty Henry and sentenced her to one month at hard labour but acquitted Duplan.[38]

The Howard and Duplan cases allow historians a small window into the world of Dawson dance hall women who moonlighted as prostitutes. For we see that while it was all too easy to convict women for prostitution or on related charges such as drunkenness, it was extremely difficult to prosecute the men who profited from their labours. When another prostitute who allegedly worked for Duplan failed to appear to testify against him, there was not enough evidence to pursue the case. The charges were dropped and Duplan was released. Presumably women who worked in Dawson's demi-monde feared the almost certain reprisals that would have accompanied such a court appearance. This appears to have been the case throughout the period; far more women prostitutes were arrested and convicted than were their pimps.

Jennie Mack was another Dawson 'dance hall woman and prostitute' arrested by the Mounted Police in 1900. Before arriving in Dawson, she had operated the Pioneer Lodging House, a small brothel in Seattle. No stranger to the police, Jennie Mack had several aliases, including Mrs Warnick, Mrs McSwain, and Mrs C.H. Furrar. She spent two years in the Dawson jail after the Mounties arrested her for 'theft from the person' of one George Blondeau. Mack, like many other dance hall performers, lived in a room over one of the dance halls, where she supplemented her income by prostitution.[39]

In addition to the headliners and chorus line women, the dance halls employed a third group of women to work the floor after the show for a small wage and commission. They recruited women from the streets of the red-light district and hired them on a casual basis. These employees also encouraged men to buy drinks before offering them 'other' entertainments in the rooms upstairs or down the street. These women were open prostitutes, a fact well known to the Mounted Police. Here, then, is the brush with which all women in this sector were tarred, for it is easy to see how dance hall performers and prostitutes 'blended' in their own world, as well as in the eyes of the public.[40]

The majority of the sex trade was conducted outside the dance halls. Here the hierarchy of the demi-monde is also in evidence. In more expensive brothels and parlour houses, madams presided in offering men cigars, liquor, and music or dancing before negotiating more intimate entertainments. Women who worked in the higher priced establishments gained a degree of privacy and 'refinement' and charged higher prices for services. Less 'refined' brothels offered their clientele a variety of lower class entertainments and a wide assortment of nationalities of women. The Bartlett, for example, was a Dawson brothel specializing in exotic women. Kept by a French couple, Luceille Martin and Jean Lucin Robert, the Bartlett employed the services of at least three other French-born women, including Martin's sister, Marceille. The rest of the payroll included one African American woman and women of English, Japanese, and Hungarian birth. Miners were accustomed to this type of 'selection,' it seems, for Mary Murphy found that a number of brothels in Montana mining camps similarly specialized in exotic women in this period. Whether they worked the mines in Montana or the Yukon, gold miners demonstrated a distinct preference for French women.[41]

Brothels also operated in a highly competitive market. In Dawson this meant more than simply offering a selection of ethnicities. Some brothels and parlour houses attempted to lure customers by offering exotic entertainments. In Dawson's demi-monde, it was the Bartlett once again that gained notoriety. The Mounted Police noted that this establishment offered 'grossly indecent' burlesque shows in addition to the more usual sexual commerce between individual women and their clients. This type of entertainment was apparently well beyond the limits of Dawson City moral tolerance, for the show resulted in the arrest of three female employees as well as one of the proprietors. The women were each convicted on the charge of being a 'prostitute participating in exhibitions of a grossly indecent nature' and sentenced to two months at hard labour. The male proprietor was convicted of 'vagrancy' and for living as a 'macque' or pimp.[42] Even in Dawson City, the community had limits to the indecencies it would allow.

Located on a rung slightly below the brothels and parlour houses of Dawson were the 'cigar stores.' Cigar stores as a rule were very small operations, usually with an independent woman proprietor, occasionally in association with a procurer. Often such operations were private apartments or cabins with a simple sign above the door. Since the operators of such establishments could not legally sell sex or liquor, the proprietors improvised and advertised cigars as the commodity for sale – hence their euphemistic title. These women set their own conditions and hours of work, and presumably also their own fees. Camille Léonard for example, worked as a dancer and also ran her own 'cigar store' at the turn of the century. Camille, who had arrived in Dawson in 1899, was by 1901 residing on Second Avenue and earning a monthly salary of $200 per month as a dancer. It would appear, however, that 'French Camille' had a hard time making ends meet as a dancer, for the city directory for the same year lists her as the proprietor of the Seattle Cigar and Tobacco Store at the same address. That she was getting rich at either occupation is doubtful, for after three years in the Yukon, the twenty-seven year old Léonard had accumulated only $100 in personal assets and held no real estate or mining property.[43] The Mounties, as noted earlier, turned a blind eye to the so-called cigar trade, considering it the lesser of many evils in town.

Perhaps the best known of the Dawson's self-described tobacconists was Marguerite Laimee. Laimee was an American woman who had followed the mining camps from California, where she was born, to Idaho, South Africa, and Australia. Arriving in Dawson in July 1898 from Sydney, she at once opened a cigar store in the Green Tree Hotel on Front Street. She later relocated to the corner of Second and Lane, where the Mounted Police monitored her activities as a prostitute. Laimee apparently prospered at her trade, for she later testified under oath that she made $60,000 in two years at her Dawson trade.[44] In 1901, Laimee realized the dream of many Dawson prostitutes, trading in the hazards of the oldest profession for marriage to a wealthy miner, George Carmack, who severed his connection with Kate at about the same time. Like many 'unrespectable' women, the new Mrs Carmack abandoned all connection with prostitution upon her marriage and later denied her previous means of employment.

If Laimee made a substantial sum of money as a prostitute in Dawson, however, she appears to have been the exception. For very few prostitutes were able to accumulate much in the way of wealth or property during the Klondike gold rush. Indeed, at the time of the census in 1901, only a tiny handful reported assets or property over $400 in value.

It is possible, of course, that these young women were reluctant to report their income to government officials, yet the records indicate that the vast majority held no real estate and no personal property of value. Just as they do today, pimps, drugs, and alcohol swallowed up a good portion of these women's income. It is also possible that women who made substantial sums of money left the Territory quickly and re-established themselves elsewhere.

Dance hall performers fared better than prostitutes, yet these women also lived close to the edge of poverty. Kate Rockwell's biographer notes that at the height of her Dawson career, the performer was pulling in 'thousands of dollars a month' but even if this was true, it was also an expensive lifestyle to maintain, and Kate was unable to retain much of her earnings. The census taker recorded Rockwell's salary at $200 per month in 1901. That this 'salary' did not include her commissions seems clear, although there is no way of calculating what the additional income would have amounted to or how much it fluctuated seasonally. Rockwell reported personal and real estate assets of $100 in 1901.[45] She later lost what little money she had saved by investing in bad business ventures with her lover, Alex Pantages. Nearly all of the other female dance hall employees reported assets and property valued at under $400, indicating that whatever their incomes, poverty was never far away.

Last in the red-light hierarchy were the women who plied their trade from the rows of cribs or hutches that lined the streets and alleys of Dawson and Lousetown. These working women are the most difficult to document, for they above all others do not speak for themselves in the sources. Early photographs of Lousetown show one street with approximately sixty cribs side by side. Contemporaries noted that each hutch was a room occupied by a single prostitute, each with her name clearly painted over the door. The usual practice was for the woman to draw the blinds when she was 'entertaining' a client, and to open them when she was available. Business was brisk, especially after spring clean-up, and the more popular prostitutes often found queues of men waiting when they pulled up the blinds.[46]

Some of these prostitutes worked the floors of the dance halls to supplement their income and solicit clients. Many split their time between prostitution and other service sector employment such as needle, laundry, or restaurant work. Elizabeth Davis Brooks is a typical example of one of these impoverished working women. Brooks reported to the census taker in 1901 that she was a 'self-employed seamstress' earning $175 per month.

Most working prostitutes in Dawson led a much less glamorous life than the popular literature depicted. Here an uncorseted group of women pose in front of their cribs. Drugs, alcohol, and poverty were common companions of Klondike prostitutes.

MIDNIGHT HOUR
OSHIWORA, OR "WHITE CHAPEL" OF DAWSON,

The romantic stereotype of the frontier prostitute almost never held true. Here in the one-room 'cribs,' working women plied their trade in Paradise Alley — an alley often clogged with both mud and men.

When the Mounted Police arrested Brooks the following year as an inmate in a house of ill fame, they left little doubt that the needle trade did not form the major source of her income. Elizabeth Brooks was a 'prostitute by occupation.'[47] However she made her living, she was barely making ends meet, for after three years in Dawson she had accumulated assets of less than $200.

Like many prostitutes of the nineteenth century, Brooks was a highly transient woman. Born in Meritz, Germany, she arrived in New York in 1877. The following year she went to Minneapolis and from there to the gold and silver camps of Colorado. Here she remained until setting out for Dawson in 1898. When she appeared in police court in 1902, the judge convicted her of residing in a house of ill fame, fined her $50, and sentenced her to two months at hard labour. The two African American women arrested in company with Brooks received lesser sentences of one month hard labour in addition to their fines. The reason for the difference in sentencing is unclear. In the predominantly Caucasian world of Dawson City, one might expect to find that the courts treated African American women more harshly than others, yet the evidence – Brooks was described in the police record as Caucasian, of 'neutral complexion' – seems to indicate the contrary.[48]

Brooks's African American partners were Josephine Arnold and Millie Wallace Brown. Arnold and Brown were sisters who had arrived in Dawson in 1898 and three years later reported themselves laundresses. It appears that they were employed in both trades, for the jail records state that each was a 'prostitute and laundress' by occupation. At the time of the census they were living together on Third Avenue, in the cabin next to Elizabeth Brooks. Like Brooks, these women had moved frequently, although they had been living in Dawson for four years by the time of the census. Arnold resided in Arizona prior to coming to the Klondike and listed an estranged husband in Vancouver. Brown reported coming to Dawson with her husband, having last resided in California. Brown's husband, Charles Wallace, also resided at the same address on Third Avenue and is listed as a bartender, a common local euphemism for pimp. He may have been acting as the sisters' procurer, although the Mounties did not arrest him at the time.[49] Like so many other red-light households – and it is worth noting that in 1901 they were once again living in the neighbourhood from which they had been ordered to remove in 1899 – the existence of this one was tenuous. Between them, Arnold, Wallace, and Brown reported a total of $400 in personal property in 1901.[50]

Scarlet Culture: Ethnicity in the Demi-Monde

If the demi-monde was hierarchical, it was also an overwhelmingly international and impoverished group of people. The dance hall performers were nearly all American; the prostitutes and their procurers in Dawson were largely European.[51] Gamblers, musicians, bartenders, and other 'sports' associated with this subcommunity were similarly of an international background. Very few of these people accumulated any wealth while in Dawson.

Although historians have made numerous estimates of the number of people who belonged to the demi-monde, there exist no reliable figures. In the dance halls alone, the figure was probably in the neighbourhood of 500 in 1898. By the fall of 1901, 110 persons were employed as performers and entertainers according to the census, and more than half of these were women. The vast majority were young Americans, but a significant number of French, Belgian, German, English, Mexican, Austrian, and Spanish women also found employment in this sector.[52]

Closer examination of the women in the sex and entertainment sector reveals much about the world within which they lived. As a group the performers were slightly younger than the average Dawson male, ranging from eighteen to forty years with an average age of twenty-six. They were also slightly more affluent, earning an average salary of $200 per month. Their incomes came and went just as quickly, however, for over 70 percent claimed personal assets equalling no more than $100. Although one might have expected dance hall performers to display a high degree of transience, by the fall of 1901, over 65 percent had been residents for three years or more, indicating that the work was steady enough and the wages high enough to encourage some stability within the ranks. The popular image of a rotating swirl of actresses and dancers remains astonishingly unchanged, but in reality a good many women lived and worked in Dawson for the duration of the rush. Only a handful of entertainers had been resident less than a year.[53]

Women who worked as prostitutes are more difficult to document than those who worked as dancers. In the fall of 1898, the Mounted Police raided the red-light district in Dawson and arrested sixty-nine women. Each woman was convicted of being an inmate of a house of ill fame and fined $50 plus court costs. That a significant group of women was living and working in 'houses of ill fame' is corroborated by numerous diaries and memoirs.[54] Building a profile of these women's lives and work proves difficult, however, for it is only when they came into prolonged contact with the law – when they were sentenced to prison – that we find detailed records for them. For the sixty-nine women arrested in September 1898, there is only a list of names. Because they were simply fined and released their records are incomplete. None of them appears in the jail registers, even at a later date, although seven appear in the 1901 census.

The *Dawson Gaol Register* contains very detailed information for fifteen known prostitutes incarcerated between 1898 and 1903. The *Register* gives inmates' place of birth, previous residences, medical and family history, as well as elaborate physical descriptions of the women themselves. By cross-referencing the police and jail records with the 1901 census, we find detailed information about another forty-three prostitutes, including seven of those who had been arrested in 1898. Altogether, using all these sources, it is possible to find fifty-eight women in the sex trade about whom more is known than simply a name. Most of them gave the usual euphemisms for their official occupations: dressmaker, housekeeper, tobacconist.

Looking at this group of fifty-eight women, we can learn much about the daily lives and experiences of Klondike prostitutes. First, they tended to be older than the dance hall performers, their ages ranging from twenty to forty-three with an average of twenty-nine. Many prostitutes followed the miners from camp to camp – from Aspen and Cripple Creek to Dawson, then to Nome and back – providing the services they knew to be in high demand. Yet like the dance hall performers, many prostitutes called Dawson their home for extended periods. Twenty of the fifty-eight – a full 35 percent – had lived in Dawson for four years or longer at the time of the 1901 census.

Prostitutes represented an ethnic diversity of significantly different proportion to the general population. Over half of the women were European born, and a full 31 percent of these were born in France. This figure may actually be a little low, for the Mounted Police noted in 1899 that the majority of the forty-three newly relocated prostitutes on Fourth Avenue were French.[55] A number of oldtimers, including Joseph Charles Dubé, Martha Black, and Ed Lung, also recalled that a large group of French-speaking Belgian prostitutes arrived in Dawson in 1898.[56] The number of French women was balanced somewhat by the African Americans and Euro-Americans – each representing about 15 percent. The other prostitutes came from a variety of nations, with Germans, English, Belgians, Swedes, Canadians, Irish, Hungarians, and Japanese together making up 40 percent. Yukon Native women did not live or work in association with any of the known brothels, prostitutes, or procurers in Dawson during the boom period.

The balance favouring French women is a curious aberration in the ethnic breakdown in Dawson, although it appears to have been similar to other frontier mining communities. During the same period, a large proportion of prostitutes on the Comstock in Nevada and in Butte, Montana, were also French born, a pattern apparently established in the 1850s in California.[57] Although we have no business records with which to verify the implication, we might infer that French prostitutes derived both a higher status and higher wages for their services.

The legends of the Klondike have often conjured up images of wealthy miners freely distributing their wealth among prostitutes, dance hall women, and faro wheels. The women prostitutes of Dawson, however, lived in almost universal poverty. Financial information taken from the 1901 census shows that the vast majority were struggling. This was little different from the other gold camps in which these women had lived; Anne Butler and Marion Goldman have found that prostitutes from Nevada to Montana were among the poorest residents of nineteenth-century mining communities.[58]

There are of course no official figures for the cost of a visit to a prostitute in Dawson. Although hundreds of Klondikers recorded all manner of events and experiences in their diaries and memoirs, only one made reference to the cost of a visit to a Dawson prostitute. Edward Trelawney-Ansell was the brave sourdough who stated in his memoir that the price generally ran to four ounces of gold dust – about $64 – for what he considered a 'very hurried entertainment.'[59] Trelawney-Ansell's memoir is silent about whether this price was standard, but presumably it fluctuated depending on the size and calibre of the brothel and the individual service requested by the client.

Certainly $64 seems an incredible fee considering that miners were making $75 per month on many claims. That most Dawson prostitutes were not realizing huge profits is demonstrated by the census, which shows that over 80 percent declared personal and real estate assets valued at less than $300, and most of these declared $100 or less. Prostitutes, of course, shared their fees with their madams, pimps, and lovers and had their own costs of living. Again, the record is silent on how these negotiations worked out for the individual women involved.

Only seven of the prostitutes identified in the 1901 census held property valued at between $400 and $1,500. Less than 1 percent owned mining claims, while 2 percent owned real estate or dogs. (Dogs were valu-able assets in the Klondike because most winter transportation was by dogsled. The Yukon census in 1901 had a separate column for dogs and the usual value was assessed at $50 each.) Given the extraordinary cost of living in Dawson and the high costs of transportation for those who chose to spend the winters outside the Yukon, even $400 would quickly have been disposed of, leaving little or no security. In an economy in which fuel for the winter months could easily exceed $150, the existence of a Yukon prostitute was tenuous at best.

Prostitutes employed various strategies to survive the high costs of liv-ing and seasonal unemployment so characteristic of life in Dawson. Hundreds of prostitutes came and went every summer, avoiding the slow winter season when living costs were highest. Some spent only a single summer in the Yukon while others spent the winters in the South, return-ing annually for spring clean-up when the miners headed back to town. The women who could not afford to travel tried to survive the long slow winter season by working as laundresses, dancers, and waitresses. Once spring clean-up began and new wealth was freed from the Yukon gravel, however, women in this industry had to be ready for the spree and the party that followed. Indeed, many prostitutes migrated to roadhouses along the creeks each May in order to gain the gold closer to its source.[60] If they had spent the winter Outside, these professionals rushed back as soon as navigation opened in order to take full advantage.

Financial security was a crucial issue for working women in the Yukon, especially as the long, harsh winter approached. The scarce sup-ply and exorbitant cost of fuel and provisions required a good deal of planning and stockpiling for winter survival – not easily accomplished in the unstable demi-monde. Given the high cost of living, many Dawsonites combined more than one occupation in order to support themselves and their families, and women within the red-light districts were no exception to this pattern. Many combined incomes drawn as laundresses, dress-makers, waitresses, performers, and prostitutes.

Some women combined the sex trade with domestic service by becoming mistresses. One woman contemporary noted, for example, that many of the men in Dawson had live-in 'housekeepers or cooks' who were really their mistresses, and that this made it virtually impossible to distin-guish the respectable from the unrespectable women in town.[61] For some, like Jeremiah Lynch, the matter was clear: 'There was no honest occupa-tion for women [in the Klondike]. Many went professedly as housekeepers to miners who were rich enough to employ one; but it was only another name.'[62] Many Dawsonites, then, felt no need to sort out which 'dressmakers' and 'housekeepers' really practised a trade that involved no needles and very little soap: they were all whores. For the women who made their livings as legitimate dressmakers or laundresses, encountering the attitudes of men like Jeremiah Lynch must have been most uncomfortable.

A number of known prostitutes in Dawson supplemented their usual wages with proceeds from other illegal activities. This was apparently common throughout the Canadian and American wests, for Anne Butler has found that the dynamics of the demi-monde – high costs of living, drug and alcohol habits, and dishonest pimps and lovers – encouraged women to engage in criminal activities. It is therefore perhaps not surprising to find that a number of Dawson prostitutes were also arrested for thieving. Maggie Richardson, for example, had 'maintained herself at different periods by prostitution' in Minnesota, Vancouver, and Seattle before the Mounted Police arrested her in Dawson in 1903. The judge convicted Richardson of relieving Edward Lecernes – presumably her client – of $185 in excess of her established price. Annie Gallina was known to her clients as the 'Irish Queen.' Gallina was a twenty-five-year-old prostitute who found herself under arrest for theft in August 1900. A naturalized American of Irish birth, Gallina left an estranged husband in Seattle in 1900 to come to Dawson, making it the eighth in a string of cities in which she had lived since 1887. Like the Irish Queen, several other women, including Eva Terry Emilson, Stella Freudenthal, and Jennie Mack, were similarly convicted of theft. The objects of their crime were usually their clients, although these seemed somewhat reluctant to report such crimes.[63]

Prostitutes used a variety of strategies to survive the Yukon winters. Mabel Larose got around her problem of seasonal unemployment by auctioning herself off for the winter of 1897-8 in the Monte Carlo Saloon. Larose reportedly received room, board, and $5,000 in exchange for her exclusive domestic services.[64] Another account claims that a Dawson paramour received $20,000 for spending two winters with the same miner.[65] More commonly, prostitutes who could afford the passage went elsewhere in the winter, plying their trade in the coastal cities of the Pacific Northwest. The remaining women found work within the local saloons, restaurants, and laundries, managing – more or less – to survive until spring clean-up and the busy season recommenced.

Women in the Klondike were a scarce and valuable commodity. There are numerous stories of men offering to buy women for their weight in gold or some such seemingly preposterous sum. Indeed, one oldtimer remembered Bob Ensley offering a woman known as Little Blanche just that if she would marry him in 1898: 'The scales were set up in the M&M [M & N] Saloon and the transaction completed.'[66] Regardless of her respectability, a woman was a commodity that could bring high returns in Dawson. But being a commodity, whatever the price, brought with it a number of potential dangers and limitations. Women under long-term theatre contracts, for example, while ensuring themselves winter salaries and employment were often considered the personal property of their managers. Similar to the European prostitutes recruited by French pimps, these women's personal and professional lives were circumscribed by their relationship with their employers and lovers.

The hazards of the scarlet life were many in Dawson. In addition to seasonal unemployment, a young prostitute's world contained poverty, disease, violence, drugs, and alcohol. Typhoid epidemics were indiscriminate in their victims but struck especially hard at those living in the close quarters of Lousetown. Venereal disease, always a professional hazard, reached epidemic proportions in 1899. Other forms of malaise appeared in the demi-monde as well. From the detailed drawings contained in her police file, it appears that Josephine Arnold attempted suicide on more than one occasion. The knife scars on her wrists bear silent testament to the despair of a young African American prostitute. Local officials committed Annie Gallina, the Irish Queen, for insanity in 1902.[67]

Personal relationships between men and women were difficult to maintain in the demi-monde of Dawson. 'Klondike Kate' Rockwell reported that most of her colleagues in the dance halls were trapped by unsteady employment and by turbulent, often violent relationships with men. Indeed, a number of violent incidents involving women of the demi-monde were reported in the local newspapers. Stella Hill, a local dance hall performer, committed suicide by swallowing strychnine in December 1898 after being jilted by a local bartender – her lover and pimp. Myrtle Brocee shot herself in her room over Sam Bonnifield's saloon after an argument with her lover, Harry Woolrich. In February 1898, Libby White, a forty-three-year-old 'promiscuous' woman, was shot by her jealous lover, who then killed himself. Such acts of violence and desperation were the extreme, but they indicate the potential dangers of daily life for women in Dawson's demi-monde.[68]

Like Stella Hill, many dancers and prostitutes had lovers who were also their theatrical agents, managers, or pimps. Others, such as Kitty

Rockwell, took up with the gamblers, bartenders, and musicians they met and worked with in the dance halls and saloons. Indeed, when Rockwell commented on the low calibre of her colleagues' boyfriends, she knew whereof she spoke. She had invested all her savings in theatrical endeavours, first in Dawson itself and then in Victoria and Seattle with her lover, the penniless and philandering Alexander Pantages. She eventually lost it all, including Pantages himself.[69]

In many instances, however, women negotiated good terms for themselves. One wealthy Italian miner in 1897 reportedly entered a written contract to pay his 'housekeeper' $500 a week. He was also reported to have 'cleaned the town out of silks and satins' in order to indulge his housekeeper's tastes.[70] What she was required to do in return and the degree to which these were her own terms is unknown, but it seems clear that as short-term employment, this was a lucrative contract.

Of course, such 'housekeepers' held their employment quite literally at the pleasure of their lovers. If her employer suspected her of flirting with another man, or tired of her for any reason, the woman might find herself out on the street without recourse. This was exactly the fate of Babe Pyne, who was living with Jack Glover in Dawson in 1899. When Glover tired of Babe's habit of 'constantly drinking Absynthe and Whiskey,' he threw her and all of her belongings unceremoniously out of his cabin.[71] Of course, women like Pyne also exposed themselves to the potential of abuse and violence in these situations.

Employment in the entertainment and sex trade offered women access to a larger pool of male clients, and among them many women found marriage partners and lovers – for better or for worse. Marguerite Laimee gave up her evening profession to marry George Carmack. Laimee gained financial security rather than social acceptance, however, for Carmack, the notorious 'squaw man,' was of questionable respectability. Despite Carmack's great wealth the couple never gained entry into polite Dawson society, although there is no reason to believe that they desired to do so.

Laimee's experience was in no way unusual. Many women of 'questionable' background married well in the Klondike, and although some may have become 'respectable,' they rarely became part of the inner sanctum. Dolly Orchard, for example, was a former dance hall performer who married Jimmy Turner, a prominent local assayer. Turner discovered that polite society no longer welcomed him after his marriage, due to his wife's former occupation. As one socialite editorialized, though many dance hall women probably made good housewives, 'very few invaded the sacred precincts of Dawson society.'[72] Once they married they also changed their names and disappeared from the record, making it difficult for historians to trace them.

One sourdough noted later that many of the dance hall women married in Dawson and lived respectable lives and 'people were not aware of their background.' While it is true that dance hall performer Babe Wallace married and then divorced Hill Barrington, and 'Dirty Maude' married Sid Barrington, it is doubtful whether Dawson society ever 'forgot' these women's earlier professional careers. Dolly Mitchell, another dance hall performer, met and married William Crawford Sime, who had arrived as a clerk for the Bank of Commerce in 1898. The Simes family, like the Barringtons, never gained access to the inner circle of Klondike life.[73]

Marriage did not always ensure escape from the demi-monde, however, for some 'scarlet women' found marriage partners within that world. Gussie Anderson, born Lillian Green, was a performer who worked at the Palace Grand Theater. She married her boss, proprietor James Hall. This match, although worse in the long run for Gussie than for Hall, was opposed by Hall's friends. After failing to talk him out of his plans, they convinced the Mounted Police to arrest and declare him insane two days before his marriage. Presumably Hall's confinement was intended to allow the prospective groom a 'cooling off' period to reconsider. The couple were wed, but Hall was a heavy drinker and the match was marked by violence and general unhappiness. Hall eventually committed suicide, leaving Gussie to fend for herself, alone once more.[74]

Lulu Mae Eads was a dance hall performer who came to Dawson with a Mexican trumpet player named Lopez in 1900. Like Gussie Anderson, she soon married her boss, Murray Eads, proprietor of the Monte Carlo Dance Hall, and together they operated a Dawson hotel for the next twenty years. Never very respectable, Lulu Mae was charged in 1907 with allowing loose women to frequent her premises.[75] Lulu and Murray remained in the hotel business until they perished in a shipwreck in 1918.

Members of the demi-monde were a close-knit community themselves. Señor Lopez, Lulu Eads's travelling companion in 1900, played in the orchestra led by Adolph Freimuth. Freimuth was a German-born musician who came to Dawson at the turn of the century with a theatrical troupe that included Kate Rockwell. Nellie Palb James, an English dance hall performer in Lousetown, married Freimuth shortly after his arrival.[76]

In general, however, family and home life were almost nonexistent for dance hall performers and prostitutes. Not only did these women travel a significant distance to reach the Yukon, but most of them were alone. A few, like Josephine Arnold and Millie Brown and Luceille and Marceille Martin lived and worked as sisters. Another, Annie Gallina, had a brother who was working for the White Pass Railway in Alaska. But most were far from home, family, and friends. A number cohabited with male lovers, but few married. Those who did seemed to enjoy little conjugal bliss, and even fewer managed to live with or near their children. Significantly, only one of the fifty-eight prostitutes identified had any children living with her in 1901.[77]

It is likely that, similar to other stampeders, women who worked as prostitutes went to the Klondike seeking higher wages and left their dependants in the care of family or friends Outside. At least one known prostitute, Stella Hunter Freudenthal, did just that. She left her child in her home state of New York in 1900 when she set out for the Klondike. She spent the winter of 1901-2 in Washington, visiting family and supporting herself during the slow winter season outside Dawson. Freudenthal returned to Dawson in March of 1902, shortly before being arrested for theft.[78] Like the more 'respectable' women, family visits for prostitutes were made only when the means were available, and what little money they managed to save they probably sent south for their children's welfare.

Of course, this tactic was not restricted to the women of the red-light district. Georgia White and Martha Black are two examples of the many 'respectable' women who left their children in the care of others in the South for extended periods while they were in the Yukon.[79]

Pimps and Procurers: The Other Side of the Scarlet Life

Dawson prostitutes were often recruited and brought to the Klondike by their pimps, lovers, and husbands. There are few references to these men who controlled and did trade in women. It seems clear, however, that procurers were early on the scene, for one stampeder noted that a number of the first Dawson prostitutes were brought in by 'polygamous bartenders' in March 1897. This commentator noted that the demi-monde was hot on the trail to Dawson that year, and the city was soon full of 'contraband whisky pedlars, gamblers, Jews, Gentiles, [and] ladies whose briefness of skirt barely equalled the briefness of their characters.'[80] Respectability was assessed and assigned to individuals as they arrived.

Although evidence is scarce on the procurers as a rule, four of the seven men arrested in connection with prostitution in Dawson City were

French born. The Mounted Police identified them as Felix Duplan, Clement Laborde, Jean Lucin Robert, and Frank Salets. Two of these worked in association with the Bartlett. The Bartlett was that infamous brothel described by the Mounties as 'a notorious house of assignation giving exhibitions of a disgusting nature.'[81]

Parisian Jean Robert and his lover, Luceille Martin, were the joint proprietors of the Bartlett. When three of Robert and Martin's French employees were arrested for their 'exhibitions,' Robert was charged with living off the avails of prostitution. The police recorded his occupation as 'macque' or procurer. Robert claimed to have been a banker in Paris, but the Mounted Police were certain that he had 'been engaged in his present occupation in London, England' before arriving in Dawson. Robert seems to have recruited a number of the women 'inmates' of the Bartlett, for Luceille and Marceille Martin arrived from France in February 1902, the same date Jean Robert and another Parisian pimp named Felix Duplan both arrived. Louise Coragod, another French prostitute, arrived a few weeks later.[82]

The link between Robert's pimping operation in 1902 and earlier French prostitution seems to have been Felix Duplan. Duplan, a Parisian-born macque, also found himself arrested for living off the avails of prostitution in 1902. Duplan had first come to Dawson in February 1898, the same time that Kitty Henry had arrived from Cripple Creek, Colorado. In 1900, he returned to Paris, arriving back in Dawson on 25 February 1902. That his return from France corresponds exactly with the arrival of Jean Lucin Robert and the three French prostitutes subsequently employed by the Bartlett indicates that he had been on another recruiting mission.[83] It is likely that Duplan and Robert, as well as Clement Laborde and Frank Salets, were part of the French Connection that brought at least some of the many other French women to Dawson for the sex trade. Men like Duplan and Robert presumably fronted the travel expenses in return for a percentage of the women's earnings in Dawson.

The Mounted Police were often unable to prosecute men on charges of procuring, for it was very difficult to obtain the testimony necessary for their convictions from prostitutes. This is not surprising, since the women were often romantically involved with their pimps, and they relied on them for protection and security. Many prostitutes were also indentured to their procurers for their passage inward. Thus, when their friends or lovers lied on the stand or refused to testify, procurers charged with living off the avails found the charges either dropped or reduced to vagrancy. Since 'vagrancy' was a charge for a host of undesirable activities, it is very difficult to distinguish the procurers from among the many other 'vagrants.'

Still, there are instances when the vagrants' specific indiscretions were recorded by the North West Mounted Police. When the police arrested eighty-two men in the Lousetown raid in September 1898, they charged them all with vagrancy. This is an inordinately high number, and it seems likely that the group included men who were associated with the sex trade, either as procurers, bartenders, waiters, or even clients, although these details are not available in the record. Between 1898 and 1903 five inmates of the Dawson jail found themselves convicted of vagrancy for living off the avails of prostitution or being a 'close associate of prostitutes.' These included all of the male members of the French Connection, as well John Henry Kimball, an American 'mulatto' and 'morphine fiend.' Another man, Enoch Emmons, found himself convicted of vagrancy and chastised for allowing his wife to be a harlot. When the police were determined to prosecute, it seems, convictions were indeed possible.[84]

The Clientele: Patrons of the Demi-Monde

If it is difficult to distinguish dressmakers from prostitutes, prostitutes from chorus line performers, and procurers from legitimate bartenders, it is even more difficult to establish the make-up of their clientele. It seems safe to say that it was male. Beyond that, there is little evidence to establish what proportion of the clientele was made up of merchants, professionals, tradesmen, or labourers. Of course, it seems likely that miners and labourers – especially during the peak period after spring clean-up – were the largest group. Still, the authors of numerous Klondike diaries and memoirs agree that the clientele came from every strata of Dawson life, from the highest ranking officials to the lowest of the down-and-out.

In the 1898 raid of the red-light district, the police arrested and charged eighty-two men and sixty-nine women. Despite their efforts to bring some moral and social control to the district by raids and arrests in 1898, the Mounted Police arrested and convicted only one man on a charge specifically related to purchasing sexual favours. One Mr F. Brown of Dawson was convicted of 'frequenting a house of ill fame'[85] and thus earns the historical distinction of being one of the very few documented clients of Dawson's numerous brothels. Of course, the Mounted Police had their own reasons for maintaining their preoccupation with prosecuting the prostitutes and their procurers rather than their customers:

clients were often men of position and influence whose arrest could prove embarrassing for both the arresting officer and the suspect himself.

Throughout the Klondike gold rush, citizens complained that Canadian officials kept company – and even cohabited – with women of questionable background. This was a source of another headache for the Laurier administration in Ottawa. Notable among the charges 'of drunkenness and lust' were that Commissioner Lithgow could be found in company 'with harlots in the dance halls' and that the civil servant Monsieur Girouard was living in 'open fornication' with one Marie ('Montreal Marie') Lambert.[86] In a number of cases, government officials were chastised for appearing drunk in public and for frequenting the dance halls. Presumably, some government officials also sought the services of Dawson's scarlet women during their Klondike postings.

Not to be outdone by the Canadians, Dawson's first American consul was also known for his penchant for liquor and as a frequent visitor to Lousetown. In one of his official dispatches, in fact, Colonel McCook had to report that he had fallen into a snow bank on the way home from Lousetown and frozen his hand one night in January 1899.[87] McCook apparently enjoyed the seamier side of Dawson, for his official correspondence also indicates that he regularly held business meetings in various Dawson saloons, a habit that resulted on at least one occasion in a law suit.[88]

The average, steady Lousetown customer, then, remains anonymous. Occasionally, miners like Frank Ogren, George Blondeau, and Edward Lecernes pressed charges of theft against prostitutes after finding themselves relieved of gold dust well beyond the expected price, but these men were very much the exception.[89] In fact, when a number of oldtimers in Dawson were interviewed in later years, they all claimed that they went to the theatres of the later period but knew little about the 'goings-on' in the dance halls, brothels, and cigar stores of the earlier period. Even well after the rush was over, few men admitted to associating with prostitutes. The clientele remains, as always, even more shadowy than the women themselves.

Conclusions

> With overhead a lamp of red I sit me down and wait;
> Until they come, the nightly scum with drunken eyes aflame;
> Your sweethearts, sons, ye scornful ones – 'tis I who know their shame;
> The gods you see are brutes to me – and so I play my game.

Klondike saloons were the centre of social life. This particular one has rather more of the de rigueur nudes on its walls than usual.

In this verse from 'The Harlot,' Robert Service summarized the relationship not only between Klondike prostitutes and their clientele but between the prostitutes and the other women of Dawson. For though gambling and prostitution were illegal in Canada – even in the Klondike – in the earliest years of the rush, these activities went largely unprosecuted. In the interest of the community order, local authorities attempted to regulate vice rather than to suppress it entirely. This seems to have been a pragmatic solution to problems within a resource-based community with a largely male population. The federal government, over 3,000 miles away in Ottawa, proved unsympathetic to such local adaptations, however, and eventually forced the closure of Dawson's dance halls and casinos, as well as tighter restrictions on the world's oldest profession.

In looking beyond the mud and muck of the red-light district, we have seen that the residents of Dawson's demi-monde were even more multi-ethnic, hard-working, and poor than the average Klondiker. In the complex hierarchy of scarlet life, individuals created an intricate web of social networks. These stretched beyond the Klondike, encouraging others to join those already there and providing the basis locally for meeting potential employers, agents, clients, business partners, and lovers.

From the vantage point of the rest of Dawson, women of the demi-monde were seen as parasites, waiting to relieve the miners of their new-found gold.[90] Some Dawson residents, like Jeremiah Lynch, believed that all working women in town were engaged in immoral activity. Such attitudes created a hostile environment for migrant working women who sought 'honest work' as dancers, domestic servants, and waitresses. For some, prostitution was the best or perhaps only alternative. Many had worked as prostitutes in other frontier communities; others, who had perhaps come to the Yukon with the goal of marrying a wealthy miner, resorted to prostitution in order to keep the proverbial wolf from the door. Whatever the motivation, it was hard work done under trying conditions.

CHAPTER 5

'Like Flocks of Migrating Geese':
Social Work and Religious Life in the Klondike

EARLY IN THE HISTORY of Dawson City local residents identified an élite who shaped and defined Klondike social life. Far from being a frontier town where all citizens were made equal by rugged conditions, a social order developed early in Dawson based on ethnicity, family, and occupation and closely resembling those in more southern cities. Throughout the period, Dawson 'society' drew its constituents from the clergy, government officials, and the growing commercial and professional sectors. This social clique excluded Native people, labourers, working women, and miners, even those like George Carmack who struck it rich but lacked the prerequisite breeding for upper class Klondike life.[1]

The establishment of churches, hospitals, schools, and charitable associations provided forums for both social and philanthropic activity, establishing a line between the providers and the recipients of charity and social reform. The development of a government bureaucracy, in addition to a stable commercial and professional sector, provided a pool of individuals not only accustomed to the strict social divisions so common in more southern nineteenth-century communities but also eager to replicate them.

The Migratory Clergy

Quite literally, the first white collar work in the Yukon was missionary work. Proselytizing first among the Native people and later among the miners, the Church of England held a monopoly on the souls of Yukoners throughout the early period. After the Bonanza strike in 1896, other Protestant denominations and the Roman Catholic church quickly followed. All of Dawson City's early social services – including hospitals, schools, and unemployment relief – were provided through the efforts of the many members of the Klondike clergy.

Beginning in the early 1880s, the Church Missionary Society (CMS) of the Church of England established its presence in Alaska and the Yukon. The CMS had as its mandate the conversion and salvation of heathen and Aboriginal souls. Their early Yukon missionaries included the reverends Kirkby, McDonald, Bompas, Sim, and Canham, who, along with their wives and assistants, formed a small but close community of educated social leaders although they lived separately in their respective missions.[2]

The Reverend William Carpenter Bompas was the pioneer missionary to work in what became the Yukon Territory. It was Bompas who established the mission for the Han people near the Fortymile mining camp in the late 1880s and who later also ministered to the Han at Moosehide and Dawson. Bompas considered it his personal duty to try to ease the impact of the non-Native deluge that Native Yukoners experienced during and after the Klondike gold rush. One of the ways he tried to do this was by building a corps of respected, committed missionaries. The Reverend and Mrs Bowen were two of these.

When the Reverend Richard Bowen arrived at Fortymile in 1896, Bompas's mission included himself, his wife Charlotte, a number of Métis children, and two young missionary women.[3] One of these young women was Miss Mellett, a Dublin-born school teacher who had come to the North in 1893 and spent her first year with Bishop and Mrs Bompas at Fortymile. Devoted to the principals of the CMS, Mellett eagerly joined the growing community of northern missionaries and spent two years under rather rough conditions at Rampart House with the Archdeacon and Mrs Canham. Mellett returned to Fortymile in 1896, where she met and soon married the newly ordained Richard Bowen. Bompas seems to have approved of the union, since he expected that it would encourage the couple to remain in the region. Thus, the community of missionaries provided itself with a social network – small though it was – from which formal and informal networks could be forged among colleagues who were also white, educated, and 'genteel.'[4]

In 1896, the CMS asked Bowen to give up his work with the Native people and establish an Anglican church for the growing non-Native community at the mouth of the Klondike River. Bowen later remembered that Bishop Bompas was only too happy to delegate responsibility for the spiritual care of the miners, since he wanted nothing to do with the people he considered detrimental to 'his beloved Indians.' Bowen and his new bride moved to Dawson, built St Paul's log church, and provided the first services in July 1897.[5] The Bowens were among the first members of 'respectable' Dawson society. Following in their wake, most of the Protestant clergy found themselves included in a wide social circle of young, well-educated anglophones in the growing town.

Bowen's new position came with its own curses and rewards. One of his immediate problems, for example, was running interference between his friend the bishop and the developing mining community. Bishop Bompas was famous for holding the non-Natives of the Klondike in great disdain – his fellow clergy excepted. Superintendent Charles Constantine of the North West Mounted Police pointed this out when he noted in his 1896 report that the bishop 'has no use for any person unless he is an Indian. [He] has the utmost contempt for the whites in general and myself in particular.' This placed a good deal of strain on young Bowen, who agreed with Constantine that by this date Bompas had 'lost both touch with and regard for the white people he met.'[6] Bowen set about walking the uneasy road between the bishop and the non-Native residents of Dawson City. It was largely due to his diplomacy and in spite of the bishop's animosity that issues of land grants and Indian policy were eventually resolved. The bishop for his part soon removed to Carcross and subsequent clergy formed a close relationship with the Mounted Police and other government officials for practical, benevolent, and social purposes.

The Bowens were the first in a long string of male and female clerics of all denominations who soon flocked to the Klondike to minister to the needs of the growing community. When the rush began in earnest and families began arriving in the district, the other churches quickly established themselves in Dawson. The church buildings, makeshift as many of them were, were still more permanent than the personnel who preached in them. As a Dawson school teacher later remembered, the Protestant ministers in Dawson, 'came and went like flocks of migrating geese in the fall. (The Roman Catholic priests, on the other hand, hung on for decades.) It was often said that the White Pass Railway and steamship line existed entirely on fares sold to the ever-changing procession of ministers, nurses, teachers and mounted policemen.'[7] The pattern of rotating social service personnel seems to have been generally accepted by the local population, since most of the posts paid very little and even young people soon found better prospects in the South.

The Presbyterians were close on the Church of England's heels, sending three ministers to the region in 1897. One of these, the Reverend Andrew Grant, was particularly well suited to Dawson life for he was both a medical doctor and an ordained minister. Unlike many of his colleagues, Grant called Dawson his family's home for over a decade and was a constant fixture among its social set. He was instrumental in founding the Protestant Good Samaritan Hospital in Dawson and also served as hospital superintendent during its first four operating years. The Presbyterian church, from its earliest Yukon inception, also held services regularly on the creeks. A succession of ministers came and went, conducting services in schoolhouses and mining cabins throughout the mining districts.[8]

One of Grant's first Presbyterian colleagues was the Reverend Alfred Hetherington, who arrived in 1898 to supervise building the Presbyterian St Andrew's Church and parsonage in Dawson. Both of log construction, the buildings were erected on a site granted from the government reserve. Hetherington, like most Dawson ministers, moved in a social circle that included other clergy, government officials, and professionals. From among this circle, much as Bowen had done, Hetherington soon found a marital partner – his organist, Alberta Swan. Swan had also come to the Klondike in 1898, accompanying her brother Anson, a mining engineer, and their mother and sister. Like the other Yukon clerics, Hetherington provided a wide array of services, from visiting scurvy victims on the creeks to performing marriage, baptism, and funeral services in town. It was a difficult and demanding life, and the Hetheringtons returned south in 1902.[9]

As was the case in many southern Canadian cities, the Presbyterian church and its Anglo-Scots members were front and centre in the 'social' world of Dawson. In November 1900, for example, the annual St Andrew's Ball was described in the *Klondike Nugget* – not immodestly – as the 'greatest social event ever recorded in history.' The soirée began with a march, complete with two pipers and led by the commissioner of the Yukon,

William Ogilvie. The toastmaster gave a Highland toast to a group that included the local judge and his wife, top-ranking government and Mounted Police officials, and a number of prominent lawyers, doctors, and their wives.[10] That the Presbyterians were well represented in the social hierarchy of Dawson is also demonstrated by the membership list of the board of managers of the Presbyterian church between 1898 and 1900, which included several of the top Yukon brass: Gold Commissioner Thomas Fawcett, Dominion Land Surveyor J.B. Tyrrell, several lawyers, two doctors (besides the Reverend Grant, who also chaired the board), and two prominent merchants.[11]

There was a notable exception to the social position that clergymen and their wives held in Dawson 'society.' Couples of mixed race did not find themselves included in the social whirl. That ethnicity was reason enough to exclude individuals is exemplified in the case of Mrs Robert McDonald. For while Mrs McDonald was the wife (and later widow) of one of the Yukon's oldest and most respected missionaries, she was Native, and for that reason was carefully excluded from most social functions. The Reverend and Mrs Totty, residents of Moosehide throughout the height of the rush and another mixed-race couple, are also notable in their absence from the lists of participants in the balls, skating parties, and other social events each season.

In 1898, the contest between the Protestant churches for the souls of Dawson began in earnest when the Methodists joined the Anglicans and Presbyterians. The first of the Methodist clergy was the Reverend Turner, sent north from the mining camps of British Columbia in 1898. Turner was followed by a series of other missionaries and evangelists, including the Baptists, the Lutherans, Christian Scientists, Theosophists, and the Salvation Army.

Rebecca Ellery led the Salvation Army's crusade to the Klondike, arriving in the stampede summer of 1898. The members of Ellery's brigade marched into Dawson with signed contracts to serve and to save the community for a period of twelve months. Taking full advantage of the midnight sun, the Salvationists built a hostel, and within two months of their arrival were open for business. A Klondike gold camp might seem like an unlikely place to hear the tambourines of hallelujah lads and lasses, yet before the hostel building opened its doors, Salvation Army revival meetings were a permanent part of the Dawson streetscape.[12]

Like many other Dawsonites, the Salvationists worried that the winter of 1898-9 would bring hardship and deprivation to many people. For

Photo by
B. Johnstone

DAWSON'S MIDWINTER Open-Air THERMO Dance.

J. GR
PAI

Dawson residents were relentless in devising creative ways to help one another through the long, dark winter months. Here a local artist captures the crowds who turned out for an outdoor dance and bonfire.

*The officers of the Salvation Army
arrived in Dawson in 1898 to battle for
the souls of the Klondike. Their Dawson
hostel for unemployed men, built within
two months of their arrival in 1898, was
nearly always full.*

despite the Mounted Police order for all travellers to bring with them a year's supply of provisions, many people arrived with nothing. Some had lost their supplies when their boats went under the Whitehorse or Five Finger rapids. Others fell victim to theft, while still others had sold their supplies in order to speculate on mining property. Anticipating high rates of winter unemployment, the Salvation Army's shelter aimed to alleviate some of the distress with thirty bunks and meals furnished at 'bedrock prices.' Early in the winter of 1898 the Army attempted to offer food and shelter in return for work at chopping wood, but when the pile grew to a mountain and they exhausted their pool of customers for firewood, they reinstated their nominal fee structure. The hostel was full to overflowing all winter.[13] Unlike the other clergy and philanthropists, however, the Salvationists were not admitted to Dawson's inner social circle, largely because their zealous public meetings, as well as the women's scarlet tunics, were viewed as 'unrespectable' by the more conservative element.[14]

With the arrival of religious institutions, a forum for respectable, middle class social and philanthropic activity was created in Dawson, helping both to create and to maintain social distinctions within the community. The Presbyterians were leaders on this front. In 1898, they formed one of Dawson's first charities, the Christian Endeavour Society. This group, the precursor to the Ladies' Aid Society, included a number of prominent Dawson men and women. Not to be outdone, the Methodists established their own philanthropic Epworth League in 1898 and a Sunday school the following year. The Epworth League appointed subcommittees to run prayer meetings and to organize missionary and evangelistic activities, relief, and visiting the sick, as well as for 'Temperance and Social Purity.' On all counts, and especially the last, the committee had its work cut out in the Klondike.[15]

By 1899, the number of women and families was also rapidly increasing Dawson City. By December of that year the Methodists alone counted forty children in regular Sunday school attendance, a number that soon increased to sixty.[16] Here women found an opportunity for 'respectable' participation in the public arena as Sunday school teachers, distributors of relief, and visitors to the ill and shut-in.

One of the more unusual facets of frontier proselytizing was the insistence on holding to southern patterns of organization. In order 'to do efficient work,' for example, the Methodists created a ladies' aid society at the outset. Unfortunately, only nine women qualified as 'ladies' in the entire Methodist congregation of 1898, so the Dawson City Ladies' Aid Society for the first two years was 'largely composed of men.'[17]

The Ladies' Aid, its membership aside, was successful in raising money from the community for the hospital and for repairs to the church, while at the same time looking after the needy and destitute. Why Methodists felt that they must call the subgroup thus charged the Ladies' Aid is unclear, although such duties had long been the responsibility of the women in southern congregations. Perhaps the board of managers was confident that more women would join the congregation as the community continued to grow. Indeed, this seems to be exactly what happened, for after 1899 there is no further mention of male membership in the Ladies' Aid Society. The Presbyterian church also organized its own ladies' aid but not until 1899, when it had a sufficient number of women to do so. Both the Catholics and the Anglicans also established their own women's auxiliaries for philanthropic and social endeavours.

The contest for the souls of Dawson was not limited to the Protestant churches, of course, for the Roman Catholic church was early on the scene. An American Jesuit priest named William Judge established the Catholic presence in 1897. Judge arrived in Dawson from Alaska and began his work in a tent in the spring of 1897, moving by midsummer to a two-storey log building that served as Dawson's first Catholic church and mission. Judge was joined the following summer by the Sisters of Ste Anne. Together these clerics established the first formal medical institutions and school. Yet like the Salvationists, the Catholic clergy remained apart from Dawson society.

By 1900, then, Dawson City boasted four main churches: Roman Catholic, Anglican, Presbyterian, and Methodist. Each congregation operated a women's group, and these were described by one local resident as accomplishing 'much good.'[18] Dawson City by 1898 was well endowed with benevolent and philanthropic endeavours, all of them much busier than they had expected to be.

'Many Heartrending and Sickening Sights':
Public Health and the Medical Profession in Dawson

The arrival of Father Judge signalled more than simply the establishment of regular mass in Dawson. Judge was also responsible for the creation of the first local hospital. To raise money for the building of St Mary's Catholic Hospital, the local community got involved, selling tickets for $50 that entitled subscribers to medical services at any time over the following year. Many Dawsonites found reason to cash in this early form of medical insurance in subsequent months. Over the winter of 1897-8, Judge provided care for up to fifty patients at a time, many of them suffering from scurvy. The hospital committee continued to raise funds, with the result that early in the summer of 1898 they were able to complete a three-storey addition to original two-storey log building hastily constructed the previous year.[19] And just in time, too.

The stampede summer of 1898 was the height of the Klondike gold rush. Dawson City, built as it was on a mud flat with no sanitation or drainage, was soon a city of 20,000 souls exposed to disease. In fact, just as the Sisters of Ste Anne – a contingent of the Grey Nuns – arrived in mid-summer to assist Father Judge, a typhoid epidemic broke out. During the epidemic St Mary's Hospital accommodated as many as 140 patients at a time, thousands over all.[20] Several more times over the next year epidemics swept the community, claiming hundreds of victims. Among these victims was the priest himself. After Judge's death in 1899, Father P.E. Gendreau of the Oblate Order arrived to preside over the parish, and he remained its priest for many years.

One of Dawson's early doctors, W.B. Barrett, also arrived during the summer of 1898 in time to assist in the big epidemic. Within a few weeks Barrett had taken over the supervision of medical services at St Mary's. Here he was soon joined by a second Canadian, Dr J.O. Lachapelle, and the two men remained fixtures in Dawson for many years.[21] The arrival of Barrett and Lachapelle was a great relief to Father Judge, who had been in a constant state of worry because the two doctors he had on staff were Americans and not licensed to practice in the dominion. With the able assistance of the Sisters of Ste Anne, the new doctors attempted to tend to the health of the local community.

The formation of a social élite in Dawson is evident in the establishment of its two hospitals, first St Mary's and later the Good Samaritan Hospital. In the process of setting up the two hospitals, we see the emergence of a complex network drawn from the ranks of Dawson's male and female missionaries, civil servants, and professionals. After the first major typhoid epidemic in 1898, the 'ladies of Dawson' organized a month-long bazaar to raise money to relieve St Mary's Hospital of its hefty debt. The 'ladies' of the nonsectarian committee were drawn from the highest levels of the community, including the wives of local Mounted Police officers, prominent civil servants, lawyers, and merchants. Only one of the organizing ladies was the wife of a miner. Mrs McDonald was the beautiful young wife of Big Alex McDonald, 'King of the Klondike,' a highly celebrated miner and speculator who was also the chief patron of St Mary's Roman Catholic church. The group was also largely anglophone, with the exception of the French Canadian wife of Justice Dugas, and her position was of an honorary nature. Faith Fenton represented another exception – as the sole professional woman – but as the *Toronto Globe* correspondent, she was something of a celebrity and accustomed to moving among the upper echelon. It is interesting to note that while Justice Dugas, probably the most influential Catholic in town, was named Patron of the Bazaar, only two other male francophones were involved: François-Xavier Gosselin, a senior government official, and a 'Monsieur De Lobel,' whose occupation is unknown. The rest of the group was made up largely of English Canadians and British Protestants (about 70 percent), with a number of prominent Anglo-American Protestants also welcomed. While the social upper crust was dominated by Protestants, religious affiliation took a back seat to community need. The profits from the charity bazaar for St Mary's Hospital totalled $12,000, clearing the hospital's debt and adding a much needed (albeit shortlived) surplus to its accounts.[22]

Similarly, the first board of managers for the Protestant Good Samaritan Hospital was also composed of prominent English Canadians. Included in the list were Bishop Bompas, the superintendent of the Mounted Police, two doctors, a lawyer, the Protestant clergy, and several merchants. It was this group who decided that the present level of medical services proffered in Dawson was insufficient and set about taking the necessary steps to create a second hospital. That the first hospital was Catholic and the second distinctly Protestant followed the pattern of medical and benevolent institutional development in most Canadian cities.[23]

Religion aside, there was a real need for the creation and maintenance of social services. The Roman Catholic hospital was sorely overloaded in its first year of operation. Partly in response to the great need and partly because it was the usual fashion, the Protestants therefore built their own, the Good Samaritan Hospital, in the fall of 1898. Far from causing the usual southern Protestant-Catholic conflict, the founding of the Protestant hospital was apparently welcomed by all. It was also highly beneficial to the community as a whole, as one of St Mary's physicians explained: 'Both hospitals were carrying a capacity load during the following two or three years, while the greatest harmony existed in a friendly rivalry – each stimulated by the other to improve its services.'[24] This sentiment was supported by the Protestants in their own statement when they set about raising money for the endeavour: 'While we admire and highly commend the noble efforts being made on behalf of the sick and disabled by the Catholic church in the hospital already in our midst, at the same time we cannot but realize its inability, by lack of room and other facilities, to supply the needs of those unfortunates among us who require medical attendance and skilful nursing.'[25] Realizing the importance of maintaining community solidarity, the Catholic and Protestant social welfare advocates displayed little animosity toward one another.

Under the direction of the Reverend Grant, the Good Samaritans opened their doors on 11 August 1898 with two nurses (members of the newly arrived contingent of Victorian Order of Nurses) and ten patients. Two years later, Grant was assisted by a matron remembered only as Miss Smith, who managed a staff of seven nurses through the typhoid and pneumonia epidemic in the fall of 1900. Between scurvy – referred to by the English stampeders as 'Canadian black leg' – and typhoid, both hospitals were full through both winter and summer for the first two years.[26]

Unfortunately, many of the victims of these epidemics were unable to pay their medical bills, and both hospitals operated in the red for much of the early period. From September 1897 until December 1898 St Mary's Hospital treated 726 patients, fewer than half of whom were able to pay. Some worked out an agreement with the hospital when they could not pay. Mrs S.J. Taylor, for example, paid off the amount she owed St Mary's for her care during the typhoid epidemic by working as a cook for the hospital.[27]

Despite the efforts of the well-meaning members of Dawson society, medical costs remained prohibitive to many Klondikers. And while individuals stricken with fatal and/or contagious disease were never turned away, others in less life-threatening circumstances sought alternatives elsewhere. When Martha Purdy (later Black) explained to Father Judge in the fall of 1897 that she was pregnant, he informed her that the fees for a hospital delivery would be in the neighbourhood of $1,000. Purdy, estranged from her husband and unable to afford such a fee, decided she would cope on her own, and like so many other Yukon women, she delivered her son alone and unattended in her cabin during the winter.[28]

In addition to creating an impetus for establishing a network to provide medical services, the epidemics of 1897 and 1898 directed attention to public health and sanitation. In an attempt to prevent another epidemic like that of the summer of 1898, the Canadian government appointed J.W. Good as medical health officer for Dawson. Beginning in the spring of 1899, Dr Good undertook a campaign to improve sanitation

A small contingent of the Victorian Order of Nurses embarks for the Yukon with Toronto Globe correspondent Faith Fenton. Left to right, they are Margaret Payson, Georgia Powell, Amy Scott, Fenton, and Rachel Hanna.

and the water supply. Soon all over town residents noticed public bulletins ordering that 'No water for domestic purposes shall be *SOLD* or *DELIVERED* from the Yukon or the Klondyke Rivers unless from a point one-half mile above the mouth of the Klondyke on the Yukon River, or from a point on the Klondyke above the mouth of Bonanza Creek.'[29] The same rule applied to the taking of ice, and the public was also informed of the necessity of boiling all water taken from other sources for personal use. The health officer also instituted new rules for cleaning privies and removing garbage, with sanitation officers 'ever vigilant' in their enforcement.[30] As well, Good ordered the immediate construction of board sidewalks and a system of drainage to prevent the knee-deep mud in the streets in the spring. The implementation of these orders improved transportation and public health simultaneously. It was also Dr Good who undertook the community health plan under which local prostitutes were required to have regular medical examinations.

Professions for women were almost as limited in the Yukon as they were in more southern parts of Victorian North America. Religion, medicine, and education were among these limited options. Some women, like Miss Mellett and Alberta Swan, found their calling in the Protestant missions. Others, such as the newly minted young nurses of the Victorian Order of Nurses, joined the Klondike stampede to assist in the care of the sick and injured. The Sisters of Ste Anne combined their religious vocation with their practical skills of nursing and teaching. Most of the women who worked in the medical field in Dawson were young and unmarried. They came to the Klondike for the same reasons given by so many others: for adventure and opportunity.

The Victorian Order of Nurses (VONs) came to the Klondike under contract, much as Salvation Army officers and public school teachers did later. These women – Georgia Powell, Rachel Hanna, Margaret Payson, and Amy Scott – all eagerly signed up for a two-year adventure before leaving Ontario in the spring of 1898. The VONs travelled for a portion of their journey in the company of the Yukon Field Force. Along the way they were surprised to encounter sexism and animosity from the men. Counter to the many tales of chivalry offered to women by men on the Chilkoot Trail, the enlisted men of the Canadian military resented having to consider the privacy of the nurses in their midst and to mind their own language.[31] Once in Dawson, Georgia Powell and Rachel Hanna went to work at the Good Samaritan Hospital, as matron and duty nurse respectively. Margaret Payson gained charge of the small hospital at Grand Forks, while Amy Scott was dispatched to the NWMP barracks hospital to assist the government surgeon. While these women remembered their excitement at taking part in the historic gold rush, none of them denied that theirs was difficult and demanding work, most of it performed under less than ideal conditions. Powell noted that they worked gruelling hours, 'witnessing many heartrending and sickening sights, improvising and planning, teaching and tending, night and day.'[32] She found that she adapted well to northern life, and like many Yukon professionals, remained in Dawson for several years beyond her original term. The other VONs from the original group returned to the South after their term expired.

The year after Father Judge founded St Mary's Hospital, the Sisters of Ste Anne sent a group of women trained as nurses, and they became the staff of St Mary's Hospital and later also of the St Mary's Roman Catholic School. Among them were Sister Mary Joseph Calasanz, Sister Mary Jean Damascene, Sister Mary of the Passion, and Sister Mary Prudentienne. Sister Mary Zeno, the senior member of the group, had gone to Juneau in 1886, where she founded Ste Anne's Hospital and served as its head for twelve years before coming to Dawson to assist in the new hospital there. Unlike the VONs, the Sisters were not certified nurses, but 'were extremely competent in caring for the sick, the result of long experience as missionary teachers.' They also came to Dawson well acquainted with the conditions of northern outpost nursing.[33]

Beyond the two public hospitals, there were other options for Yukon nurses. A few women in the early period ran small nursing homes or private hospitals with a few beds, which were not, as a rule, especially prosperous. Yet some private duty nurses seem to have made very good wages, for in two separate instances they reported earnings of $10 per day. This compares well with the average wage of restaurant workers, which was less than half that sum. Still, it was not steady work – patients recovered, after all – and frequent unemployment was often the plight of these private nurses. Georgia White, for example, worked as a private duty nurse whenever she could find employment, yet she was often forced to work as a waitress to sustain herself. This situation reflects the difficulty of finding steady work even for professionals in Dawson society.[34]

Not all Klondike nurses were women, of course. During the typhoid epidemic of 1898, St Mary's Hospital employed anyone who claimed even the smallest amount of medical training. An American veterinarian and an English nurse – both men – were thus recruited and took their orders from the nuns and doctors.[35] Another young male nurse named Mr Cunningham was fired by the Good Samaritan Hospital on September 1898, less than a month after the institution opened its doors. He was soon replaced by one 'Miss Latta,' who was engaged at a salary of $100 per month.[36]

Klondike nurses worked closely with a large pool of physicians. By the summer of 1898 doctors were sufficiently numerous to prompt the formation of the Yukon College of Physicians and Surgeons, which boasted fifty members in its first year. The college formally established the presence of the medical profession in Dawson and soon implemented – for better or worse – a regulated fee structure for services. The most controversial aspect of the college was that it required the registration of all 'qualified' physicians.[37] This effectively barred many local doctors from practising since it admitted only those who held degrees from 'recognized' institutions – almost none of them American. American-trained physicians could not practise, 'as their licenses did not bear the stamp of the Crown.'[38] By the time of the census in 1901, for example, fourteen doctors were practising in Dawson City and only one of these was an American, Dr U.F. Horn, who had been a resident since 1898. Of the remaining thirteen, ten were Canadian born and three originated in Great Britain.[39] While there were obvious public benefits to licensing medical doctors, the move to institute licensing may well have been a deliberate attempt by Canadian professionals to increase their own status and prestige while diminishing the competition for patients.

Dr Luella Day was one of many American doctors barred from practising medicine in the Klondike. A graduate of the Chicago Medical School, Day had come to the Yukon in 1897. In May 1898, she had attempted to deliver the baby of a miner's wife. The woman died, and while the crown dropped the charges against Dr Day, she was prevented from practising medicine in the Yukon after that date.[40] The death of Day's patient occurred just a few weeks before the creation of the Yukon College of Physicians and Surgeons, and may very well have been responsible for its organization. Day had to content herself with practising medicine as a nurse for the rest of her Klondike sojourn.

The new licensing system for physicians was not particularly problematic in the town, which contained a good number of Canadian- and British-trained physicians, but on the creeks, where scurvy, typhoid, smallpox, and measles were common, there was a definite shortage of medical help. As a result, many miners suffered alone in their cabins and many

PIONEER MEDICAL FRATERNITY.
Dawson. Y. T.

Dawson City established its own College of Physicians in 1898 to ensure that only properly licensed doctors could practise. Shown here are many of its early members.

women delivered their babies without attendance or travelled outside the territory to avoid exorbitant delivery and hospitalization fees.

Most of the local physicians moved among the social set of Dawson. Indeed, of the eighteen physicians and surgeons listed in the 1902 directory, half are immediately recognizable as civic leaders. Dr Bourke, for example, was also the proprietor of Hotel Metropole, one of the better establishments in town. Likewise, doctors Barrett, Cassels, Grant, Richardson, and Thompson were all prominent members of local churches and charities. All of these men remained in Dawson for many years, as did the popular French Canadian physician Dr Lachapelle, who was still a resident at the time of his death in 1924.[41]

Like so many others, doctors were not immune to gold fever. Randy McLennan, a local doctor of many years, gained his patients' respect for both medical and mining expertise. He was appointed mining recorder for the Duncan district in 1909 and was still mining and doctoring when he moved to the Mayo district in 1915. That McLennan was not unusual in his dual occupation is supported by reports of the first US consul, who noted that 'in Dawson and at the mines one finds Doctors, Lawyers, professional men of all descriptions, U.S. politicians out of jobs all found working at anything they can find to do.'[42]

Most of the more prominent local physicians seem to have restricted their participation to the financial side of mining. The Reverend Dr Grant and Dr Lachapelle, for example, were both known for their willingness to invest in promising mining ventures. Dr Alfred Thompson, a leading member of Dawson society and later a member of parliament, was president of the Eldorado Dome Quartz Mining Company. Among his partners were two brokers, a jeweller, a hotelkeeper, a merchant, and a dance hall proprietor.[43] Thompson's list of partners indicates that while Dawson City drew very clear lines for social circles, it threw a much wider net for business purposes.

A Ruler and a Good Evening Dress: Public Education in Dawson
From the beginning, miners, merchants, and professionals alike brought their families to the Klondike, and with them came the need to establish schools. As early as 1896, Mounted Police Commander Constantine noted that miners at Fortymile were bringing in their families, 'some leaving them in the settlement, others taking them to the creeks with them.' He remarked then that within a year it would be necessary to open a school for non-Native children and that this might induce still more families to

follow. He cautioned his superiors, however, on the question of staffing the new school: 'Wages are very high, consequent on the cost of provisions. Salaries paid to a teacher in the east would be of no use here, a teacher would starve on it.' Furthermore, he noted that any teachers brought in should be women, since the salaries necessary to prevent male teachers from contracting gold fever would be 'extravagant.' Constantine's advice was heeded, although it was three years before the authorities managed to establish a public school. One oldtimer, Martha Louise Black, later noted that the finest teachers in Canada were drawn to work in the Yukon 'because of the large salaries and adventurous atmosphere.'[44]

Similar to the pattern by which churches developed, the first schools in the Yukon served the Native and Métis populations. Schools for non-Native children were begun first by private individuals, then by Catholic and Protestant groups. By 1901, there were three private and two publicly supported schools in Dawson City, and by 1907 the total number of 'white' children attending school was approximately 500, although only 325 of these attended with any regularity.[45]

One of the first private schools in Dawson operated in the new Anglican church and began receiving students in August 1898. Missouri teacher Lulu Craig operated the school, which she advertised in the local newspaper. Like Alberta Swan, Craig had come to Dawson with her brother earlier that summer. Not content to sit idle, she seized the first opportunity to offer her services to the younger residents of Dawson. By 1901, three such private schools were operating in Dawson.[46]

The Sisters of Ste Anne established St Mary's Roman Catholic School in 1899, and in spite of its name the school operated as a nonsectarian institution. In its first year of operation, St Mary's registered nearly sixty children of all faiths. Sister Mary Joseph Calasanz was the school's first teacher, and she was assisted by a lay teacher named Miss Marie Connor. Sister Mary Edith and Sister Mary Zenaide took up the teaching at St Mary's in 1900 and were followed by reinforcements sent periodically from the Mother House in Montreal.[47] The staff at St Mary's had Quebec certificates, and while they counted a good many French Canadian pupils, the usual language of instruction was English. The Protestants soon followed the Catholic lead, opening a public school in 1900. The public school was larger than St Mary's, boasting almost 200 students in its second year of operation.[48]

The schools in town were fed and supported by smaller schools on the creeks, for many families continued to live on or near their mining claims well into the twentieth century. Serving these families were small schools at Grand Forks, Bonanza, Gold Bottom, Hunker, Caribou, and Gold Run creeks.[49] Teachers for the creek schools often seemed to come to their positions by accident. In the summer of 1899, for example, a Miss Lind arrived at Eldorado Creek near Dawson to visit her sister, wife of one of the miners there. She did not return to her teaching job Outside that autumn but she stayed to teach the children on Eldorado Creek in a tent schoolhouse. Among her charges were the Becker children, Willie Mellish, James Gibbs, and Harry Arndt – all offspring of local mining couples.[50]

Similarly, young Nova Scotia teacher Winifred McLellan came to join her brother, Gordon, in Dawson in 1900. He had recently established a grocery business there, and Winifred 'kept house for Gordon in the apartment over the store.' She later gained employment as a teacher on the creeks. In 1905, she taught at Caribou Creek, where she had about a dozen pupils. Like the Sisters of Ste Anne, McLellan had a mixed group of pupils, for the village of Paris was three miles from her school. She taught six 'French children' the first semester.[51]

Not all the teachers were women, of course, and a number of men who were not persuaded by the mines were thus employed. The teachers, nurses, and clergy made up a small social group of their own, as McLellan also noted: 'The gentlemen teachers had returned a few days before I left [Dawson] – one of them Mr Smille brought back a wife. Miss Zinkan is not going out as she intended, much to her sister's delight. The two nurses left last Sunday. Bella and I went down to see them off. So you see our crowd is somewhat broken up.'[52]

Within this social clique of lay teachers and nurses individuals found opportunities for social interaction and leisure. A few years later, Laura Thompson (later Berton) found in this 'crowd' a ready-made social network in which she was both welcomed and expected to participate. In fact, when the future Mrs Berton left Toronto in 1907, she was advised by an acquaintance who had just returned from Dawson to ensure that she packed a 'good evening dress.'[53]

Berton was accompanied on her trip to Dawson by a number of other professionals who would soon become part of her social set. These included the new science master, two other women teachers (there were four women teachers on the Dawson public school staff that year), three new nurses for the Good Samaritan Hospital, three Protestant ministers, the Anglican bishop, and a government telegrapher.[54] Here were members of the flock of 'migrating geese' who came and went in service of Dawson's residents.

The Klondike was a family affair from the start, and small private schools sprang up to serve the needs of Dawson families, followed by the Catholic school in 1899. Residents constructed Dawson's first public school, seen here, in 1901.

Laura Thompson Berton was one of many public school teachers to travel to Dawson under contract, although there does not appear to have been any formal channel for this recruitment. In Berton's case, the Yukon superintendent of schools contacted the superintendent of Toronto's kindergartens, who in turn asked Berton if she was interested in the position of kindergarten mistress in Dawson. Berton was eager to visit the fabled gold fields and agreed to try it for a year at more than four times her Toronto salary. She accepted the contract over and above her parents' objections that such a posting was not appropriate for a young lady of her background.[55]

Her parents needn't have worried, however, for Dawson City was a place of propriety, whatever its reputation, and Victorian rules of behaviour were not abandoned with the rush. 'Respectable' single women did not live alone, and the women teachers and nurses generally lodged together. Locating adequate housing was often a problem for single women, although by the time Berton and her companions arrived in 1907 there was an abundance of property for rent.[56] Once the four young teachers had set up housekeeping, they did entertain gentlemen callers, for there were few other respectable arenas available for such activity.

This is not a trivial observation, for just as the absence of men's clubs had the effect of leading all men, regardless of social status or ethnicity, to congregate in dance halls and saloons, there were few places for respectable young couples to socialize, and even fewer to court. It was unseemly for respectable women to visit men in their boarding houses and, of course, unheard of for them to enter a saloon.

Many Klondikers commented on the problems this created for both social and business life. United States Consul James McCook, a man accustomed to the privileges of the Philadelphia Manufacturers Club, conducted a number of his business meetings in local saloons and dance houses, a practice that landed him in hot water on at least two occasions. McCook opted for the saloon in part because he lacked a proper 'salon' in his home in which to conduct business dinners or drinks. Indeed, Henry Woodside estimated that 50 percent of Dawson's residents kept house only as a place to sleep, daily visiting the city's restaurants and saloons for their meals and entertainments. If Arthur Godfrey's testimony is anywhere close to typical, this was due in part to the poor accommodation available. He and his mercantile partner were sleeping in an attic that he described as 'the coldest place I've ever seen.' Men like Godfrey lined up for invitations to respectable women's homes, although Martha Louise Black remembered that in the early years the number of single

Cabin on Quartz Creek, Y.T.

Wealthier miners could afford to hire domestic help, demonstrated here by the anonymous African American housekeeper employed by Swiftwater Bill Gates (seated) and his wife (in floral print), on their Quartz Creek claim, 1898.

women with homes in which to entertain were so few that they could be counted on the fingers of one hand.[57]

Class and ethnic divisions were strict in Dawson, and many occupations were dominated by particular ethnic groups. Like the clergy, the lay teachers were predominantly Protestant, Anglo-Canadian or British, and about evenly split between males and females, with the exception of the staff at St Mary's, who were Catholic religious and lay women. Many anglophone professionals employed domestic help from other ethnic groups. In particular, African American housekeepers and Japanese cooks were symbols of status in Dawson society from the earliest period. By 1907, even the public school teachers 'had a Japanese cook, as many Dawson people had.' The 'little Japanese cook' soon left the teachers' employ and was replaced by a 'stolid Swedish woman named Ida.' The Yukon commissioner and his wife also had 'immaculate' Japanese servants to serve at Government House functions in the opening years of the twentieth century.[58]

Automatic membership to the inner sanctum of Dawson society was part of a young school teacher's package. This membership came with certain responsibilities, however, including that of 'holding a day.' Every woman in the social set held a day, and her measure of social success 'was calculated in direct ratio to the number of people who turned up. *Thus it was possible to compute the social standing of the entire upper crust of Dawson mathematically.*'[59] This must have been a rather cumbersome obligation for the members of the set who, like the teachers, put in a full day's work before coming home to entertain.

Still, these women moved within a social world similar to the one they had been accustomed to Outside, and many of them found marriage partners from within their new circle. Laura Thompson Berton was one of these, although Frank Berton, as a miner and lowly government clerk, had little standing, a fact her friends hastened to point out. Similarly, Ida Hastings, also a young school teacher met and married Walter Hamilton, a miner turned postal clerk.[60] Like the missionaries and ministers who married members of their congregations, school teachers often chose marital partners from among their 'crowd.'

Capturing the Era: Artists in the Klondike
Like so many others, a number of artists caught the gold fever. These people often did not really 'fit' into the social élite, yet they were definitely not part of the labouring classes. Often artists came to the Klondike as entrepreneurs, as did Ernest Keir. Keir was a photographer from

Wisconsin who combined mining with his original profession. Over the winter of 1898-9, Keir took photographs of the claims, cabins, and businesses up and down Hunker, Dominion, and Bonanza creeks, selling the prints back to the owners. In this way Keir 'cashed in' on the Klondike, making his living by selling portraits. Many photographers found the Klondike a lucrative place for business, and they aggressively competed for clients through advertisements.[61] Although large numbers of stampeders brought along their newly acquired Kodaks, the services of professionals remained in high demand. Testimony to this can be found in the hundreds of studio portraits taken in Dawson, which survive in family albums and public archives. As well, several professional photographers published Klondike albums that sold very well in the South.[62]

Painters also formed part of the general crowd who caught gold fever. Guy Lawrence's father was one of these. Mr Lawrence was a portrait painter and gambler who set out with his son for the Klondike from England in 1898. The Lawrences set about working a claim, but bad luck plagued the venture and the mine did not pay. Always a gambler, the senior Lawrence took a serious risk when he playfully wrote to his wife that he had just had his picture taken with 'Ruth,' although he failed to explain that she was a river steamer. When Mrs Lawrence received this letter in England, she was convinced that her husband was 'sleeping with a dancehall girl,' and began preparations to sell the family home and come to Canada. Realizing his folly almost too late, Mr Lawrence quickly cabled his wife, sold his claim, and returned to England with his painting supplies.[63] This incident indicates the sense of insecurity many men instilled in their families when they dropped everything to join the gold stampedes. Given the slow and unreliable communication facilities of the period, such misunderstandings were probably not unusual.

Access to Dawson's conservative inner sanctum, as a rule, was not extended to artists. Certainly Guy Lawrence's father was not extended any invitations to society functions. The famous poet Robert Service was also largely unknown in Dawson except to those who knew him as the clerk at a downtown bank. The 'bard of the Yukon' was widely acclaimed in the South, but it was only at the request of honoured guests from Outside that he was occasionally invited to attend social events.[64]

Accidental Tourists: Ladies and Gentlemen of Leisure

In addition to the large professional sector, the upper echelon of Dawson City included a number of 'ladies and gentlemen' of no apparent occupation. Unlike the loafers who hung around the dance halls, however, these people were unlikely to be picked up by the Mounted Police on charges of vagrancy. Rather, they might well invite the senior officers of that establishment to dinner. Two such ladies were sisters from Boston, Ella Hall and Lizzie Cheever. These two young socialites left Boston (and Cheever's husband) behind in March 1898 amid much fanfare. When they arrived at Dyea, they joined forces with several other people with means, and the party hired packers to transport their goods over the Chilkoot. This left the women free to enjoy the trail, and Ella Hall's account of her climb over the Chilkoot is unique among hundreds of others only in that she reported that her 'sides ached from laughter' from rolling, tumbling, and sliding down the other side of the Chilkoot.

Ten miles upstream from what they decided was a very dirty Dawson, these two 'hired a cabin built.' Here they apparently remained for at least two winters. Hall remembered it all as a great adventure, and noted that they suffered few real hardships: 'We were not entirely cut off from the fashionable world. People were coming in all the time, and we received fashion papers a few months old to be sure, but they kept us fairly well in touch with our sister countries. We didn't change our way of dressing in particular.'[65]

Similarly, Nevill Armstrong was of that class of men 'manifestly unused to the life of a miner.'[66] Armstrong, an English gentleman through and through, was more excited by the 'first blood' drawn in the Yukon – a seagull shot from the deck of river steamer – than he was by the gold fields.[67] He was so unimpressed with Dawson, in fact, that he remained only a few weeks.

Two of Armstrong's companions on the river steamer were Edith Van Buren and Mary Hitchcock. Van Buren was the niece of the former American president and Hitchcock was from similar American pedigree. Together these ladies travelled the globe, sparing no expense and leaving a trail of champagne bottles in their wake. They left New York for their Klondike adventure decked out in outlandish costumes, accompanied by a menagerie of animals and a steamer full of goods. Once in Dawson they established themselves in a huge circus tent on the banks of the Yukon River. Here they set about discovering 'who was who' in town and were soon entertaining 'Dawson's finest.'[68] Numbered among their guest list were the American consul and the commander of the Mounted Police. That the two ladies perceived the existence of the 'finest' and that they set about finding and participating in the set are clear indications that the developing town was not without obvious class distinctions.

Conclusions

By 1901, Dawson City boasted the institutions and services expected in like-sized southern cities. It had two large hospitals and schools as well as several private operations of each. It had two libraries, four new church buildings (each with a substantial congregation), and a new system of drainage, sidewalks, and public health. It also had a well-developed social set, drawn from the official, professional, and commercial sectors, which was responsible for seeing that such institutions and services were provided and maintained. These three groups each played a part in the institutional and social development of the community. The clergy and professionals together established and maintained the community's hospitals, schools, and poor relief. The officials and civil servants coordinated the legal and bureaucratic development. The mercantile sector was involved in similar activities and also promoted the city to others.

The three groups formed the basis of what might be loosely termed the upper and middle classes of Dawson, beginning with the commissioner and his inner circle and ending with the small entrepreneurs and teachers and nurses. This social scale had some fluidity as people moved from professions to labour (doctors who became miners, for example) and from labour to vast wealth (miners who became wealthy entrepreneurs). Still, in general, the community determined its members' social standing by ethnicity and occupation. From this formula was established what a local physician referred to as the 'Nucleus of 400,' a group of couples and families of similar backgrounds who entertained and socialized together.[69]

Sterling Reputations and Golden Opportunities: The Professional and Business Sectors of Dawson

T HE SOCIAL ÉLITE that included so many medical professionals, teachers, and tourists also extended a warm welcome to the lawyers,
civil servants, and merchants who flocked to Dawson City during the
Klondike gold rush. Just as the community depended on labouring people,
a white collar sector was also necessary. The white collar world offered a host
of positions to aspiring men – and a tiny few women. Lawyers, surveyors,
civil servants, mounted police, and merchants formed a large and influential group that was predominantly white, Anglo-Saxon, and Protestant.

Mining the Miners: Lawyers and Surveyors

Gold rushes always conjure up images of masses of labouring men toiling
at their mines, but they also created a high demand for a number of professionals. One of the most necessary was the lawyer. While historians have
often claimed that it was the prostitutes and camp followers who 'mined
the miners,' in Dawson City much of the miners' dust ended up in lawyers'

Many businesses established their operations first in tents, then in more permanent and substantial structures, as can be seen by the earlier and later Bank of British North America buildings.

pockets. And legally, too! For many professionals who did not want to dirty their hands with the day-to-day business of mining found that there were much more dependable alternatives. John McDougal made an apt analogy when he commented on the success of his brother's Dawson law practice in 1899: 'Frank has already located the pay streak and is fast approaching bed-rock ... I would venture to say (between ourselves) that his business for this year will be much larger than that of any lawyer or law office in Ottawa ... and I see no reason why it should not increase in the future.'[1] The saloons and dance halls were not the only places where miners were fleeced.

Naturally, most Dawson lawyers filled their agendas with cases related to mining. Since mining claims were in effect real estate transactions, transfer of ownership, surface rights, and the creation and dissolution of partnerships had to be prepared by a lawyer. As well, a large proportion of legal cases involved settling suits for defaulted wages – most of them for work on mines that did not 'pan out.' Defaulted wage cases were a problem from the earliest period, for Mounted Police Inspector Constantine noted as early as 1896 that there was no 'machinery by which small debts may be collected except that of force.' Considering force a less than satisfactory way of settling such disputes, Constantine urged the federal government to create a court system, and once established, the Yukon courts were clogged with cases for defaulted wages and breaches of contract, most of them pursued with the assistance of a licensed barrister.[2] Dawson lawyers less frequently took on criminal cases, finding themselves defending residents and clients of the demi-monde against charges that included theft, prostitution, procuring, and assault.

For these and other legal situations, lawyers had sliding fee scales based on what they thought clients could pay and the costs of operating their practice. Running an office was expensive in Dawson, regardless of the profession. Office space could not be obtained at any price, and staff for office work, when they could be obtained, drew wages of $150 to $200 per month.[3] It was a good thing, then, that Frank McDougal's legal practice was doing so well in 1899, for his overhead was probably extremely high by southern Canadian standards. McDougal was one of a number of lawyers who called Dawson their home for many years. Establishing his practice in 1898, he was still working in Dawson in 1901.[4]

Like medical professionals, the vast majority – 80 percent – of Dawson's lawyers were Canadian or British born, and most of them were Protestant. And just as for the local physicians and surgeons, this was no accident, for most American lawyers did not qualify to practise British law in the dominion. American lawyers contented themselves with practices on the Alaska side of the border, where there was plenty of work in the smaller gold camps and transportation centres. Meanwhile, some of the most prominent citizens in Dawson were English Canadian lawyers, among them George Black, F.C. Wade, Bert Pattullo, W.C.W. Tabor, and Harry Ridley.[5]

Members of the legal profession also participated in the social whirl of Dawson. Ridley and his wife were members of Dawson's early upper crust; it was Mrs Ridley who, once back in Toronto, informed Laura Thompson Berton of the need to take an evening gown on her trip north to teach school. Indeed, Mrs Ridley apparently showed Berton a whole rack of evening gowns she had worn in Dawson. Accustomed to taking a prominent role in civic affairs, lawyers littered the list of board members of the churches and hospitals of Dawson, while their wives and daughters were well represented among the charitable dames of the women's auxiliaries.

A number of lawyers, like so many other Klondikers, remained after the initial rush period to establish themselves permanently in Dawson. Charles Tabor, for example, was a New Brunswick-born lawyer who arrived at the height of the 1898 rush. Tabor maintained his well-respected law firm and was still living in Dawson nineteen years later when he was killed in an accident. Tabor married while living in Dawson, and his wife continued to reside there after his death.[6] Likewise George Black, another New Brunswick lawyer, maintained his law practice after the boom waned and went on to become both a member of parliament and commissioner of the Yukon. An active member of the local business and social community, he remained a resident of the Yukon for the rest of his life.

Roderick Ashbaugh was a similar case. Ashbaugh was a young Winnipeg lawyer who gave up his practice in that city to try his luck in Dawson in 1899. Here he remained for the rest of his life, establishing a successful practice that specialized in mining matters. Ashbaugh committed himself to the community as an active member of the Methodist congregation and the Liberal party. He was elected to serve on the first wholly elected Yukon Council in 1909, although he died in Dawson the following year before he could fulfil his term. Ashbaugh was probably typical of Dawson lawyers who represented claim owners, for in addition to acting on their behalf in the sale and acquisition of thousands of claims, he owned several himself.[7]

Surveyors also made a good living from the mining industry in the Klondike. One claim owner reported that he had paid $120 to have a forty-six foot fractional claim surveyed in 1899. This caused him to remark, 'By Jove, I would like to be a good lawyer or a good ... DLS [Dominion Land Surveyor] for the next two years out here ... The surveyors have more work than they can do here at $50 per day.'[8] This was a princely wage indeed when compared with the $6 per day of the average miner.

They were not all in it for the money, however, as the case of William Cautley clearly shows. Cautley was a twenty-four-year-old Yorkshireman who was working as a dominion land surveyor (DLS) near Cranbrook, British Columbia, when Sifton sent him to Dawson in 1897. The DLS men were appointed at a wage of $150 per month and a modest living allowance.[9] Private surveyors, meanwhile, could earn as much as three or four times that salary. Private surveying was not for Cautley though, for he preferred to work for the government. Although a surveyor by profession, Cautley worked in a variety of roles, helping Thomas Fawcett in the chaotic Office of the Gold Commissioner and occasionally acting as administrator on intestate deaths.[10] Like so many others, Cautley seems to have come under the spell of the Yukon, for three years later when the Department of the Interior reduced the number of surveyors on staff, Cautley took an appointment as the mining inspector for the Indian River District rather than leave the Yukon for another DLS position.[11]

Private surveyors found plenty of work surveying contested mining claims, residential and commercial lots, and timber berths. Six of these advertised themselves as actively seeking business in 1901, and their advertisements indicate that many of them were themselves involved in mining. One, the Canadian James Edward Beatty, worked on the construction of Yukon rail lines since he was also a civil engineer.[12] Government surveyors seem to have fit in socially with the civil servants and downtown crowd, while private surveyors floated on the fringe between the mining and mercantile crowds. Still, combining their mining interests with their surveying expertise, many private surveyors found a good living in Dawson's early years. As claims were bought up and consolidated by large companies after the turn of the century, however, the demand for surveyors diminished and not a few left for greener pastures.

The Downtown Crowd: The Commercial Sector of Dawson
At the end of the nineteenth century, the mercantile sector in both Alaska and the Yukon was dominated by two large trading companies. Throughout the period, the North American Trading and Transfer Company and the Alaska Commercial Company owned the majority of the river steamers

and thus held an obvious advantage in supplying goods. The two big companies, by one observer's estimate, together accounted for about half of all the trade along the Yukon River during the Klondike gold rush. Because the transportation season was so short – from late May to early October – Dawson's merchants relied on these large companies not only to transport wholesale goods but also for storage, since they also held a monopoly on the warehouses lining Dawson's riverfront.[13]

Individual traders and merchants always existed, although pressure from the commercial companies often forced them to the more remote outposts and mining camps. Joseph Ladue was Dawson's first commercial entrepreneur. Ladue was an American-born trader and grubstaker who came to the Yukon in 1888 when he was forty-two years old. It was Ladue and his partner Arthur Harper who staked claim to the townsite they named Dawson City in 1896. Within a couple of weeks of the Bonanza discovery, the two men were selling town lots from their trading post *cum* real estate office. Ladue had an enviable monopoly, owning not only the lots on which to build a town but also the sawmill to supply the lumber.[14] The Harper-Ladue Townsite Company also operated the city's first trading post and saloon.

Not surprisingly, Ladue did very well with this business and two years later he was ready to expand. With backing from New York financiers, Joe established himself as president and managing director of the Joseph Ladue Gold Mining and Development Company in 1898. They opened the company store in Dawson in September 1898, and although Ladue did not survive to see the enterprise mature, the firm remained one of 'Dawson's [most] reliable general supply firms and steam sawmills' for another thirteen years. Neither Harper nor Ladue, as we saw earlier, survived the rush to enjoy their wealth after many years of prospecting and trading in the harsh Yukon environment. Arthur Harper died of tuberculosis the year after the Bonanza strike and Ladue of the same disease four years later.[15]

Later Dawson mercantile operations varied in size from small specialty stores to the more substantial general merchants. Joseph Gandolfo, for example, was a well-known fruit and candy merchant formerly of the Cripple Creek gold camp in Colorado. Gandolfo was a naturalized American of Italian birth. He had arrived in Dawson in 1898 when he was fifty-two years old, and he was joined by his wife the following year and by his younger brother Alexander in 1901. The Gandolfo family did well in Dawson, where in 1898 their 'first shipment of eight tons of oranges, lemons, bananas and cucumbers arrived in an untouched market at $1 apiece.'[16] In a city where people were dying of scurvy every winter, the family had cornered a highly lucrative market. Running a business, however, was not cheap: Joseph Gandolfo reportedly paid $120 per month to rent five feet of street frontage for his shop in 1898.

Despite high costs of overhead, enterprising merchants who managed to establish themselves early in the marketplace often realized very healthy profits. The Gandolfos became prosperous and prominent, remaining in Dawson for a number of years after the rush. Active in the Roman Catholic church and regular contributors to a number of local charities, they invested their profits well and managed to maintain a very comfortable life style. According to the census, by 1901 Joseph and Josephine Gandolfo owned $15,000 worth of real estate, $8,000 worth of mining claims, and $10,200 in personal property. This was a tidy poke indeed.

Insurance rates were also high – in some cases insurance could not even be obtained – as a result of Dawson's frequent fires, further adding to merchants' overhead. Fires destroyed large districts several times. The fire of 26 April 1899 was one of the worst, with damages totalling over $1,000,000. It destroyed the Bank of British North America, along with several hotels and commercial buildings in the business district.[17] Still, despite high rents, insurance rates, and the costs of rebuilding after fires, a good profit could be turned by capturing a corner in this highly competitive market. Luxury items such as fruit, canned oysters, and salted nuts brought a brisk trade to specialty merchants.[18]

Little was known about Dawson's merchant class until Margaret Archibald produced a detailed study of the commercial development of the Klondike for Parks Canada in 1981. Archibald speculated that most of the 300 stores and saloons operating in Dawson during the summer of 1898 probably came and went that same season. Yet careful examination of the newspapers, city directories, and census data indicates that these businesses were more stable than they at first appeared. Of the nearly 300 Dawsonites who reported themselves merchants in the 1901 census, 62 percent had arrived in 1898 or earlier. Merchants and their families, like miners, labourers, and professionals, also demonstrated a tendency to make Dawson their home for extended periods.[19]

Local butcher Christophe Authier was one of these tenacious merchants. Authier came to Dawson from Quebec in 1898 and remained there until his death in 1917. One of a very few French Canadian merchants, Authier established a butcher shop in Dawson during his first summer.

As fast as the miners could stake claims, small merchants eagerly established businesses catering to their every need and fancy.

He raised his own animals, butchered the meat, and dabbled in mostly doomed mining ventures on the side. Likewise, Albert Lobley went to Dawson in 1897. He established a produce business and operated scows on the Yukon River between Dawson and Whitehorse until 1916, when he moved Outside. These small businessmen might have come to Dawson on a whim, but they remained long after the rush was over, serving the needs of their community and trying their hand at numerous schemes in their quest for fortune.[20]

The mercantile sector also demonstrated a high degree of ethnic clustering. Over 90 percent of Dawson's male Jewish population, for example, reported themselves merchants. Numbering thirty-eight in 1901, nearly 70 percent of these men were of Eastern European or Russian birth. This group also tended to cluster in their living arrangements, similar to the pattern observed among French Canadians miners in Dawson and at Paris Creek. Local merchant Abraham Isaacs, for example, a young Jewish-American merchant who came to Dawson in 1900, was living at the time of the census with three other single Jewish merchants: Max Steinfeld, Daniel Levy, and Max Krause. That they were living collectively was probably as much a function of economics as of culture, for excepting the cabin owned by Isaacs, the group had between them $400 in personal property. Levy and Steinfeld had arrived in 1897 and 1898 respectively, while Krause had only just arrived in 1901.[21] All of these men became active in the local community, although they did not move within the inner sanctum. Isaacs became a leader within the Jewish community of Dawson and acted as secretary of the 'Hebrew Congregation of Dawson' in the opening years of the twentieth century.[22]

Many anglophone merchants who established themselves at the height of the rush became fixtures of the social and political core of Dawson City. Henry Macaulay, a 'wholesale importer' from Ontario, for example, established his business in Dawson in 1898 and three years later became the city's first mayor. He was succeeded in 1902 by P.H. McLennan, a Dawson hardware merchant since 1898, who became mayor by defeating general merchant Thomas Adair. In addition to the mayor, 50 percent of the first elected city council was composed of merchants, including Horace Norquay, James F. McDonald, and Thomas Adair. The other councillors included a bookkeeper and two miners. In fact there is a high degree of overlap between early city councillors and members of the Dawson Board of Trade, including all of the above mayoral candidates and most of the councillors.[23]

From the earliest date, the commercial sector was concerned with promoting Dawson's reputation as a viable and healthy place to do business. To this end, the merchants gave aid generously in hard times. During the winter of 1898-9, when a combination of high costs of food and fuel, epidemic disease, and seasonal unemployment created a pool of destitute families and indigent sick, the commercial sector readily donated time, money, and goods. Dr Barrett of the Relief Committee reported that Dawson's merchants were quick to respond to requests for donations because they were adamant that appeals for government funds be avoided. Insisting that it was bad for the city's image – and therefore also for business – to accept government relief, the merchants insisted that Dawson was willing and able to 'look after its own.' They did so in spite of reports that 'the season's output of gold was largely sent out,'[24] leaving few resources on which to rely in order to relieve distress within the community.

Other business owners did their part to offset some of the social problems associated with high seasonal unemployment. Saloons and dance halls provided shelter at night for the 'hundreds of idle men [who] have been in Dawson during the winter.'[25] After the last drink had been served, many local saloon owners fed cold and hungry men and allowed them to sleep on the warm floors, bars, and gaming tables. Here was Dawson's unofficial social welfare system; a system badly needed during the long winter months.

The commercial sector could also form a powerful lobby on issues that affected their businesses. In 1900, for example, local merchant Charles Reichenbach spearheaded the lobby in favour of maintaining theatres and dance halls in Dawson. Reichenbach, who arrived in Dawson in 1898, was a German-born Jewish merchant operating a prosperous clothing business with his son.[26] The petition accompanying his letter to the commander of the Mounted Police was signed by nearly a hundred local businessmen, including most of the city's merchants, hotel proprietors, and contractors. The merchants vigorously protested interference with the operation of the dance halls, arguing that their businesses would be sorely hurt should this element be thrown out of work. They won their case and the dance halls remained operational, southern opposition notwithstanding. Seven years later it was again the merchants who exerted the extra pressure required to gain (at least temporarily) a reprieve in the closure of the dance halls in Dawson.[27]

In a similar battle, the commercial sector lobbied on its own behalf for fair freight rates. After the completion of the White Pass and Yukon

Railway, the Alaska Commercial Company and the North American Transfer and Trade Company shared the transportation monopoly on the river during the summer, while the railway took most of the business during the rest of the year. Taking full advantage of their monopoly, the White Pass and Yukon hiked freight rates in 1899 and again in 1900. Mounting a vociferous campaign to preserve Dawson's reputation for business, the merchants boycotted the railway, forcing both government intervention and a lowering of rates in November 1901.[28]

Of course, just as lawyers and doctors dabbled in various other businesses in Dawson, merchants also tended to engage in diverse activities. Several, including McLennan and Hein TeRoller (who succeeded James McCook in the position of US consul), sat on boards of directors for various trust companies, stage transfer lines, and power and telephone companies. Nellie Cashman mined her own claims and operated a small grocery store at the corner of Second Street and Third Avenue in the Donovan Hotel. She was one of only two women grocery store proprietors in 1901; the remaining twenty-seven groceries were owned by men though often these were family enterprises. Cashman operated her grocery to finance her mining ventures, although by her own admission, she was not a shrewd businesswoman. Upon arriving in Dawson in the spring of 1898, 'I started a short order restaurant, which I called the Delmonico,' she remembered, but 'I didn't make any fortune. Part of the reason, though, was because if a young fellow was broke and hungry I would give him a meal for nothing.'[29] All too familiar with being flat broke, Cashman always provided for those less fortunate than herself.

Other merchants, as we have seen, did not engage in the daily business of mining but got richer by investing in mining and real estate. Belinda Mulrooney was one of these. Mulrooney, among the most famous rags-to-riches Dawsonites, owned one of the largest hotels in Dawson. Like the Gandolfo family, Mulrooney increased her substantial wealth through a variety of lucrative mining investments. Still other small business owners, including Cashman and Ladue, continued the age-old practice of grubstaking miners in exchange for partial interest in a claim.

The men and women who came to Dawson to establish businesses, like those who came to mine, probably failed as often as they succeeded, and numerous accounts relate the stories of fortunes never realized. Entrepreneurs landed in a highly competitive market, and most had to make it or break it in relatively short order. Yet some, Gandolfo and Cashman among them, stayed on for many years, convinced that as long as there were miners still looking for the mother lode, there would surely be a demand for flour, beans, and oranges.

Perhaps a typical small entrepreneur was Billy Nightingale. When Nightingale 'made a failure of mining' in 1900, he started a modest hotel in Dawson. It was nothing fancy. He rented out bunks at fifty cents per night for guests with their own blankets and $2 for those without. He seems to have made a failure of hotelkeeping as well, for by the following year he was working for wages as a clerk. Nightingale had been seeking his fortune in the Klondike since 1897 and the struggle had taken its toll, for although he was only forty-five, one of his friends wrote that after four years of northern life, Billy was 'looking very old.'[30] Billy's story was probably not an uncommon progression of affairs, for many unsuccessful entrepreneurs lost both their fortunes and their savings before their Klondike adventure was over. Countless would-be Klondike millionaires ended their Dawson sojourn working for others long enough to purchase a ticket homeward.

The families of these men and women may have suffered more than the individuals themselves. Arthur Godfrey was a hardware merchant from Vancouver who suffered the separation from his wife and children in order to try to support them. He established his hardware business in Dawson in the summer of 1900 and was satisfied that he was doing well, averaging sales of $100 per day. He was optimistic that in Dawson he 'was bound to make a living' for his family. Unfortunately, his goal was never realized for he died suddenly of pneumonia in 1901 before returning home.[31] Like Hattie Godfrey, many wives waited back home for fortunes and husbands who never re-materialized.

A similar fate befell Joseph Clearihue. He had been supplying British Columbia's miners in Glenora and the Stikine during the rush of 1898 before establishing a general merchandise store in Dawson in 1900. Clearihue was attempting to support his wife and children, as his letters show: 'I have got to provide for you all and I must not throw up the sponge.' Unluckily, Clearihue got 'fixed pretty good' by his shop manager, who sold all the stock while Clearihue was out of town and then absconded with the proceeds. Discouraged, Clearihue sent his wife his last $30 and assured her he wanted 'no more of the Klondike.' The couple's bad luck did not end there, for the thirty-dollar money order went down with the ship the *Islander* and Annie Clearihue did not receive it.[32] Clearihue later successfully re-established his business in Victoria.

Many stampeders who were disillusioned with the prospects of the

Klondike sold their outfits soon after arriving in order to buy their out-bound passage. Overnight, dozens of commission agents were born, clear-ing great profits through 'buying from the downhearted and selling to the stout-hearted.' This was the motto on which the firm of Taylor and Drury based its business at Bennett in 1899.[33] These agents did very well, and by the end of the summer of 1898, the market was completely flooded with merchandise ranging from rubber boots, woollen underdrawers, and beds to caviar and champagne. Some commission agents turned their profits into permanent businesses, as did Taylor and Drury who became a per-manent institution in Yukon mercantilism from their entrepreneurial beginnings at Lake Bennett.

A small but equally hard-working group of women operated their own businesses in Dawson's competitive market. Serving the needs of Dawson's growing female population, there were eight clothing and hat shops owned and operated by women in 1901.[34] Mary Anderson, for exam-ple, had been a retail grocer and provision dealer in Chicago before the gold rush. Anderson had come with her husband in 1899 to Dawson, where they opened a lodging house. The marriage, never very stable, did not survive the relocation and Mary started her own business, a ladies' clothing shop on Second Avenue, which she ran from 1901 until 1905.[35]

Another well-known millinery and dress shop was Summers and Orell. Catherine Summers was a young seamstress who came from Ontario to join her sister, Mrs Jane Orell, in 1900. Orell had arrived in Dawson City the previous year to establish her millinery and dress shop. Following local conventions of respectability, the sisters lived together with another Ontario seamstress, Minnie Walker, who also worked in their shop.[36]

As Dawson's ethnic groups did, women tended to cluster in certain occupations. Women entrepreneurs concentrated their efforts in the restau-rant and lodging businesses in particular, most likely because minimal cap-ital outlay was required for such operations. Women often established these enterprises first in their homes and, as the business grew, expanded into more commercial surrounds. Eleven of Dawson's sixteen lodging houses were operated by women, as were seven restaurants, cafés, and lunch counters at the turn of the century. Only two women owned 'hotels' in the usual sense of the word by 1901. None of Dawson's women mer-chants sat on the Board of Trade or held any political office in the period.

The professional and mercantile groups overlapped socially. Managers and owners of the large commercial companies, for example, gained automatic entrance to the inner circle of Dawson society, as did many of the smaller but equally influential business owners in town.[37] Members of the professional and mercantile class reinforced their relationships through social and familial connections. The Yukon Tennis Club, formed during the summer of 1900, illustrates this relationship very well. The members of this exclusive club were all either merchants, professionals, or wives of the same. Nellie McLennan, for example, the wife of local merchant James P. McLennan, played tennis with Maria Starnes, wife of the commander of the NWMP. Links between the 'downtown' crowd and the civil service élite were common occurrences. Likewise for the Dawson Curling Club, as evidenced by the 1901 bonspiel in which the Yukon commissioner's rink played a rink of merchants for the championship title.[38]

The union of dentist A.J. Gillis and lodging-house keeper Frances Dorley also illustrates the connection between the professional and commercial sector. Alexander Gillis was a Nova Scotia-born dentist who came to Dawson in 1898. He established a successful practice and through it, met and married Frances Dorley. Dorley was a Seattle dressmaker and milliner who went to the Klondike on her own in 1898 when she was twenty-six. At the junction of Eldorado and Bonanza creeks she started a roadhouse, where she 'baked tons of bread and pies and made millions of doughnuts.' Moving to Dawson in the spring of 1899, she went into partnership with a Mrs Moore, investing her roadhouse profits in the Professional Men's Boarding House, 'a pleasant hostelry which catered to the more respectable element of Dawson commerce.'[39]

That Frances Dorley Gillis saw herself as having married 'up' seems clear. After she married Alex Gillis, she remembered that they were 'an active and happy part of Dawson society' for many years. The couple formed a social bridge between the professional and commercial sectors, claiming among their close friends Dr Alfred Thompson as well as Belle and Marie McCormick, daughters of the proprietor of the Portland Restaurant. Prominent himself, Alexander Gillis was instrumental in founding the first Masonic Lodge in Dawson City, and Frances became the first officer of the women's auxiliary, Daughters of the Eastern Star. The Gillises moved Outside in 1918.[40]

Martha Purdy Black, like Dorley, also entered Dawson society from the commercial sector. Tagging along with her brother on his mining ventures, Black went on to manage the saw and quartz mill financed by her father in 1901. Raising two young boys and managing the mill, Black left no doubt of her social class, for she employed a 'French housekeeper, wife of the mill watchman.' She was also part of the 'set' in Dawson, attending card and skating parties in the winter and playing tennis in the summer. Like Ella Hall and Lizzie Cheevers, the two young Boston socialites, Black had the latest and 'most beautiful clothes,' which she purchased from a local dress shop in Dawson, possibly Summers and Orell.[41] Many social events, including the annual Arctic Brotherhood and St Andrew's balls, required elaborate fashion. These, like the commissioner's dinners, were black-tie and evening-gown affairs, attended by everyone of good social standing. Presumably the ability both to obtain and to afford such attire was a means of establishing the hierarchy of the social élite, for it is mentioned often in the women's memoirs. It was from among this social set that Martha chose her second husband, the New Brunswick lawyer and later Yukon commissioner, George Black.

The mercantile and professional communities became bound together by common interests as well as by business, ethnic, family, and church connections. Gordon McLellan, a Nova Scotian and small businessman, for example, was a pillar of the Presbyterian church. Starting out as a miner in 1898, he went on to become the proprietor of 'Mac's Grocery.' McLellan also brought his sister, Winifred, to the Klondike, and she became one of the first school teachers on the creeks, as noted earlier. Winifred, Gordon, and many of their friends were active members of the church, and Gordon was superintendent of St Andrew's Sunday School for many years.[42] This type of community involvement consolidated the links between the professional and the mercantile classes, for the Presbyterian Reverend Pringle was a close friend of Winifred and Gordon McLellan.

The Personal and the Political: Government, Politics, and the Civil Service in Dawson

The first civil servants that Ottawa sent to the unorganized Yukon Territory were George Dawson and William Ogilvie in 1887. The Canadian government commissioned them to survey the area drained by the Yukon River. Due to the ever-increasing mining activity, Ogilvie and Bishop Bompas were both suggesting by 1893 that the government establish a permanent presence in the region. The men provided different rationales: Bompas saw the need to control the selling of liquor to Indians; Ogilvie considered the need for general law enforcement and collection of customs. As a result of their proposals – and one suspects that Laurier was swayed by the latter argument – the federal government sent the first

Like many young men, Gordon McLellan, proprietor of Mac's, came to the Klondike to make his fortune. He arrived alone in 1898 and soon invited his school-teacher sister Winifred to come to Dawson to keep house for him.

permanent representatives of the dominion in the form of the North West Mounted Police under the command of Charles Constantine.

Arriving in 1894 to administer sovereignty over the territory, Constantine was both commander of law enforcement and general government administrator for the next three years. The wives of Constantine and his fellow officers and the clergy formed a tiny group of genteel women who 'helped for the betterment of the social and religious life' in the region.[43] This was the forerunner of Klondike 'society.'

Constantine and his men soon established a system for the collection of customs and established British law in the region.[44] Two years later, in 1896, Constantine found himself so weighed down with administrative duties that he had little time to oversee his police force. He reported to his superiors the urgent need for civil and criminal courts and an office 'for the registration of deeds of title, Bills of Sale, Chattel mortgages and papers of that description.'[45] Clifford Sifton, Laurier's minister of the interior, created the Office of the Gold Commissioner to oversee these matters the following summer.

Federal authorities reinforced this early contingent of police with a second contingent sent in under Colonel Sam Steele and with the newly created Yukon Field Force, which arrived late in the summer of 1898. The Yukon Field Force was a force of 200 regular army men sent to the Klondike to maintain Canadian law, order, and sovereignty. Mounted Police Superintendent P.C.H. Primrose reported relief at the arrival of these reinforcements, noting that the Field Force 'assisted us by furnishing sentries in the guardroom and Bank of Commerce, head office, gold escorts and sometimes prisoners' escorts, which duties, with the small numbers of our men in Dawson, it would have been impossible for us to perform.'[46] In addition to their Dawson City detachment, the Mounted Police operated a number of other posts along the route to Dawson, including those at the Chilkoot Summit and Tagish Lake.

Of course, the young male members of the police and field forces were not exempt from the many temptations of the gold camp life. Bill Morrison, in his study of the northern Mounties, notes that the 'letterbooks of the Dawson detachment are full of records of police who were punished for visiting brothels, being drunk in dance-halls and the like.' Indeed, the Mounted Police surgeon noted that venereal disease was common among the members of the force. Such behaviour on the part of the renowned Canadian police did not seem to draw much criticism from the community; that it did not has two possible explanations. Morrison argues that such 'crimes of the flesh' (drinking and consorting with prostitutes) were easily tolerated within the frontier atmosphere of the Klondike. Yet it seems likely that such behaviour would breed resentment among, at the very least, those citizens who were themselves being arrested for drunkenness and for visiting disorderly houses. More probably, the community trusted the commanding officer to deal with such offenders appropriately. Deal with them he did, for the police records show that recalcitrant constables were generally fined $15, suspended from duty, and given two months hard labour (chopping wood) when they were found drunk and disorderly or consorting with known prostitutes.[47]

In 1896, just in time for the Bonanza strike, Ogilvie returned to the territory and was kept busy surveying building lots and mining claims. Constantine and Ogilvie were joined by Thomas Fawcett in June of 1897. Fawcett took over the supervision of mining matters as the Yukon's first gold commissioner, relieving Constantine of these extra duties. For the next two years the Office of the Gold Commissioner was the centre of political and administrative conflict. Establishing as it did a central place for miners to purchase licences and register claims, it processed tens of thousands of people in a very short span of time and without a coherent plan. Thus, as political historian David Morrison observed, many of the mining disputes that arose in connection with this office were a result of sheer chaos: 'Records were lost; claims were recorded in the names of two different miners; and on one occasion the gold commissioner actually registered two discovery claims on one creek.'[48]

Laurier and Sifton filled the Office of the Gold Commissioner and most of the subsequently created government offices through patronage appointments. Realizing the importance of the new region, Laurier sent a small group of handpicked officials to provide administration late in the summer of 1897, with James Walsh as the first Commissioner of the Yukon. Walsh was a prominent ex-Mountie, Liberal, and personal friend of Clifford Sifton. Walsh was accompanied by Judge T.H. McGuire, entrusted with the responsibility of establishing the new Provisional District Court of Yukon. 'Laurier's old friend,' J.E. Girouard – the same man later accused of living with Montreal Marie – was appointed registrar of lands in 1898.[49]

Because it was a federally administered territory, the Yukon's inner sanctum was usually dominated by the stripe of the reigning party in Ottawa. When William Ogilvie became Commissioner of the Yukon, he tried to appoint a few well-known Conservatives to temper local hard feelings. Sifton immediately informed him that this was not acceptable, for 'under our system of Government we cannot appoint our opponents to office.'[50] In Dawson, the stripe remained Liberal until after the election of 1911 and the appointees included many friends of Laurier and Sifton. In fact, the list of Laurier subscribers in 1904 – the list of people donating to the federal Liberal Party – reads like the payroll of the Dawson civil service.[51]

The Pattullo brothers are a good example of Laurier and Sifton's patronage appointments in the Yukon. Dufferin and Bert Pattullo were sons of George Pattullo, an influential Ontario Liberal referred to by Wilfrid Laurier and Ontario Premier Oliver Mowat alike as 'my Dear Pattullo.'[52] George Pattullo called upon his friends in Ottawa on his sons' behalf, with the result that both obtained promising positions in Dawson. Dufferin Pattullo – later premier of British Columbia – soon found himself accompanying Major Walsh to the Yukon as his secretary. Shortly after arriving in Dawson, Walsh appointed Duff as a clerk in the Gold Office. Here over the next several years he moved steadily through the ranks of the civil service. Bert Pattullo's first position in Dawson was as a government lawyer. He was promoted to the position of crown prosecutor after writing to his father to 'see what you can do' to further his chances in this regard.[53] Likewise, all the Yukon commissioners and their top assistants before 1912 were Liberal party faithful: William Ogilvie, James Ross, Judge Dugas, Thomas Fawcett, François-Xavier Gosselin, Napoleon Laliberte, and others.[54]

Meanwhile, from the day of he arrived in 1897, the New Brunswick lawyer George Black led a small core of Dawson Conservatives.[55] After the defeat of the Laurier government in 1911, Ottawa Conservatives conducted a general purge in the civil service, and a number of Black's friends and associates replaced the Liberal faithful. In one of many letters documenting this purge, the Department of the Interior announced its decision 'to appoint Mr Albert E. Lamb, B.A., L.B., [sic] of Dawson, as Registrar in the Gold Commissioner's Office there, in place of Napoleon Laliberte, whose services are to be dispensed with for political partizanship.'[56] Lamb, a long-time Conservative, upheld the tradition of Yukon patronage appointments.

Mutual friends in Ottawa notwithstanding, the first group of Klondike mandarins was not always congenial. With Major Walsh came a Liberal lawyer named F.C. Wade, another friend of Sifton's. Wade was an outspoken critic of Walsh, condemning him for wintering at Tagish and not arriving with the others in Dawson in the fall of 1897. This attack was levelled at Walsh on the assumption that his presence at Dawson might have somehow alleviated the winter of 1897 food shortage. He openly criticized Gold

Commissioner Thomas Fawcett for the disorganization and ineffectiveness in his office. Wade even came into conflict with Mounted Police Commander Constantine, whom he reportedly called down over issues of liquor licensing. When another member of the group, Judge McGuire, tried to pull Wade back into line, Wade turned his acid pen in that direction, accusing McGuire of having the 'unhappy faculty of sticking his nose into everything that does not concern him.'[57] Such internal conflict within the new administration did little to instil confidence in the locals, and there were daily complaints of fraud and mismanagement of government affairs. A number of scandals followed, implicating some of the highest ranking officials, including Walsh, Fawcett, and even Wade himself.

That many allegations of fraud and bribery were substantiated is perhaps to be expected. Low salaries and high costs of living tempted a number of civil servants to take advantage of their positions, much to Laurier's and Sifton's great embarrassment. Yukon officials were paid only slightly higher wages than civil servants in the South. The usual salary for a junior clerk in the Office of the Gold Commissioner, for example, was $900 per year, while a more senior clerk could draw $1,200. This was only $10 per month more than a comparable clerk drew in the South. Taking in huge amounts of gold dust and currency every day, several young clerks gave in and helped themselves to a 'golden opportunity.' Two such clerks, Conklin and Layfield, were investigated for mishandling government funds in 1898.[58] Another was Thomas Middleton, who had been appointed to the Gold Office in 1898. This young English-born clerk misappropriated nearly $6,000 in mining claim fees. A scandal ensued when, upon being discovered, Middleton committed suicide by slitting his throat.[59]

Government officials earned much higher wages than did their clerks, yet this did not preclude them from occasionally taking advantage of their positions. James Langlois Bell of Quebec, for example, was appointed assistant gold commissioner in 1899 at an annual salary of $4,000, in addition to $1,200 in annual living expenses. Bell was removed from this position after an investigation into his handling of information and sale of mining claims. Thomas Fawcett was also removed from his position as gold commissioner, although it is unclear whether he was corrupt or simply overwhelmed by the volume of work.[60]

Still others found themselves accused not of misappropriation but of conflict of interests. F.C. Wade was charged in 1899 with acting in conflict of interest while he was crown prosecutor because he also privately represented several mining firms – sometimes acting as counsel for the prosecution and defence on the same case. Reports that Wade had grown rich on mining revenue led the Laurier cabinet to pass an order restricting all officials from staking, purchasing, or sharing profits from mining claims. J.E. Girouard and W.H.P. Clement both conducted private legal practices outside of their civil service positions. As well, Girouard and another French Canadian, Judge Dugas, were both chastised by the commissioner for devoting 'too much time to the acquirement of [mining] claims.'[61]

For many young Liberals, appointment in the service of the government was an opportunity for an expense-paid adventure to the Klondike. Caught up in the spirit of the rush, these men occasionally participated in the boisterous social life that Dawson offered. The young clerk William Beattie, for example, arrived once too often at the Gold Office in a 'state of Intoxication' and acting 'in a profane and riotous manner.' Claiming connections in Ottawa, Beattie refused to be reprimanded by his supervisor. Commissioner Ogilvie handled the matter by suspending and fining Beattie before transferring him out of Dawson to the mining office at Hunker Creek, where he was presumably expected to 'dry out.' Even the estimable Dufferin Pattullo, clerk in the Gold Office and later Premier of British Columbia, demonstrated an affection for Dawson's night life such that Sifton found it necessary to reprimand him personally when Duff visited Ottawa. Still others, notably Philip Holliday, were removed from their positions after being convicted of supplementing their incomes by criminal activity, in Holliday's case by selling whisky to Indians.[62]

Informal networks based on place of origin operated within the ranks of the civil service in a way similar to that among miners and labourers. Business and family connections 'back home' provided a ready basis for friendship and assistance in finding employment. George Nash, a young clerk, wrote home about the number of members of the 'Ottawa crowd' he encountered when he arrived in Dawson. Nash's father, Patrick, journeyed to Ottawa where he called in favours by seeking government appointments for himself and a number of the other members of the 'Ottawa crowd,' which Sifton later awarded.[63]

Though many Dawsonites, especially those looking for work, regarded government positions with envy, civil servants themselves found it difficult to maintain a comfortable life style. In 1898, the average government clerk was making about half the wage of clerks in the private sector in Dawson – $60 per month for a government clerk and upward of $125 per month for a clerk in a private law firm. That such salaries were hardly enough to survive on is clear from the volume of correspondence over living allowances. Civil servants in Dawson employees received room and board in government housing in addition to their salaries. After October 1899, the government found it too expensive to provide these services and gradually phased them out. By 1900, the government was no longer supplying meals or lodging, and civil servants received instead a monthly living allowance of $100, a sum increased by $50 after many complaints of hardship in 1902.[64] In 1904, grumbling over civil servant living allowances erupted into a formal petition for increases. Employees from all ranks made submissions the Department of the Interior detailing the myriad reasons why the allowances were insufficient. They were supported in their petition by the Bank of British North America and a number of other local businesses. In a community where groceries were easily triple the southern cost, and where dentists, barbers, and doctors charged fees five to six times the rate elsewhere, living allowances could hardly keep up.

The civil servant petition was supported by the Yukon commissioner himself, who wrote that the living allowances were 'ridiculously small.'[65] This position is well substantiated, for statements of monthly expenses sent by the commissioner to the minister of the interior ranged from $170 for a clerk supporting his wife and child to $456 for the territorial registrar to support his wife, five children, and a servant. Wrote F.A.H. Fysh, 'My wife does her own house work and is very economical and only by living this way are we [the couple and their three children] able to live within the salary and living allowance ... I receive.'[66] Married men received slightly higher living allowances than did single men – $300 more per year. As a result, many men did not bring their families in, arranging instead to have the Department of Interior pay a portion of their salaries to their wives at home.

The merchants of Dawson supported their friends and colleagues in the civil service with a petition of their own. Always a strong lobby, the merchants' petition argued that 'the salaries, reduced as intended, will not permit any of those officials and employees who are married and have to sustain their families, to meet their current expenses.' Signed by approximately forty merchants and businessmen, the petition also contended that maintaining adequate salaries would ensure that officials would not be tempted to speculate in other affairs.[67] The petitions resulted in moderate increases, but living allowances remained a contentious issue in Dawson for years.

William Cautley, a dominion land surveyor, left a memoir that reveals much about the life of single male civil servants in Dawson at the turn of the century. He remembered, for example, that the social life of Dawson offered rather less than they were accustomed to in the more southerly cities of the dominion: 'In those days there were no clubs, no private houses to which one might be invited, no place to which one could invite one's friends. My own quarters ... consisted of a small roughly-boarded room in the Gold Commissioner's staff house.' Instead, even the most respectable single men unwound at the M & N, the North Star, the Aurora, the Monte Carlo, and the Alhambra saloons. Each of these establishments had the attraction of some combination of bar, gambling room, dance hall, or vaudeville theatre. On the creeks social life was even more restricted and another surveyor, John McGregor, remembered a long stint on Hunker Creek, when 'the evenings were long and dreary' and there was 'nothing to read except a Bible.'[68]

Politics and Yukon Political Structures

The Yukon was officially made a territory by Parliament in 1898, complete with executive, legislative, and judicial bodies. A commissioner and six appointees became the Yukon Council. The council formed the top level of the civil service hierarchy, looking after the day-to-day operations of the administration and forming the upper stratum of 'society.' When William Ogilvie succeeded Major Walsh as Yukon commissioner in the late summer of 1898, his council included F.C. Wade as legal adviser, J.E. Girouard as registrar of lands, T.H. McGuire as judge, and Sam Steele as commander of the NWMP. After the scandals of 1898, however, Wade and McGuire were replaced both on council and in office by W.H.P. Clement and C.A. Dugas, respectively.[69]

In both appointed and elected positions throughout the period, a French-English tension existed, much as it did in central Canada. Just as elsewhere in Canada the French Canadian mandarins appointed by Laurier did not always get along with the English appointees of Sifton. Dugas and Girouard, for example, were the lowest paid members of the council, a matter of contention that they did not hesitate to bring to Laurier's attention, urging him both to increase their pay and to appoint more French Canadian civil servants.[70]

The French-English fact was also noticeable in political lobbies. Max Landreville and E.J. Livernash, for example, represented francophone and anglophone miners respectively in the lobby to have the mining laws changed in 1898. Meanwhile, George Armstrong and Colonel Donald McGregor, two Scots Canadians, led the 1898 movement to secure representation in Ottawa. This group soon realized that in order to gain full support and strengthen their case they needed a francophone presence; in March 1900, the exclusively anglophone membership of this committee was augmented by the addition of Auguste Noel and Alex Prudhomme.

The French-English fact was an early feature of Yukon elections, as we can see by the first two elected members of the Yukon Council in 1900, Alex Prudhomme and Arthur Wilson. Wilson was a Liberal who joined the rush in 1897 from Nanaimo, where he had been a coal miner and municipal councillor. Prudhomme was a Conservative from Quebec who arrived in 1897 and had been a miner before establishing himself as a contractor and builder. Prudhomme and Wilson were opposed in the election by a pair of independents, Thomas O'Brien and Auguste Noel. Noel was a local barrister and closet Liberal; O'Brien was one of the wealthiest hotel and saloon owners in Dawson, boasting private assets in excess of $142,000.[71] Each political ticket in subsequent elections had one English-speaking and one French-speaking candidate, indicating the importance of the French Canadian component within the community throughout the period. More than 80 percent of the men who successfully contested these positions represented the professional and commercial sector between 1901 and 1908.[72]

One of the links between the commercial and political worlds in Dawson, and a member the inner circle, was the US consul in Dawson. Colonel James Church McCook was an Irish-born entrepreneur with close ties to President McKinley, who appointed him to the post in 1898. Since Dawson's largest and most prominent mercantile operations were headed by American interests, McCook's business and manufacturing background made him a logical choice for the post. The American consul gained automatic entrance to the inner sanctum of Dawson, for McCook and his successors attended all the major social functions, including the annual St Andrew's Ball and the gala 'Bal Poudre,' held in the winter of 1904. McCook was particularly well integrated in the social and political world of Dawson society, presiding over the farewell banquet of Thomas Fawcett, the gold commissioner who left under a cloud of accusations.[73] McCook lived alone, but the wives of subsequent consuls socialized with wives of the other top Dawson officials, including the Yukon commissioner, the commander of the Mounted Police, and the gold commissioner.[74]

Soon after his appointment as the first US consul, McCook found it necessary to appoint a vice consul to assist him. He chose Ronald Morrison, a well-connected man of the inner circle. Morrison was a naturalized American of Canadian birth and a veteran of the Colorado mining camps. He was also a partner of Big Alex McDonald and a board member of the Presbyterian church.[75] His background made him an ideal candidate to assist McCook in resolving the many disputes that Dawson's American miners brought him. As an Americanized Canadian, a miner, and a public official, Morrison formed a bridge between several key components of the growing community.

Conclusions

By 1901, Dawson City boasted the institutions and services expected in Canadian cities of similar size. It had a system of courts, a jail, and a growing civil service. It counted literally hundreds of small business operations, including hotels, saloons, and shops, which depended on a handful of larger transportation and wholesaling companies. Within this growing community, many aspiring professionals established successful careers and found a place for themselves within the newly created administrative structures. Most of these were young, Protestant, English Canadian men who had come to Dawson, like so many others, seeking adventure and opportunity. With them came a corps of business entrepreneurs, and together the two groups set about erecting a political system that closely paralleled those of more southern communities. Lawyers and other professional men dominated the territorial council and government, while members of the mercantile sector dominated the municipal government they had set up.

Ambitious young professionals, then, found plenty of opportunities to advance their careers in Dawson. Some of these men were ethical, while a few were not. Yet clearly the Klondike adventure was not an event limited to the men and women who laboured in the mines. Lawyers and surveyors 'mined the miners,' while doctors, nurses, teachers, and clerics attended to their physical, intellectual, and spiritual needs. Grocers and hardware merchants aggressively fought for a share of the local market, both as suppliers and as lenders of grubstakes.

Together, the mercantile and professional residents of Dawson formed a social and political elite. The upper stratum began with the highest officials and ended with the small entrepreneurs, government clerks, teachers, and nurses. The social scale had some fluidity as people moved from professions to labour – doctors who became miners, for example –

2360. BANQUET BY THE U.S. CONSUL DAWSON JULY 4TH 99.

Banquet of the US consul. Though Americans never constituted the majority of Dawson's population, they were a large and visible component of the community. The United States established a consulate in Dawson in 1898.

or from small business to the ranks of the professionals – boarding house owners such as Frances Dorley, who married the local dentist. Still, the 'upper crust' of Dawson remained largely the preserve of the professionals who were predominantly Canadian or British Protestants. Thus, the 'downtown crowd' or mercantile sector, which remained predominantly American throughout the period, operated a social and business network of their own. At times these two groups came together to form a powerful lobby – as we saw with the protests over dance hall closures – but for the most part they carved out their own arenas of influence.

CHAPTER 7

Women, Men, and
Community in the Klondike

I N MANY WAYS Dawson City was an 'instant' city. Displacing a Han fish camp, a town of 30,000 sprang up in the space of little more than a year. Almost all of these people were newcomers, not just to Dawson but to the Yukon as well. They came from the four corners of the world, the majority of them from outside Canada's borders. Together they built a city in the wilderness, a lasting community in which many of them settled permanently. By 1901, this community was relatively stable, boasting a full-time population of nearly 10,000 people.

In this work I set out to identify the average Klondikers and to learn something about what it meant to them to have been part of the great Klondike gold rush. For it seems clear from the hundreds of memoirs and diaries written in the period that Klondikers were well aware of their status as participants in an historic event. I also looked beneath the surface of the community by asking questions about where these people came from and what role they played in establishing a community in the far northern wilderness. To do so, I examined four components of the new

TENT TOWN, DAWSON, 1898,

KEIT. Photo.

The early Dawson City was a sea of
canvas tents, as pictured here in 1898.

It did not take long for log cabins and frame houses to replace the sea of white canvas tents. Within three years, Dawson's streetscape began to resemble those of more southern, well-established cities.

community: Native people, miners and other labourers, prostitutes and other residents of the demi-monde, and the professional and business sectors. The results demonstrate that many of our assumptions about the Klondike are incorrect.

Klondike society was cosmopolitan. The assumption by several authorities on the Yukon that the vast majority of Klondikers were Americans is a false one. And while Canadian-, British-, and American-born residents together made up over three-quarters of the population, fully 20 percent reported other countries of origin. This figure remained constant throughout the period under study, and it makes Dawson look quite different from western mining towns in the United States, boasting as they did American-born populations of at least 80 percent.

Furthermore, despite at least one report that described the Yukon as 'a community of men,'[1] Dawson City was always home to a significant number of women and children. Although the ratio of men to women remained high throughout the gold rush, the potential effect of such a preponderance of males was mitigated by a surprisingly large number of families. Family life was important to the residents of Dawson City, and they moved to establish it as a permanent feature very early.

Families also tended to migrate as a unit. While most of us have come to imagine the 'golden trail' as a male migration, it turns out that thousands of women also made the long trek north. Some travelled alone; others accompanied their husbands, fathers, and sisters. It was through the combined efforts of the men, women, and families of all ethnicities that a well-ordered and cohesive community emerged by the turn of the century.

For many men and women, the journey to the Yukon constituted their first contact with Native people, and they recorded their impressions at length. From these records, it is clear that racism was a mainstay of Yukon life, an attitude that individuals did not shake off in the Klondike experience. The Native community was disrupted by the gold rush, and its development proceeded entirely separate from Dawson's. The Han, especially, attempted to minimize their interaction with the newcomers throughout the period, remaining separate from the non-Native community. Indeed, they were unwelcome in that other community.

Miners and other labouring people constituted the majority of Dawson residents. They performed most of the work in the mines and provided the necessary labour for the service sector. The group looked very much like the rest of the population although it tended to be even more overwhelmingly male and unmarried than other occupational groups.

Within its ranks, ethnic subcommunities developed, forming important social and economic links in a strange and unfamiliar place.

In an established community, individuals normally draw upon long-standing familial and occupational connections for their business and social networks. In Dawson's early years, when nearly everyone was a new-comer, familial networks existed but were largely limited to one or two individuals – a brother, a father, a sister, or a spouse. Although long-standing extended family links did not exist, familial chain migration did take place, creating small familial networks.

Klondikers also created new networks based on culture, class, and place of origin. A significant proportion of Dawson's population was made up of people who had participated in other gold rushes, including not only miners but also prostitutes, merchants, and saloon owners. Their shared background assisted individuals by providing another basis on which they could forge social and business networks. Indeed, many Klondike stampeders remarked upon reaching Dawson City that it was 'a very small world,' for they were constantly bumping into friends and acquaintances from back home. Remarks such as 'Who do you think I met the other day?'[2] are liberally sprinkled throughout the letters and diaries of Klondikers. This back-home phenomenon often proved helpful when an individual was looking for lodging or employment or learning a new language, as a number of French Canadians were. Place of origin often replaced kin networks, as John McDougal noted in a letter back home: 'There are a number [of others] from Ottawa here but not many seem to be doing very well. I have been able to give jobs as miners to a few of them so as to help them out.'[3] Small subcommunities chose to meet daily at a favourite watering hole or lived in the same boarding house or hotel, offering each other financial, fraternal, and moral support. Dawson's single French Canadian men, for example, regularly met at the Ottawa Hotel owned by Joseph Cadieux.

A significant number of French Canadians settled in the Klondike during the gold rush. Like other ethnic groups, francophones showed a strong tendency to cluster both in occupation and in choice of living space. From the earliest period the French Canadian presence helped shape the cultural, religious, and political structure of the Yukon. Other subcommunities, such as the ones that developed within the red-light district and among Eastern European Jews, were equally important to their constituents.

Dawsonites, then, often established new networks based on family, culture, and place of origin. In a society where mail was slow or nonexistent, people depended on newcomers to bring information from Outside. Thus, news brought to an individual from his or her home town or village was often the starting point for a friendship or business partnership. In this way, place of origin – even when the individuals had not been acquainted back home – replaced kin as a kind of mitigating factor. As well, Klondikers often came in waves of chain migration. At times this was a forced chain, as in the case of indentured prostitutes, whereas others came voluntarily to join friends, family members, and business partners. These links in turn fostered further chain migration.

People in Dawson City demonstrated a strong sense of community. This can be shown, in part, by their terms of residence. Popular stereotypes of the Klondike emphasize the highly transient nature of the population, but we have seen that fully 65 percent of Dawson's population had been resident for three or more years by 1901. Their commitment to and involvement in the establishment of services, businesses, and government institutions demonstrates that these people were not just 'passing through,' challenging previous assumptions about the inherent instability of mining communities.

A stable core of local residents contributed to the emergence of a highly stratified community in Dawson. A local physician noted this phenomenon as early as 1898, when residents established an exclusive group of upper and middle class membership in which 'good fellowship flourished to a degree unthought of in older Canadian communities.'[4] Dr Barrett leaves us in no doubt that he thought of Dawson as a 'community' and that within this community he found a group of social peers. Indeed, Dawson residents, newly arrived and feeling displaced, moved very quickly to establish a social world within which they could feel a sense of community and belonging. Thus, Klondikers quickly established local chapters of fraternal associations including the Masons, Elks, and Oddfellows, as well as familiar church-based groups such as the Epworth League and the ladies' auxiliaries of various denominations. Dawson rewarded and took pride in local conditions and the achievements of its constituents, as demonstrated by the creation of two uniquely northern fraternities, the Arctic Brotherhood and Yukon Order of Pioneers. The latter, the earliest fraternal association in the Yukon, based its prestigious membership on individuals' length of residence in the territory – their commitment to northern life. Like other fraternities, this one provided aid to members in hard times, arranged and attended funerals, and provided assistance to widows and children of deceased members. They were, and remain, an exclusively male order.

Dawson residents drew class lines early, and the upper crust created an elaborate social life that made those class distinctions very clear. Contrary to the myth of an egalitarian mining frontier, members of the Klondike inner circle 'were determined to keep up appearances' despite their remote location. It was fashionable, for example, for families of high standing to employ Japanese cooks or African American housekeepers. The commissioner of the Yukon was a leader within this circle and he maintained a staff of servants that included 'an immaculate Japanese servant [dressed] in white'[5] and a gardener – a rare commodity and a difficult job with such a short growing season. Martha Black, another member of the set, remembered that until her husband became Yukon commissioner in 1910, Government House had never received miners and labourers in its parlours, for the commissioner and his associates moved in an entirely different circle. Numerous women remembered ordering the 'latest' fashions from Toronto, New York, and Paris for the many society functions they attended in Dawson.

Dawson City thus contained a clear and familiar social structure from the start. The hierarchy began with the commissioner and moved down incrementally through the ranks of the professional and mercantile sectors to the miners and labourers on which they all depended. The lowest rungs of this ladder were reserved for prostitutes, Métis, and Native people. According to one commentator, in fact, Dawson residents computed each others' social status according to a mathematical formula.[6] Patterns of social distinction established early in the formation of the community became only more entrenched as it stabilized

The upper crust also eliminated potential members on the basis of ethnicity. Like other Victorian cities of the era, Dawson made social distinctions based on race and culture. Jews, Catholics, French Canadians (with a few notable exceptions), Native people, Japanese, and African Americans, for example, were excluded from the inner circles of Dawson life, leaving a white, Anglo-Protestant core. That ethnicity was deemed reason enough to exclude individuals is demonstrated by the absence of Native women in the social whirl of Dawson, despite the fact that several of them married prominent non-Native men such as the reverends Robert McDonald and Benjamin Totty. Few non-Native women dared defy social pressure, as Mrs Stringer did, by befriending Native women and inviting them to social functions.[7]

Membership in the upper stratum was strict, and members could be expelled for breaking the rules and crossing the lines. The respectable

Jimmy Turner found this out, for example, after making an 'honest woman' out of dance hall performer Dolly Orchard. If the couple had any illusions about their new social status, these disappeared when they found themselves unwelcome in 'the sacred precincts of Dawson society.'[8]

Like most cliques, Dawson society accommodated fringe dwellers who were not really accepted as members yet were too important for a variety of reasons to be excluded. Admission of some of these people provides insight into the importance of community to Dawson residents. One of the fringe dwellers was 'Big Alex' McDonald, who gained entrance to the club less because of his wealth – many very rich miners were never admitted, witness George Carmack and his Tagish relatives – than for his active community involvement with the churches and hospitals in Dawson. Like Robert Service, Big Alex became a famous Klondike symbol to the outside world, and both men retained membership at the outer edge of the set.[9]

A number of other social patterns also persisted in the Klondike, albeit sometimes in a strange form. The existence of a Methodist Ladies' Aid Society heavily male in composition, for example, indicates a stubborn inclination to replicate southern structures and institutions regardless of local conditions. That individuals set out to create a familiar world in a harsh and remote wilderness is perhaps not at all surprising, yet Dawson also adapted laws and social mores to suit local conditions.

Yukon officials walked a fine line between what the community would accept and the orders imposed from afar. Over time they created a system that accommodated both community interests and needs and their own mandate to maintain order. The Mounted Police allowed gambling and prostitution to operate in a reasonably open and orderly fashion. It was widely acknowledged that the prostitution trade was brisk in Dawson, and for the most part, the NWMP turned a blind eye. Periodically, to show that vice was not completely unrestricted, they carried out a raid of the red-light district and arrested large numbers of prostitutes, pimps, and even clients. Still, this required much time, energy, and paperwork, and the raids were few and far between. Even in Dawson, however, there were limits to the indecencies tolerated, and the NWMP were sensitive to this fact as well. As the community grew and stabilized, local authorities encouraged women in the sex trade to take their business indoors and outside the city limits. Still, unless they were particularly blatant, the women were allowed to conduct their business unmolested.

The system of mutual tolerance and accommodation that evolved depended on changing needs. When the health of the predominantly male population was jeopardized by an outbreak of venereal disease, authorities moved to protect the health of the community by ordering medical examinations for prostitutes. Similarly, aware that outlawing gambling would drive it underground and set the stage for crooked and rigged games, authorities allowed saloon owners to operate casinos in plain view. The system operated as a compromise between what was strictly defined as legal and what the community believed was appropriate. When a distant and unsympathetic federal government some 3,000 miles away ordered an end to all this, local opposition was vigorous.

Just as in more southern cities at the end of the nineteenth century, poverty was widespread in Dawson. In mining communities where fortunes could be made overnight, millionaires such as Clarence Berry and Big Alex McDonald were the exception. Most Klondikers left home with little money and returned with even less. They encountered high costs of living in Dawson, and although wages were also high it was a difficult place in which to save money. Local residents from all social levels therefore worked to provide at least the minimum social safety net to provide for fellow Yukoners who fell on hard times. Organized charity was not just an outlet for social-minded upper and middle class women but a needed and valued contribution to community stability.

When my grandparents established their mining claim and trap line on the Sixtymile in 1935, they intended to stay for only a short while. Like so many individuals and families before them, they remained for the rest of their lives. My grandmother has now spent more than sixty winters in her beloved Yukon. She can tell you, as can most Yukoners, that the transience and impermanence that still characterizes northern life are tempered by stability and local commitment. The Klondike gold rush brought many people on a brief sojourn, but it also brought hundreds more who put down roots and set about the work of creating and maintaining a community in which they could live, work, and raise their families. Dreamers from more than forty countries brushed the gold dust from their eyes and shouldered the loads of firewood, snow, and ice that were a part of daily life in the northern mining community that was – and is – Dawson City.

Appendix:
Quantifying the Klondike

THE MOUNTED POLICE undertook the first Yukon census in 1898. Seeking largely security and electoral information, they asked questions only about Klondikers' sex and citizenship. The results indicated that the population was overwhelmingly male and American. That is, of the 15,000 people counted, over 9,000 reported themselves American citizens. Nearly 5,000 were British – they counted Canadians and other British subjects together – while 360 people reported themselves citizens of foreign countries. This then, seems to be the basis for assumptions about the American make-up of the Klondike.

The federal government followed the 1898 head count with a full and detailed census in 1901. For the purposes of this study, I compared the North West Mounted Police census of 1898 with the federal 1901 manuscript census for Dawson. I began by compiling an electronic database of all thirty-eight census districts of Dawson City proper, Klondike City, South and West Dawson, and Moosehide Village. In my data collection, I recorded each Dawson resident's name, sex, date of arrival in the Yukon, age, religion, place of birth, and marital status in 1901. After culling the database for duplicate entries, I found detailed information for 7,503 people living in greater Dawson in September 1901. I also compiled a separate database – which I refer to as the master database – in which I recorded information about the many individuals I came across in published and unpublished manuscripts on the Klondike between 1896 and 1905.

When I first compared the tabulations from the three sets of data – the police census, the manuscript census, and the master database – the results appeared to conflict. According to the Mounted Police, over 60 percent of Klondikers were Americans. Yet the manuscript census and the master database both produced figures of only 40 percent. Closer examination of the figures revealed that the Mounted Police asked only about Klondikers' *citizenship* while the other two data sets contained information about both nativity *and* citizenship.

The figures that the Mounted Police compiled for citizenship closely corresponded with the master database figures for Klondikers' last stated place of residence. Sixty-eight percent of Klondikers listed in the master database had last lived in the United States, 30 percent had come from other parts of Canada or Britain, and 2 percent came from other foreign countries (see Table A2). When I compared citizenship with ethnicity, however, I found that less than half of Klondikers were American born. In both the master database and the 1901 census, I assessed ethnicity based on the combination of place of birth, native tongue, and reported skin colour. Where the records indicated that a person was American born and identified by his or her contemporaries as 'Black' or 'Coloured,' for example, I recorded his or her ethnicity as African American. Similarly, I recorded Quebec-born francophones separately from Quebec-born anglophones. Lumberjacks who were born in Sweden and who had lived in Washington State, where they had become naturalized, I recorded as Swedish in ethnicity and American in origin. In this way I hoped to build a much more detailed portrait of the community.

I compared the results of the ethnicity and place-of-origin tabulations from the master database and the 1901 census and immediately discovered that while the majority of Klondikers might have been American *citizens* they were not Americans by birth. Indeed, less than half of all Klondikers were American born. That is, over 20 percent of individuals in both the 1901 census and the master database who reported their last outside residence as the United States were either temporary residents or naturalized citizens. Correspondingly, the figure for those who last resided in other parts of Canada and those born in Canada was almost exactly the same – about 30 percent. The figure that changed was the non-North American born. When I compared the ethnicity and place-of-origin figures for non-North Americans, the picture changed dramatically. The number of people born in the British Isles, Scandinavia, and Continental Europe was at least double that of people claiming citizenship in those places. Overall then, the figure for the non-North American born rose almost exactly in proportion to the drop in the American citizenship/origin figure (Tables A2 and A3). Since the other figures in the master database and the 1901 census so closely correspond, it seems clear that the proportion of Americans in relation to Canadians and Europeans remained at a constant 40 percent in Dawson from at least 1896 to 1905. Outside of town, the figure changed, for in 1901 only 25 percent of all Yukon residents were native-born Americans. The major results of the tabulations are presented in the tables that follow.

Table A1

Birthplaces reported by Klondikers, 1885-1914

Country	1901 census	Master database	Country	1901 census	Master database
Australia	40	15	Palestine	3	1
Austria	66	16	Italy	47	17
Baltics	1	0	Japan	61	6
Belgium	18	8	Lapland	1	0
Brazil/Peru	3	0	Mexico	2	3
Canada	2,206	648	New Zealand	22	5
Chile	2	1	Norway	177	27
China	5	0	Poland	12	5
Costa Rica	1	0	Portugal	3	1
Cuba/Bermuda	3	0	Romania	2	3
Denmark	62	9	Russia	43	6
Egypt	2	0	S. Africa	6	0
England	490	69	Scotland	202	14
Finland	43	6	Spain	7	0
France	90	19	Sweden	220	34
Germany	324	34	Switzerland	24	5
Greece	9	2	Turkey	2	0
Holland	8	1	United States	3,022	804
Hungary	7	3	Wales	29	3
Iceland	6	0	West Indies	1	0
Ireland	195	60			

Source: 1901 manuscript census and master database.

Table A2

Citizenship of Dawson residents, 1885-1914

Citizenship/origin	NWMP 1898 census		Master database, 1885-1914	
	Number	Percent	Number	Percent
United States	9,534	63	2,260	68
Britain (British subjects)	4,911	32	988	30
Continental Europe	360	2	26	1
Other/unknown	398	3	25	1
Total	15,203	100	3,299	100

Note: Origin is defined here as an individual's last stated place of residence before Yukon and taken as a rough equivalent to citizenship. Citizenship is asked in the NWMP census but not always known in the other databases.

Table A3

Nativity of Yukoners, 1885-1914

Place of birth	1901 census (Dawson)		1901 census (Yukon)		Master database, 1885-1914	
	Number	Percent	Number	Percent	Number	Percent
United States[1]	3,022	40	6,707	25	804	43
Canada[2]	2,026	27	8,163	30	648	36
British Isles	1,030	13	2,416	9	146	8
Continental Europe	587	8	1,395	5	101	6
Scandinavia	509	7	1,442	5	76	4
Australia and other British possessions	62	1	253	1	19	1
Russia and Eastern Europe	76	1	296	1	17	1
Asia	66	1	97	0.5	6	0.5
Other/unknown	125	2	6,450	23.5	7	0.5
Total	7,503	100	27,219	100	1,824	100

1 American figures include African Americans.
2 Canadian figures include Native people.

Table A4

Occupations of Klondikers, 1885-1914

	1901 census	Master database, 1885-1914
Professional/white collar		
Accountant/clerk	380	71
Architect	4	0
Banker	7	30
Civil servant	35	478
Dentist	9	30
Doctor	14	84
Druggist	8	14
Government official	15	81
Journalist	17	13
Lawyer	37	128
Newspaper editor	3	14
Nun/female clergy	9	29
Nurse	28	15
Optician	1	0
Photographer/artist	13	18
Priest/male clergy	10	24
Salvation Army officer	4	7
School teacher	8	26
Sheriff	0	1
Telegraph operator	8	2

Occupations of Klondikers, 1885-1914, *continued*

	1901 census	Master database, 1885-1914
Undertaker	2	7
Veterinarian	3	2
Total	615	1,074
Commercial		
Bath house proprietor/manager	1	8
Bicycle dealer	0	1
Broker (customs/insurance)	38	80
Contractor/builder	20	23
Dance hall or saloon proprietor	18	97
Entrepreneur/real estate broker	10	17
Hotel/restaurant keeper	162	399
Livery stable/wagon shop owner	13	5
Manufacturer	1	11
Merchant	268	636
Miller	1	0
Mining company owner/manager	4	8
Sawmill owner/manager	6	18
Steamship owner	4	2
Trader	13	9
Utilities company manager	4	12
Wood/lumber merchant	19	42
Total	582	1,368
Skilled trades		
Baker	51	122
Blacksmith	48	49
Butcher	56	11
Carpenter	246	39
Electrician	17	6
Engineer/surveyor	144	88
Firefighter/fire chief	30	3
Florist	4	0
Furrier	7	2
Gunsmith	0	3
Jeweller/goldsmith	36	53
Mechanic/machinist/metal worker	83	36
Painter	58	34
Plumber	3	2
Police officer	75	198
Printer	23	14
Ship master/captain	31	6
Stonemason/bricklayer	15	3
Tailor/shoemaker/milliner	104	53
Total	1,031	722

Occupations of Klondikers, 1885-1914, *continued*

	1901 census	Master database, 1885-1914
Semi-skilled trades		
Army/Yukon soldier	1	38
Barber/hairdresser	56	38
Farmer	29	30
Mail carrier	8	4
Miner	2,414	3,292
Railway worker (chainman, switchman, telegraph lineman)	4	31
Seaman/sailor	68	365
Warehouse worker	233	227
Trapper/hunter/logger	83	22
Wood chopper/sawmill worker	90	46
Total	2,986	4,093
Unskilled labour and service		
Cook/waiter/bartender	377	49
Criminal	32	43
Dancer/actor/entertainer	84	59
Dog catcher/pound keeper	0	1
Domestic servant	108	12
Fisher	2	1
Gambler	10	25
Laundry worker	88	21
Manual labourer	247	23
Musician	26	10
Peddler/vagrant	6	3
Pimp/procurer	0	4
Prostitute	0	15
Peddler	71	5
Scavenger	2	5
Theatrical agent	1	1
Wife	564	169
Total	1,618	446
Total workforce	6,832	7,703
Child	462	467
Occupation not given	209	7,185
Total population	7,503	15,355

Table A5

Occupational groupings, 1885-1914

Occupational category	Master database		1901 census	
	Number	Percent	Number	Percent
Manual labour and service sector	446	6	1,618	24
Semi-skilled trades	4,093	53	2,986	44
Skilled trades	722	9	1,031	14
Commercial and mercantile	1,368	18	582	9
Professional	1,074	14	615	9
Total	7,703	100	6,832	100

Note: These figures exclude children and those for whom there was no information about occupation or employment.

Table A6

Cross-tabulations of occupation and ethnicity of Dawson residents, 1901

Ethnicity	Unskilled	Semi-skilled	Skilled	Commercial	Professional
American	794	1,004	385	252	257
British	192	429	154	52	72
Canadian	281	891	290	141	245
Continental European	153	226	114	65	21
Japanese/Chinese	50	3	2	10	1
Native	2	31	0	0	1
Other British subjects	7	42	9	6	3
Russian/East European	17	21	8	27	3
Scandinavian	104	304	64	26	5
Other	18	35	5	3	7
Total	1,618	2,986	1,031	582	615

Source: 1901 manuscript census.

Table A7

Workforce participation by men and women of Dawson, 1901

Occupational category	Men	Women	Total
Service sector/unskilled[1]	807	811 (564)	1,618
Semi-skilled	2,963	23	2,986
Skilled	938	93	1,031
Commercial	514	68	582
White collar	531	84	615
Total	5,753	1,079	6,832[2]

1 These figures include women's unpaid labour. Figure in parentheses represents women who reported their occupation as 'wife.'
2 The total adult workforce excludes children under fourteen and those for whom there was no information.
Source: 1901 manuscript census.

Table A8

Sex of Yukoners, 1898-1921

| | Men | | Women | | |
Source	Number	Percent	Number	Percent	Total
NWMP Census, Yukon (1898)	13,147	92	1,195	8	14,342
NWMP Census, Dawson (1898)	4,516	88	646	12	5,162
1901 Census, Yukon	23,084	85	4,135	15	27,219
1901 Census, Dawson	6,098	81	1,405	19	7,503
1911 Census, Yukon	6,508	77	2,004	23	8,512
1921 Census, Yukon	2,819	68	1,338	32	4,157

Table A9

Marital status of Yukoners, 1901-21

Marital status	1901 census[1] (Dawson City)		1901 census (all of Yukon)		1911 census (Yukon)		1921 census (Yukon)	
	Number	Percent	Number	Percent	Number	Percent	Number	Percent
Single	4,215	57	20,011	74	5,506	65	2,390	57
Married	2,432	32	6,691	24	2,635	31	1,311	33
Widowed	206	2.5	482	1.8	304	3	230	5
Divorced	23	0.5	36	0.2	60	0.7	26	0.5
Not stated	627	8	-	-	7	0.3	200	4.5
Total	7,503	100	27,220	100	8,512	100	4,157	100

1 Figures for marital status of Dawson residents not available after 1901.

Table A10

Religious affiliations of Dawson and Moosehide residents, 1901

Religion	Number	Percent
Protestant	4,541	60
Catholic	1,683	23
Nonbelievers	552	7
Unknown	445	6
Other	136	2
Jewish	95	1
Orthodox	51	1
Total	7,503	100

Source: 1901 manuscript census.

Table A11

Religious affiliations of Klondikers, 1885-1914

Affiliation	1901 census	Master database
Baptist	229	4
Buddhist	1	0
Church of England	889	24
Confucian	9	0
Congregationalist	80	2
Episcopalian	208	12
Free Thinker[1]	51	0
Jewish	95	21
Lutheran	731	17
Methodist	801	165
Mormon	5	0
Native religion/Pagan	67	0
Nondenominational Protestant	337	139
Presbyterian	1,249	263
Quaker	2	0
Roman Catholic	1,683	823
Russian or Greek Orthodox	21	0
Salvationist	8	0
Seventh Day Adventist	4	1

1 This category is self described.

Table A12

Migration patterns of Dawson families, 1896-1901

Arrival in Yukon	Number	Percent
Whole family together	222	42
Wife and children joined husband one year after his arrival	123	23
Wife and children joined husband two years after his arrival	94	18
Wife and children joined husband three years or more after his arrival	81	15
Wife arrived before husband	6	1
Total	526	100

Source: 1901 manuscript census.

Table A13

Dawson citizens' length of residence, 1885-1901

Length of Yukon residence	Number	Percent
Five years or longer (arrived 1896 or earlier)	419	5
Four or five years (arrived 1897-8)	3,314	44
Three years (arrived 1899)	1,142	15
Two years (arrived 1900)	1,522	20
One year or less (arrived 1901)	1,202	16
Total	7,599	100

Source: 1901 manuscript census.

Notes

Abbreviations

NA	National Archives of Canada, Ottawa
NAUS	National Archives of the United States, Washington, DC
NL	National Library of Canada, Ottawa
PAA	Provincial Archives of Alberta, Edmonton
PABC	Provincial Archives of British Columbia, Victoria
YTA	Yukon Territorial Archives, Whitehorse

Preface

1 My grandparents' story has been ably told by my aunt, Ellen Davignon, in *The Cinnamon Mine: Memories of an Alaska Highway Childhood* (Whitehorse: Studio North 1988). For the story of the scientific expedition that brought Bob from Greenland and Elly from Denmark in the first place, see Dick North's *Arctic Exodus: The Last Great Trail Drive* (Toronto: Macmillan 1991).

Chapter 1: Gamblers of a Hundred Hells and Dreamers from the Seven Seas

1 NL, G36, reel 1, United States Consul Records, Dawson City, Yukon, McCook to Hill, 8 June 1899. See also: PABC, Add. MSS 2719, reel A-1659, James Cran Papers, diary entries 7 July and 23 July 1898; YTA, MS 87/104, Albert Edward Hetherington Papers, diary entry 9 Mar. 1899; and YTA, MS 82/53 F-5, Georgia White Papers, diary entry 8 July 1898.

2 Anna DeGraf, *Pioneering on the Yukon* (Hamden, CT: Archon 1992), 54.

3 YTA, MS 82/224 F-1, part 1, Garner-Knott Family Papers, recollections.

4 PABC, Add. MSS 2711, reel A-1650, A. Scott Gillespie Papers.

5 Ibid. See also: YTA, MS 82/224 F-39, Garner-Knott Family Papers, 'Klondike Gold Rush Prospectors through Edmonton by Land and Water Routes, 1897-1898.' See also J.G. MacGregor, *The Klondike Rush through Edmonton, 1897-1898* (Toronto: McClelland and Stewart 1970).

6 For a sense of how perilous the Stikine route could be, see Larry Pynn's *Forgotten Trail: One Man's Adventures on the Canadian Route to the Klondike* (Toronto: Doubleday 1996). The poem is from YTA, MS 82/390 F-119, James Edward Beatty Papers, undated diary entry 'written on a tree near Moss Lake on the Teslin Trail, 1898.'

7 See, for example, Pierre Berton, *Klondike: The Last Great Gold Rush, 1896-1899* (Toronto: McClelland and Stewart 1972) and David Morrison, *The Politics of the Yukon Territory* (Toronto: University of Toronto 1968).

8 YTA, CR 81/45, part 1, file 3, Sisters of Ste Anne Collection, W.B. Barrett, memoir, 6.

9 Laura Thompson Berton, *I Married the Klondike* (Toronto: McClelland and Stewart 1985), 46.

10 Agnes Dean Cameron, *The New North: An Account of a Woman's 1908 Journey through Canada to the Arctic* (Saskatoon: Western Producer Prairie Books 1986), 38.

11 PABC, Add. MSS 947, Edward Durban Sheringham Papers, memoir, 2; M. Zaslow, 'The Yukon: Northern Development in a Canadian-American Context,' in *Regionalism in the Canadian Community*, ed. M. Wade (Toronto: University of Toronto 1969), 181; ibid., reprinted in

Interpreting Canada's North, ed. K. Coates and W.R. Morrison (Toronto: Copp Clark 1989), 133-48.

12 See Thomas Stone *Miners' Justice: Migration, Law and Order on the Alaska-Yukon Frontier, 1873-1902* (New York: Peter Lang 1988), 2; William R. Morrison *Showing the Flag: The Mounted Police and Canadian Sovereignty, 1894-1925* (Vancouver: University of British Columbia 1985); Morris Zaslow, *The Opening of the Canadian North* (Toronto: McClelland and Stewart 1971), 139; and David Breen, 'The Turner Thesis and the Canadian West,' in *Essays on Western History*, ed. L.H. Thomas (Edmonton: University of Alberta 1976).

13 Ella Lung Martinson, *Trail to North Star Gold: A True Story of the Alaska-Klondike Gold Rush* (Portland: Binford and Mort 1984), 88.

14 See Ralph Mann, *After the Gold Rush: Society in Grass Valley and Nevada City, California, 1849-1870* (Stanford: Stanford University Press 1982); Leanne Sander, '"The Men All Died of Miners' Disease": Women and Families in the Industrial Mining Environment of Upper Clear Creek, Colorado' (PhD diss., University of Colorado at Boulder, 1990); and Elizabeth Jameson, 'High-Grade and Fissures: A Working-Class History of the Cripple Creek, Colorado, Gold Mining District, 1890-1905' (PhD diss., University of Michigan, 1987), 543.

15 See Leroy McQuesten, *Recollections of the Yukon* (Anchorage: Alaska Historical Society 1986), 18 and Anna DeGraf, *Pioneering on the Yukon* (Hamden, CT: Archon Books 1992), 33, 67.

16 Canada, *Census, 1901* (hereafter cited as 1901 census).

17 See, for example, Blaine Williams, 'The Frontier Family: Demographic Fact and Historical Myth,' in *Essays on the American West*, ed. Harold Hollingsworth and Sandra Myers (Austin: University of Texas 1969), 63-5 and Paul Voisey, *Vulcan: The Making of a Prairie Community* (Toronto: University of Toronto 1988), 18.

18 For Anglican influence, see the 1901 census; for information about Roman Catholicism, see Marthe F. Beauregard, *Baptêmes, mariages, sepultures de Ste. Marie de Dawson City, Yukon, 1898-1956* (Montreal: Editions Bergeron et Fils 1976).

19 See also Stephen Thernstrom, *The Other Bostonians: Poverty and Progress in the American Metropolis, 1880-1970* (Cambridge: Harvard University Press 1973), 6-7.

20 Michael Katz, *The People of Hamilton, Canada West: Family and Class in a Mid-Nineteenth Century City* (Cambridge: Harvard University Press 1975), 20 and Ralph Mann, *After the Gold Rush*, 210-2.

Chapter 2: The Original Yukoners and the Klondike Gold Rush

1 Julie Cruikshank, *Reading Voices / Dän Dhá Ts'edenintth'sé: Oral and Written Interpretations of the Yukon's Past* (Vancouver: Douglas and McIntyre 1991), 78.

2 A. McFadyen Clark, 'Koyukon,' in *Handbook of North American Indians*, vol. 6, ed. June Helm (Washington: Smithsonian Institution 1981), 585-6.

3 P.A. Tikhmenev, *A History of the Russian American Company*, trans. and ed. Richard A. Pierce and Alton S. Donnelly (Seattle: University of Washington Press 1978), 383-4.

4 Clifford Wilson, *Campbell of the Yukon* (Toronto: Macmillan 1970), 70.

5 Cruikshank, *Reading Voices*, 83.

6 See Kerry Abel, 'William Carpenter Bompas,' *Dictionary of Canadian Biography*, vol. 13 (Toronto: University of Toronto Press), 92-4; and H.A. Cody, *An Apostle of the North: The Memoirs of the Right Reverend William Carpenter Bompas* (Toronto: Musson 1908).

7 Catherine McClellan, *Part of the Land, Part of the Water* (Vancouver: Douglas and McIntyre 1987), 76-7. See also Cruikshank *Reading Voices*, 129, 104.

8 Thomas Stone, *Miners' Justice: Migration, Law and Order on the Alaska-Yukon Frontier, 1873-1902* (New York: Peter Lang 1988), 8.

9 Cruikshank, *Reading Voices*, 91. See also Robert G. McCandless, *Yukon Wildlife: A Social History* (Edmonton: University of Alberta Press 1985), 32.

10 YTA, MS 80/89, reel 47, George Snow Papers, 38.

11 Beardslee, as quoted in *Chilkoot Trail: Heritage Route to the Klondike*, ed. David Neufeld and

Frank Norris (Whitehorse: Lost Moose 1996), 43.

12 Neufeld and Norris, eds., *Chilkoot Trail,* 38-43.

13 Melody Webb, *The Last Frontier: A History of the Yukon Basin of Canada and Alaska* (Albuquerque: University of New Mexico Press 1985), 26-37, 47. For a detailed discussion of how this process of alliances worked, see Sylvia Van Kirk's *Many Tender Ties: Women in Fur-Trade Society, 1670-1870* (Winnipeg: Watson and Dwyer 1980) and Jennifer Brown's *Strangers in Blood: Fur Trade Company Families in Indian Country* (Vancouver: University of British Columbia Press 1980).

14 Webb, *The Last Frontier,* 64-6.

15 Ibid., 55; E. Callahan, 'A Yukon Autobiography,' *Alaska Journal* 5 (Spring 1975): 127-8; Webb, *The Last Frontier,* 172.

16 Kenneth S. Coates, *Best Left As Indians: Native-White Relations in the Yukon Territory, 1840-1973* (Montreal: McGill-Queen's University Press 1991), 77.

17 NA, MG 17 B2, Church Missionary Society Papers, Bompas to Gould, 13 Jan. 1896. See also Cruikshank, *Reading Voices,* 6.

18 Kenneth Coates and William Morrison. 'More than a Matter of Blood: The Federal Government, the Churches and the Mixed Blood Populations of the Yukon and the Mackenzie River Valley, 1890-1950,' in *1885 and After,* ed. F.L. Barron and J.B. Waldram (Saskatoon: Canadian Plains Research Center 1986), 263; quotation from NA, MG 29 C92, Reverend Richard J. Bowen Papers, memoir, 99.

19 Cornelius Osgood, *The Han Indians: A Compilation of Ethnographic and Historical Data on the Alaska-Yukon Boundary Area* (New Haven: Yale University Press 1971), 17; quotation from Frederick Palmer, *In the Klondike, Including an Account of the Writer's Journey to Dawson* (New York: Scribner 1899), 70.

20 Coates and Morrison, 'More than a Matter of Blood,' 263.

21 Richard Slobodin, 'The Dawson Boys,' *Polar Notes* 5 (June 1963): 28.

22 Cruikshank, *Reading Voices,* 132.

23 This story is related in many memoirs, including William Ogilvie, *Early Days on the Yukon and the Story of Its Gold Finds* (Toronto: Bell and Cockburn 1913), 125-31 and George Carmack's own, *My Experiences in the Yukon* (n.p.: Marguerite Carmack 1933), 9.

24 Kitty Smith reflecting on the life of Shaaw Tláa (Kate Carmack), quoted in Cruikshank, *Reading Voices,* 132; Webb, *The Last Frontier,* 62; Allen A. Wright, *Prelude to Bonanza: The Discovery and Exploration of the Yukon* (Sidney, BC: Gray's Publishing 1976), 292-3.

25 For a full description of this impact, see Neufeld and Norris, eds., *Chilkoot Trail,* 22-48.

26 NA, MG 30 C41, William R. Elliott Papers, diary entries for August through October 1902. See also Palmer, *In the Klondike.* For non-Native observations of Native peoples, see: YTA, MS 78/18, John Grace Papers; PABC, Add. MSS 1158, Ronald E. Weir Papers (John McGregor memoir); NA, MG 29 C62, Clayton Scoins Collection (Alden Smith diary); PABC, Add. MSS 1323, Thomas Wilson Papers; YTA, MS 80/89, reel 47, George Snow Papers; YTA, MS 82/53 F-5, Georgia White Papers; Della Murray Banks, 'Rainbow's End,' *Alaska Sportsman* 9, 10 (1945): 14-5, 21-7; William Haskell, *Two Years in the Klondike and Alaska Goldfields* (Hartford: Hartford Publishing 1898); John Secretan, *To the Klondike and Back* (New York: Hurst and Blackett 1898); Robert Oglesby, *The Klondyke Gold Region: Account of a Six Months Trip through the Yukon Gold Fields* (n.p.: 1899); Robert C. Kirk, *Twelve Months in the Klondike* (London: William Heinemann 1899); A.E.I. Sola, *Klondyke: Truth and Facts* (London: Mining and Geographical Institute 1897); and Palmer, *In the Klondike.*

27 Neufeld and Norris, eds., *The Chilkoot Trail,* 43-8; YTA, MS 80/89, reel 47, George Snow Papers, memoir, 4; Ogilvie, *Early Days on the Yukon,* 153-7.

28 PABC, Add. MSS 1158, Ronald E. Weir Papers, John McGregor memoir. McGregor and his party had left Nanaimo, BC, in late July 1897 and crossed the summit early in August 1897.

29 F. La Roche, *Photographic Views en route to the Klondike via the Skaguay and Dyea Trails* (Chicago: Henry O. Sheperd 1897).

30 Kirk, *Twelve Months in the Klondike*, 42; Secretan, *To the Klondike and Back*, 41; Oglesby, *The Klondyke Gold Region*, 523.

31 Kirk, *Twelve Months in the Klondike*, 41-2; Ogilvie, *Early Days on the Yukon*, 153; Secretan, *To the Klondike and Back*, 56; and Palmer, *In the Klondike*, 8-9.

32 Sola, *Klondyke: Truth and Facts*, 55.

33 Josiah Spurr, *Through the Yukon Gold Diggings: A Narrative of Personal Travel* (Boston: Eastern 1900), 46.

34 NA, MG 29 C62, Clayton J. Scoins Collection, Alden Smith to Mother, 8 Apr. 1898.

35 YTA, MS 80/89, reel 47, George Snow Papers, memoir, 11.

36 Cruikshank, *Reading Voices*, 129; Sola, *Klondyke: Truth and Facts*, 59.

37 Frederick Funston, 'Over the Chilkoot Pass to the Yukon,' (Canadian Historical Images on Microfiche, No. 14295, 1896), unpaginated; William Morrison, *Showing the Flag: The Mounted Police and Canadian Sovereignty, 1894-1925* (Vancouver: University of British Columbia Press 1985), 12, 36.

38 Cruikshank, *Reading Voices*, 129-31.

39 Veazie Wilson, *Glimpses of the Yukon Gold Fields and Dawson Route* (Vancouver: Thompson Stationery 1897), unpaginated, photo 47.

40 Secretan, *To the Klondike and Back*, 138.

41 Sola, *Klondyke: Truth and Facts*, 66-7; NA, MG 29 E105, Edward Lester Papers, diary entry 10 Mar. 1899. See also Palmer, *In the Klondike*, 4-7. For a discussion of the Tutchone mobility see Catherine McClellan, 'Tutchone,' in *Handbook of North American Indians*, vol. 6, *Subartic*, ed. June Helm (Washington: Smithsonian Institution 1981), 493.

42 Kirk, *Twelve Months in the Klondike*, 82.

43 Osgood, *The Han Indians*, 25-8. There may well have been four bands, for Osgood points out that anthropologists have had some trouble distinguishing between 'Charlie Village' and 'Johnny Village' of the lower river before 1890.

44 Stone, *Miners' Justice*, 13.

45 For a general survey of this pattern of wildlife depletion in Han territory, see McCandless, *Yukon Wildlife*, 30-3 and J.R. Lotz, *The Dawson Area: A Regional Monograph* (Ottawa: Department of Northern Affairs 1966), 150-1. See also John R. Crow and Philip R. Obley, 'Han,' in *Handbook*, vol. 6, *Subarctic*, ed. Helm, 511.

46 Webb, *The Last Frontier*, 78; NA, MG 29 C92, Reverend Richard J. Bowen Papers, memoir, 188.

47 For Bompas's letters, see NA, MG 30 E-2, vol. 3, Constantine Papers, Bompas to Daly, May 1893 and 9 Dec. 1893. For full discussion of the police presence, see Morrison, *Showing the Flag*. For Charles Constantine's remarks, see NA, MG 30 E55, vol. 4, Constantine Papers, Constantine to the Commissioner, 5 Jan. 1896 and Constantine to Ogilvie, 19 Nov. 1896.

48 Coates, *Best Left As Indians*, 82-5.

49 NA, MG 30 E55, vol. 4, Constantine Papers, Bompas to T.M. Daly, May 1893; NWMP, 'Report of Inspector Constantine, 1894,' *Sessional Papers*, 1895, vol. 30, 76.

50 NA, MG 29 C92, Reverend Richard Bowen Papers, memoir, 99.

51 NA, RG 18 A-1, vol. 140, Constantine to Commissioner Herchmer, 6 Dec. 1896.

52 YTA, CR 81/16 f. 73-7, St Paul's Anglican Church Papers, J.A. Smart to Bishop of Selkirk, 12 Aug. 1897.

53 YTA, YRG 1, series 1, vol. 7, file 1187, Ogilvie to Secretary of the Interior, 11 Dec. 1900 and Ogilvie to Bompas 27 Sept. 1900. For a fuller discussion of federal government policies and Yukon Native people, see Coates, *Best Left As Indians*, 159-86. For a discussion of how this period has complicated the comprehensive land claim negotiations ever after, see Council for Yukon Indians, *Together Today for Our Children Tomorrow* (Whitehorse: Council for Yukon Indians 1977).

54 1901 census; J.E. Spurr, *Through the Yukon Gold Diggings* (Boston: Eastern 1900), 105; Crow and Obley, 'Han,' 506.

55 Coates, *Best Left As Indians*, 46; NA, MG 29 C91, W.C.E. Stewart Papers, McDougal to Stewart [ca. Nov. 1899], 6; NL, G36, reel 1, Despatches from United States Consuls, McCook to Moore, 31 Mar. 1899; McCandless, *Yukon Wildlife*, 32.

56 1901 census.

57 Julius M. Price, *From Euston to the Klondike* (London: Sampson, Low, Marston 1898) 191; 1901 census.

58 Coates, *Best Left As Indians*, 84-5. See also Coates and Morrison, 'More than a Matter of Blood,' 155.

59 NA, MG 29 C92, Reverend Richard J. Bowen Papers, memoir, 56.

60 NA, MG 30 E55, vol. 4, Constantine Papers, Constantine to Commissioner, 24 Mar. 1896; Oglesby, *The Klondyke Gold Region*, 530; for Native pilots see, for example, Haskell, *Two Years in the Klondike*, 217 and Secretan, *To the Klondike and Back*, 138; for the pioneer's comments, see YTA, GR82/86, vol. 1313, Department of Indian and Northern Affairs, Historic Sites, Victoria Faulkner files, oral interview with Ray Stewart, n.d.; for the variety of employment on river steamers, see NAUS, State Department Records, Despatches from United States Consuls in Dawson City, Canada, 1898-1906, reel 1, 'Information and Complaint,' sworn before S. Steele, 28 June 1899. See also Slobodin, 'The Dawson Boys,' 29.

61 Slobodin, 'The Dawson Boys,' 29; 1901 census.

62 1901 census.

63 NA, RG 18 D4, reel C2152, North West Mounted Police Gaol Register.

64 Reverend Richard Martin, oral testimony collected by Richard Slobodin, 'The Dawson Boys,' 33.

65 When Slobodin visited Moosehide in the early 1960s, the Reverend Martin was still living there. See his 'The Dawson Boys,' 33.

66 NA, MG 17 B2, series C.1/o, Church Missionary Society, Reeve to Gould, 23 July 1900; NL, G36, reel 2, Despatches from the United States Consulate, Dawson City, McCook to Hill, 19 Sept. 1901. For forest fires, see, for example, NA, MG 29 C88, Ernest F. Keir Papers, journal entry, 41; Josiah Spurr, *Through the Yukon Gold Diggings*, 102; and Price, *From Euston to the Klondike*, 248-9. For efforts to prevent famine, see Coates, *Best Left As Indians*, 173.

Chapter 3: The Thrill of the Chase

1 1901 census. Of a total workforce of 6,832, 4,604 were employed in unskilled or semi-skilled occupations.

2 Among the many stampeders to comment on non-Native packers at length was Josiah Spurr, *Through the Yukon Gold Diggings: A Narrative of Personal Travel* (Boston: Eastern Publishing 1900), 39-42. For George Carmack's involvement in the packing trade, see William Ogilvie, *Early Days on the Yukon* (Toronto: Bell and Cockburn 1913), 133. See also Anna DeGraf, *Pioneering on the Yukon, 1892-1917* (Hamden: Archon 1992), 51-6.

3 PABC, Add. MSS 1188, file 1, George R. Pattullo Papers, Duff Pattullo to G.R. Pattullo, 27 Sept. 1897.

4 Wendy Jones, *Women Who Brave the Far North* (San Diego: Grossmont 1976), 96.

5 DeGraf, *Pioneering on the Yukon*, 123-4. See also David Neufeld and Frank Norris, *Chilkoot Trail: Heritage Route to the Klondike* (Whitehorse: Lost Moose 1996), 145.

6 See for example, YTA, MS 79/98, Dorothy Wass Papers, Joseph Tanner to Mother, 24 June 1901; and NA, MG 29 C92, Reverend Richard Bowen Papers, memoir, 180.

7 DeGraf, *Pioneering on the Yukon*, 106.

8 1901 census.

9 YTA, MS 79/98, Dorothy Wass Papers, Joseph Tanner to Mother, 24 June 1901; NA, RG 85, vol. 1608, file 7034, Northern Administration Branch Records, William Galpin, 'Report Regarding the Mining Operations on Quartz Creek during the Year Ended 1st November 1909.'

10 For employment statistics, see Maria Ferguson, *Dawson City, Yukon and Alaska Directory and Gazetteer* (Seattle: M.L. Ferguson 1901) and the 1901 census. For Tanner's remarks, see YTA, MS 79/98, Dorothy Wass Papers, Joseph Tanner to Mother, 24 June 1901.

11 Ferguson, *Dawson City, Yukon and Alaska Directory and Gazetteer* (1901) and the 1901 census.

12 1901 census.

13 NL, G36, reel 1, United States Consul Records, Dawson City, Yukon, McCook to Hill, 12 Sept. 1899, and McCook to Adee, 9 Sept. 1901; 1901 census.

14 Sam Dunham, 'The Alaska Gold Fields,' *Alaska Journal* 14, 1 (Winter 1984): 7-64.

15 *Yukon Midnight Sun*, 11 July 1898.

16 DeGraf, *Pioneering on the Yukon*, 106.

17 Ibid., 42-3.

18 NA, RG 85, vol. 655, file 3005, Congdon to Sifton, 21 Mar. 1904; 1901 census.

19 1901 census; YTA, MS 87/83 F-198, Elizabeth Jones Papers, Elizabeth to Bertha, 10 Jan. 1902.

20 DeGraf, *Pioneering on the Yukon*, 20, 50.

21 YTA, MS 82/53 F-5, Georgia White Papers, diary entries 21 Feb. to 29 June 1898.

22 Tappan Adney, *The Klondike Stampede of 1897-1898* (New York: Harper 1900).

23 1901 census; NL, G36, reel 1, United States Consul Records, Dawson City, Yukon, McCook to Hill, 24 May 1899 and Report of the Meeting of the Citizens' Relief Committee, 21 Dec. 1898.

24 YTA, MS 82/240 F-39, Henry Dow Banks Papers, diary, and Elisabeth Banks Nichols to W.D. McBride, 20 Sept. 1960. See also YTA, MS 90/56, Andrew Norelius Papers, memoir.

25 For statistics on marriage and gender, see 1901 census.

26 See Melody Webb, *The Last Frontier: A History of the Yukon Basin of Canada and Alaska* (Albuquerque: University of New Mexico Press 1985), 82-4; Michael Gates, *Gold at Fortymile Creek: Early Days in the Yukon* (Vancouver: UBC Press 1994), 20-2; and Kenneth Coates and William Morrison, *Land of the Midnight Sun: A History of the Yukon* (Edmonton: Hurtig 1988), 55.

27 NA, MG 30 C49, Ella Hall Papers, memoir.

28 YTA, MS 83/156 F-8, Mabel Moore Papers, notes written in 1937 by Moore about her life in Alaska and Yukon.

29 The male pronoun is used here advisedly, for 99 percent of Dawson's miners were male, even as late as 1901.

30 For a record of the fee, see NL, G36, reel 1, United States Consul Records, Dawson City, Yukon, McCook to Hill, 8 June 1899. For charges of corruption, see Sir Charles Tupper, *Charges against the Government and Its Officials in Connection with the Yukon Administration* (Ottawa 1899). This was a speech given in House of Commons, 14 Apr. 1899. See also, David R. Morrison, *The Politics of the Yukon Territory, 1898-1909* (Toronto: University of Toronto Press 1968), 10-7 and Morris Zaslow, *The Opening of the Canadian North, 1870-1914* (Toronto: McClelland and Stewart 1971), 113. For a more scathing attack by a contemporary Dawsonite, see Labelle Brooks-Vincent, *The Scarlet Life of Dawson and the Roseate Dawson of Nome: Personal Experiences and Observations of the Author* (San Francisco: Brown, Meese and Craddock 1900), all.

31 PABC, Add. MSS 1323, file 1, Thomas Wilson Papers, diary entry 27 July 1898. See also Adney, *Klondike Stampede*, 435.

32 PABC, Add. MSS 1323, file 1, Thomas Wilson Papers, diary entry 9 Aug. 1898; NL, G36, reel 1, United States Consul Records, Dawson City, Yukon, McCook to Moore, 6 Aug. 1898.

33 YTA, MS 79/98, Dorothy Wass Papers.

34 YTA, MS 82/190 F-18, file 47, R.L. Ashbaugh Papers, Morrison to Ashbaugh, July 1901.

35 Ibid., Etta Endl to Ed Morrison, n.d. (ca. summer 1901).

36 NL, G36, reel 1, United States Consul Records, Dawson City, Yukon, W.P. Clement to H. TeRoller, 26 Nov. 1900.

37 YTA, MS 78/18, John Grace Papers, memoir, 1-3.

38 1901 census; YTA, MS 82/390 F-119, James Edward Beatty Papers, Certificate of indenture between Marie Richer and George Rice, Dawson, 31 Jan. 1901.

39 NA, RG 85, vol. 664, file 3885, Northern Administration Branch Records, Thomas Fawcett to Deputy Minister of Interior, 16 July 1897.

40 Ibid., Lock to LeCapelain, 22 Mar. 1950.

41 See John M. Findlay's *People of Chance: Gambling in American Society from Jamestown to Las Vegas* (New York: Oxford University Press 1986), 79-109.

42 YTA, MS 82/1, part 2, file 2, Margaret Waddington Collection, petition by Robert Craig to probate will, 22 Jan. 1909; Also see the affidavit of Edward O. Finlayson and R.J. Love to Lawrence Lake, 28 Dec. 1940. The list of mining properties owned by McDonald at the time of his death included claims on Clear, Eldorado, Squaw, Granite, Hunker, Adams, and Sheep creeks.

43 NA, RG 85, vol. 1608, file 7034, Northern Administration Branch Records, William Galpin, 'Report Regarding the Mining Operations on Quartz Creek during the Year Ended 1st November 1909.'

44 NA, MG 30 E55, vol. 4, 'Constantine Papers,' Constantine to Commanding Officer, 15 Aug. 1896. See also Pierre Berton, *Klondike: The Last Great Gold Rush: 1896-1899* (Toronto: McClelland and Stewart 1972), 76.

45 For a lively and entertaining account of this family's experiences, see Edna Berry's memoirs, *The Bushes and the Berrys* (San Francisco: C.J. Bennett 1941).

46 NA, RG 85, vol. 658, file 3318, Report of Receipts and Disbursements of the Public Administrator's Office, 1917; and 1901 census.

47 PABC, Add. MSS 698, vol. 1, file 10, J.B. Clearihue Papers, John Finlayson obituary (news clipping no title or date, probably the *Victoria Colonist*, ca. 1918).

48 NA, RG 85, vol. 658, file 3318, Report of Receipts and Disbursements of the Public Administrator's Office, 1912-3; and 1901 census.

49 NA, MG 29 C27, Joseph Charles Dubé Papers, transcript of oral interview with Dubé; Ella Lung Martinson, quoting her father, Ed Lung in *Trail to North Star Gold: A True Story of the Alaska-Klondike Gold Rush* (Portland: Binford and Mort 1984), 113. See also 1901 census, section F-17 of Dawson City.

50 YTA, MS 82/32 F-1, part 2, file 4, Winifred McLellan Papers, Winifred McLellan to Maggie Electa, 8 Sept. 1905.

51 NA, RG 85, vol. 1608, file 7036, Northern Administration Branch Records, 'Report by Fiset for Glacier Creek, 1907-1908.'

52 YTA, MS 82/327 F-59, part 2, Blanche Pépin Lambert Papers, memoir.

53 NA, MG 29 C27, Joseph Charles Dubé Papers, transcript of oral interview with Dubé.

54 Quoted in Suzann Ledbetter, *Nellie Cashman: Prospector and Trailblazer* (El Paso: University of Texas 1993), 47

55 *Dawson Daily News*, 15 Dec. 1899; 1901 census.

56 For the number of women involved in mining, see Barbara Kelcey, 'Lost in the Rush: The Forgotten Women of the Klondike Stampede' (MA thesis, University of Victoria, 1989), 30. Kelcey based her figures on the *Index to Original Locator Claims* (to 1901) held by the Yukon Territorial Archives. For a description of women's work see, for example, Ethel Anderson Becker, 'Little Girl on the Klondike Gold Fields,' *Alaska Sportsman* 27, 11 (1962), 36. For Mrs. Shand's claim, see Margaret Clark Shand and Ora Shand, *To the Summit and Beyond* (Caldwell, ID: Caxton Printers 1959), 167-9

57 For Gédéon Pépin's recollection, see YTA, MS 82/327 F-59, part 2, Blanche Pépin Lambert Papers. For Martha Black's experience, see Martha Louise Black, *My Ninety Years* (Edmonds, WA: Alaska Northwest Publishing 1980). For Mae Melbourne's, see *Klondike Nugget*, special edition, 1899, 31; cited also in Kelcey, 'Lost in the Rush,' 152. For Annie May Enright's, see YTA, MS 82/190 F-18, file 7, R.L. Ashbaugh Papers, Ashbaugh to anonymous, 28 Apr. 1909. Also file 6, Agreement between Mitchell and McPhail, 1909, and file 24, Enright correspondence and contracts.

58 Cited in David J. Hall, *Clifford Sifton*, vol. 2, *The Lonely Eminence* (Vancouver: University of British Columbia Press 1985), 131.

59 Ibid., 133. See also Morrison, *Politics of the Yukon Territory*, Chapter 6.

60 NA, RG 85, vol 1608, file 7033, Northern Administration Branch Records, John Fraser,

'Annual Report of the Mining District of Dawson for Year Ending 31 December 1914.' For a full discussion of the economic and technological changes that took place in the Yukon gold industry in this period, see Lewis Green, *The Gold Hustlers* (Vancouver: J.J. Douglas 1972).

61 Frederick Palmer, *In the Klondike, Including an Account of the Writer's Journey to Dawson* (New York: Scribner 1899), 140.

62 Spurr, *Through the Yukon Gold Diggings*, 134: Spurr described her as looking tired and lonely.

63 Ibid., 47.

64 For details about domestic chores, see Ethel Berry, 'How I Mined for Gold on the Klondyke,' *The Examiner Sunday Magazine*, 1 Aug. 1897, 1. Quotation from Becker, 'Little Girl on the Klondike,' 36.

65 PABC, Add. MSS 698, vol. 6, file 4, J.B. Clearihue Papers, Joseph to Annie Clearihue, 8 Sept. 1901.

66 NA, MG 30 E55, vol. 4, Constantine Papers, Constantine to Commanding Officer, 15 Aug. 1896.

67 1901 census.

68 Ibid.

69 YTA, MS 83/156 F-8, Mabel Moore Papers.

70 Della Murray Banks, 'Woman on the Dalton Trail,' *Alaska Sportsman* 9, 1 (1945), 27-8.

71 YTA, MS 80/89, reel 47, George Snow Papers, brochure advertising Snow's Company of Players from Victoria, Sacramento and San Francisco (n.d.), featuring Mr George T. Snow and Miss Anna Edes Rablen, along with 'a strong company of undoubted reputation.'

72 YTA, MS 82/454, Yukon Order of Pioneers Collection, article from *The Pathfinder* (Feb. 1922). See also DeGraf, *Pioneering on the Yukon*, 33-4.

73 Helen Berg, 'The Doll of Dawson,' *Alaska Sportsman* 8, 2 (1944), 26-30.

74 1901 census. Madame Forget was forty-five years old and the daughters were nineteen and fifteen respectively.

75 Michael J. Piva, *The Condition of the Working Class in Toronto, 1900-1921* (Ottawa: University of Ottawa Press 1979), 52, 45.

76 YTA, MS 80/503, box 2, file 3, Emil Joseph Forrest Papers, recollections, unpaginated.

77 Becker, 'Little Girl on the Klondike,' 36.

78 PABC, Add. MSS 698, vol. 6, file 4, J.B. Clearihue Papers, Joseph to Annie Clearihue, 18 Sept. 1901. Clearihue was himself separated from his wife Annie and hastened to assure her of faithfulness.

79 Sarah E. Patchell, *My Extraordinary Years of Adventure and Romance in Klondike and Alaska* (London: Arthur H. Stockwell, n.d.).

80 NL, G36, reel 1, United States Consul Records, Dawson City, Yukon, McCook to Hill, 12 Sept. 1899, and McCook to Adee, 9 Sept. 1901.

Chapter 4: The Scarlet Ladder

1 NA, MG 30 E55, vol. 4, Constantine Papers, Constantine to Walsh, 17 Mar. 1898; William B. Haskell, *Two Years in the Klondike* (Hartford, CT: Hartford Publishing 1898), 371, 377; YTA, MS 80/89, reel 47, George Snow Papers, brochure advertising Snow's Company of Players from Victoria, Sacramento and San Francisco (n.d.), featuring Mr George T. Snow and Miss Anna Edes Rablen, along with 'a strong company of undoubted reputation.'

2 Haskell, *Two Years in the Klondike*, 355. Hal Guest, 'City of Gold: Dawson, Yukon Territory, 1896-1918' (PhD diss., University of Manitoba, 1982), 245, offers the figure of 500 workers, while the American Consul, James McCook, suggests 1,000. See NL, G-36, reel 2, United States Consul Records, Dawson City, Yukon, McCook to Hill, Consular Dispatch No. 93, 24 May 1899.

3 Guest, 'City of Gold,' Chapter 8.

4 NA, RG 85, vol. 658, file 3417, Sifton to Ogilvie, 6 Jan. 1900 and Ogilvie to Sifton, 14 May 1900. See also RG 18 D1, vol. 3055, Sam Steele Report, 12 Oct. 1898; and MG 27 II D15, Clifford Sifton Papers, reel C493, A.B. Perry to Sifton, 7 Nov. 1899. It should also be noted that

in 1898 and 1899 there were severe typhoid and smallpox epidemics in Dawson, and thus the authorities were indeed extremely concerned about the general sanitary conditions and health of the residents. As well, a number of the members of the Mounted Police in Dawson were themselves treated for venereal disease in the period. See, for example, 'Report of the Police Surgeon at Dawson for Year Ending November 1899,' *Sessional Papers*, 1900, 33, no. 15, p. 73.

5 NA, RG 85, vol. 658, file 3417, Sifton to Ogilvie, 6 Jan. 1900. In the telegram, Sifton ordered 'the immediate discontinuance' of granting certificates of health to 'women of bad repute.' See also Ogilvie to Sifton, 14 May 1900.

6 NA, RG 18 D4, reel C2152, *Dawson Gaol Register*, May 1903 (hereafter the *Dawson Gaol Register*). The pimp and proprietor of the notorious Bartlett brothel was also convicted of vagrancy in this raid.

7 See NL, G-36, reel 2, United States Consul Records, Dawson City, Yukon, McCook to Hill, 24 May 1899.

8 See NA, RG 18 D1, NWMP records, vol. 1445, file 181, part 6, McPhail Report, 10 Nov. 1899; and Wood to Ogilvie, 5 Nov. 1900. For a discussion of the real estate speculation involved in this removal, see Guest, 'City of Gold,' 245-8.

9 Guest, 'City of Gold,' 239-48.

10 In a raid conducted over three nights, the NWMP arrested and fined twenty-two 'inmates of houses of ill fame.' The fine in each case was set at $50 plus costs. See *Klondike Nugget*, 15 Apr. 1902, 16 Apr. 1902, and 17 Apr. 1902. Throughout the period, however, only one man was arrested for 'frequenting' a house of ill fame. See 'Report of Superintendent Constantine,' *Sessional Papers*, 1899, no. 32, 15.

11 For a full discussion of the complexities of the relationship between mining and gambling, see John M. Findlay's *People of Chance: Gambling in American Society from Jamestown to Las Vegas* (New York: Oxford University Press 1986), 79-109.

12 NA, RG 85, vol. 658, file 3417, Ogilvie to Sifton, 12 Sept. 1900.

13 See, for example, ibid., Kate Heaman, Women's Christian Temperance Union (London, Ontario) to Clifford Sifton, 27 June 1900.

14 Ibid., Sifton to Ogilvie, 14 Aug. 1900.

15 Ibid., Ogilvie to Sifton, 12 Sept. 1900.

16 Ibid., Ogilvie to Sifton, 12 Sept. 1900.

17 Ibid., Smart to Ogilvie, 22 Nov. 1900.

18 Ibid., Smart to Ogilvie, 22 Nov. 1900.

19 Ibid., O'Brien and Jackson to Wood.

20 Ibid., T. Eggert to Major Wood, 24 Nov. 1900.

21 Ibid., Reichenbach to Major Wood, 26 Nov. 1900. Letter of petition, same date and file, states that if the new order were 'strictly enforced it will virtually close the theaters and thus be detrimental in many ways to the business people of Dawson.'

22 Ibid., Telegram, McAulay and Clayton to Sifton, 26 Feb. 1901. Another telegram of almost identical content was dispatched to Sifton by the Canadian Bank of Commerce, Bank of British North America, Alaska Commercial Company, Alaska Exploration Company, North American Transportation and Trading Company, Harper and Ladue Townsite Company and McAulay Brothers, 29 Feb. 1901.

23 Ibid., Smart to Wood, 11 Mar. 1901.

24 Ibid., Ogilvie to Sifton, 19 Mar. 1901.

25 Ibid., Rev. Andrew Grant to Ogilvie, 19 Mar. 1901.

26 Ibid., Lithgow to Secretary of the Interior, 16 Apr. 1907.

27 Ibid., Oliver to Henderson, 6 Sept. 1907.

28 Ibid., Wood to Acting Commissioner, 16 Apr. 1907. When asked for their version, the proprietors of the two establishments protested that they were an important and integral part of Dawson's social life and that there was a deliberate move afoot to drive them out of busi-

ness. And while they conceded that cases of prostitution might have occurred, whenever it was discovered the offenders were dismissed from the hotel. See J. McDonald, M. Nelson, J.M. Eads and M. Eads to Minister of Justice, 25 Apr. 1907.

29 Ibid., petition to Minister of Justice, 25 Apr. 1907.

30 NA, RG 85, vol. 659, file 3632, Henderson to Oliver, 7 Dec. 1907. How the Flora Dora managed to stay in business without selling alcohol was a mystery, and although the NWMP were watching the Flora Dora very carefully, they claimed they could not detect the illegal sale of alcohol on the premises.

31 Ibid., Major Wood to Henderson, 7 Dec. 1907.

32 Martha Louise Black, *My Ninety Years* (Edmonds, WA: Alaska Northwest Publishing 1980), 47.

33 See Barbara Kelcey, 'Lost in the Rush: The Forgotten Women of the Klondike Stampede' (MA thesis, University of Victoria, 1989); Melanie J. Mayer, *Klondike Women: True Tales of the 1897-1898 Gold Rush* (Ohio: Swallow/University of Ohio Press 1989); and Frances Backhouse, *Women of the Klondike* (Vancouver: Whitecap 1995).

34 Mary Murphy, 'The Private Lives of Public Women: Prostitution in Butte, Montana, 1878-1917,' *The Women's West*, ed. Susan Armitage and Elizabeth Jameson (Norman: University of Oklahoma 1987).

35 Ellis Lucia, *Klondike Kate, 1873-1957* (New York: Hastings House 1962), 73; NA, RG 85, vol. 658, file 3417, Ogilvie to Sifton, 14 Aug. 1900.

36 Rockwell's comment is found in Lucia, *Klondike Kate,* 74; Mounted Police records in *Dawson Gaol Register,* 11 Nov. 1902.

37 Quotation from NA, MG 29 C91, W.C.E. Stewart Papers, undated letter from John McDougal to Stewart written during his trip to the Yukon in the summer and early fall of 1899; salary figure from 1901 census.

38 *Dawson Gaol Register,* 25 Mar. 1902.

39 See ibid., 11 Sept. 1902, for the charge against Jennie Mack. For her living situation, see NA, RG 85, vol. 658, file 4316, Wood to Sifton, 30 Nov. 1900.

40 Lucia, *Klondike Kate,* 71, 73; NA, RG 85, vol. 658, file 3417, Wood to Sifton, 22 Nov. 1900.

41 1901 census; Murphy, 'The Private Lives of Public Women,' 201.

42 *Dawson Gaol Register,* May 1903.

43 1901 census; Maria Ferguson, *Dawson City, Yukon and Alaska Business Directory and Gazetteer* (Seattle: M.L. Ferguson 1901).

44 James Albert Johnson, *Carmack of the Klondike* (Seattle: Epicenter Press/Horsdal and Schubart 1990), 115, 215

45 Lucia, *Klondike Kate,* 85, 87; 1901 census.

46 One of the more commonly reproduced photographs of the 'White Chapel' or alley of cribs in 1899 appears in Anne Butler's *Daughters of Joy, Sisters of Misery: Prostitutes in the American West, 1865-1890* (Urbana, IL: University of Illinois 1985), insert before p. 25; and also in Stan Cohen's *Queen City of the North: Dawson City, Yukon a Pictorial History.* (Missoula, MO: Pictorial Histories 1990), 116. Ella Lung Martinson remarks on the queues of waiting clients in *Trail to North Star Gold: A True Story of the Alaska-Klondike Gold Rush* (Portland: Binford and Mort 1984), 82.

47 *Dawson Gaol Register,* 18 Apr. 1902.

48 Ibid. Hal Guest argues that 'black' women were in fact treated more harshly than 'white' women by the courts. See his 'City of Gold,' 248.

49 *Dawson Gaol Register,* 18 Apr. 1902.

50 1901 census. It is worth noting here that in examining the working conditions and social lives of Dawson's working women, I could find no evidence that prostitutes and dance hall performers were any less honest in reporting their incomes and valued assets than other Klondikers. I have taken the women at their word, assuming they were telling the census taker the truth, just as I have for the miners, lawyers, accountants, and small business owners discussed elsewhere in this text.

51 1901 census. Guest states that the majority of prostitutes were also American. See his 'City of Gold,' 148

52 For the estimated number of people in the demi-monde, see Labelle Brooks-Vincent, *The Scarlet Life of Dawson and the Roseate Dawson of Nome: Personal Experiences and Observations of the Author* (San Francisco: Brown, Meese and Craddock 1900), 77; for comments about Belgian immigrants, see NA, MG 29 C27, Joseph Charles Dubé Papers, transcript of oral interview with Dubé.

53 1901 census.

54 The convictions are recorded in 'Reports from the North West Mounted Police at Dawson,' Appendix L, Return of Criminal and Other Cases Tried in the Yukon Territory, 1 Dec. to 30 Nov. 1898, *Sessional Papers*, 1899, vol. 33, no. 15. Among the diaries and memoirs are Laura Thompson Berton, *I Married the Klondike*; Black, *My Ninety Years*; Mary Lee Cadwell Davis, *Sourdough Gold: The Log of a Yukon Adventure* (Boston: M.A. Wilde 1933); and Haskell, *Two Years in the Klondike,* among others.

55 NA, RG 18, vol. 1445, file 181, part 6, McPhail Report, 10 Nov. 1899.

56 Martinson, *Trail to North Star Gold,* 82; NA MG 29 C27, Joseph Charles Dubé Papers, transcript of oral interview with Dubé.

57 Marion S. Goldman, *Gold Diggers and Silver Miners: Prostitution and Social Life on the Comstock Lode* (Ann Arbor: University of Michigan Press 1981), 71.

58 See Anne Butler's *Daughters of Joy* and Marion Goldman's *Gold Diggers and Silver Miners.*

59 Edward C. Trelawney-Ansell, *I Followed Gold* (New York: Lee Furman 1939), 171.

60 Brooks-Vincent, *Scarlet Life of Dawson,* 74.

61 Ibid., 73.

62 Jeremiah Lynch, *Three Years in the Klondike* (London: Edward Arnold 1904), 58.

63 Butler, *Daughters of Joy,* 45. For Maggie Richardson's conviction, see *Dawson Gaol Register,* 11 Feb. 1903; for Annie Gallina's, see 14 Oct. 1900. Eva Emilson Terry and Stella Freudenthal were charged with theft on 20 Mar. 1902, Jennie Mack on 11 Sept. 1902, Amanda Manson on 25 Aug. 1900, and Maggie Johnson and Maud Westwood on 11 Feb. 1903.

64 Pierre Berton, *Klondike: The Last Great Gold Rush: 1896-1899* (Toronto: McClelland and Stewart 1972), 172.

65 Maud Parrish, *Nine Pounds of Luggage* (London: Hutchman 1940), 21.

66 YTA, MS 82/97, R.W. Cautley Papers, memoir, 53.

67 *Dawson Gaol Register,* 18 Apr. 1902; 11 July 1902.

68 Lucia, *Klondike Kate,* 98-100; *Klondike Nugget,* 24 Dec. 1898, 10 Dec. 1898, 4 Feb. 1898. See also P. Berton, *Klondike,* 369.

69 Lucia, *Klondike Kate,* 86-112.

70 Haskell, *Two Years in the Klondike,* 359.

71 *Klondike Nugget,* 16 Aug. 1899.

72 Berton, *I Married the Klondike,* 48.

73 YTA, GR 82/86, vol. 1313, Department of Indian and Northern Affairs, Historic Sites, Victoria Faulkner files.

74 *Dawson Daily News,* 9 Dec. 1899.

75 Kenneth Coates and William Morrison, *The Sinking of the Princess Sophia* (Toronto: Oxford University 1990), 12; and Charlene Porsild, 'Lulu Mae Eads,' *Canadian Dictionary of Biography,* vol 14 (Toronto: University of Toronto 1995).

76 1901 census.

77 1901 census.

78 *Dawson Gaol Register,* 20 Mar. 1902.

79 See YTA, MS 82/53 F-5, Georgia White Papers; and Martha Louise Black, *My Ninety Years.*

80 John Secretan, *To the Klondike and Back* (New York: Hurst and Blackett 1898), 58, 52.

81 *Dawson Gaol Register,* 12 May 1903.

82 Ibid., 12 May 1902.

83 Ibid., 12 May 1902 and 25 Mar. 1902.
84 For the Lousetown raid, see 'Return of Criminal and Other Cases Tried in the Yukon Territory, 1 December 1897 to 30 November 1898,' *Sessional Papers*, vol. 31 (1899). For details about Robert and Duplan's procuring activities, see *Dawson Gaol Register*, 5 Dec. 1903 and 2 Mar. 1902 respectively. For chronology of the migration routes and employment history of Luceille and Marceille Martin and Louise Coragod, see corresponding entries in *Dawson Gaol Register*, 5 Dec. 1903.
85 'Return of Criminal and Other Cases Tried in the Yukon Territory, 1 December 1897 to 30 November 1898.'
86 NA, RG 85, vol. 659, file 3632, Rev. Pringle to Frank Oliver, Jan. 1904 and Pringle to Oliver, 31 July 1907.
87 NL, G36, reel 1, United States Consul Records, Dawson City, Yukon, McCook to Moore, 31 Jan. 1899.
88 Brooks-Vincent, in her *Scarlet Life of Dawson*, 48-9, notes that McCook's (she calls him McDuff) exploits were well known to the locals.
89 *Dawson Gaol Register.*
90 Spurr, *Through the Yukon Gold Diggings*, 74.

Chapter 5: 'Like Flocks of Migrating Geese'

1 Laura Thompson Berton, *I Married the Klondike* (Toronto: McClelland and Stewart 1985), 46.
2 See S.A. Archer, ed., *A Heroine of the North: Memoirs of Charlotte Selina Bompas* (London: Macmillan 1929).
3 NA, MG 29 C92, Reverend Richard J. Bowen Papers, memoir, 57.
4 Ibid., 100.
5 Ibid., 100-1.
6 NA, MG 30 E55, vol. 4, Constantine Papers, Constantine to Commissioner, 5 Jan. 1896; MG 29 C92, Reverend Richard J. Bowen Papers, memoir, 100.
7 Berton, *I Married the Klondike*, 17.
8 PAA, MSS 75.387, vol. 171, file 5121, Dawson City United Church Papers, essay by D.E. McAllister, Recording Steward, Whitehorse United Church, n.d.
9 Ibid.
10 *Klondike Nugget*, 30 Nov. 1900; YTA, MS 77/51 F-59, part 2, Walter Hamilton Papers.
11 YTA, CR 82/51, part 2, reel 57, United Church Papers, Session Record, St Andrew's Presbyterian Church, Dawson, 25 May 1898. See also *Minutes*, 29 Jan. 1900.
12 G. Bloss, 'Saga of the Klondike: The Diaries of Rebecca Ellery,' *Canadian Home Leaguer* 19, 5 (1972), 10.
13 NL, G36, reel 1, United States Consul Records, Dawson City, Yukon, Report of the Meeting of the Citizens' Relief Committee, 21 Dec. 1898.
14 For an extended discussion of the debate over 'respectability' and the Salvation Army in Canada, see Lynne Marks, 'Hallelujah Lasses: Working-Class Women in the Salvation Army in English Canada, 1882-92,' *Gender Conflicts*, ed. F. Iacovetta and M. Valverde (Toronto: University of Toronto Press 1992), 67-117.
15 For the Christian Endeavour Society, see YTA, CR 82/51, part 2, reel 57, United Church Papers, *Minutes*, 10 Jan. 1899; for the Epworth League, see PAA, MSS 75.387, vol. 171, file 5114, Dawson City United Church Papers, *Minutes*, 31 Oct. 1898.
16 YTA, MS 87/104, Albert E. Hetherington Papers, *History and General Information Booklet, First Methodist Church, Dawson City*, pamphlet (ca. 1901).
17 Ibid.
18 Maria Ferguson, *Dawson City, Yukon and Alaska Directory and Gazetteer* (Seattle: M.L. Ferguson 1901), 58.
19 YTA, MS 78/18, John Grace Papers, memoir, 13.
20 PABC, Add. MSS 686, Otto Nordling Papers, essay on St Mary's Hospital by O. Nordling. See

also clipping from *Montreal Gazette* (n.d., ca. 1948).

21 YTA, CR 81/45, part 2, Sisters of Ste Anne Collection, *St. Mary's Hospital, Dawson, 1897-98 to 1947-48,* unpaginated pamphlet (1948). See also Berton, *I Married the Klondike,* 163.

22 YTA, CR 81/45, part 1, file 4, Sisters of Ste Anne Collection, reminiscences of Sister Mary Joseph (undated).

23 YTA, CR 81/16 folder 75, St Paul's Anglican Church Papers, *Minutes of the Board of Managers for the Good Samaritan Hospital,* 12 Feb. 1898. For an excellent discussion of this pattern of Protestant-Catholic institutional rivalry, see P. Rooke and R. Schnell, *Discarding the Asylum* (Washington: University Press of America 1983).

24 YTA, CR 81/45, part 1, file 3, Sisters of Ste Anne Collection, W.B. Barrett, memoir, 6.

25 YTA, CR 85/22, Good Samaritan Hospital Papers, open letter from the Board of Managers to the People of the Klondike, 31 Jan. 1898.

26 For the hospital's staffing, see PAA, MSS 75.387, vol. 171, file 5121, Dawson City United Church Papers, essay by D.E. McAllister, Recording Steward, Whitehorse United Church (undated). The term 'Canadian black leg' is noted in PABC, E/E C81, Ernest Corp Papers, memoir (undated), 15.

27 NL, G36, reel 1, United States Consul Records, Dawson City, Yukon, Statement from St Mary's Hospital, submitted by Father Judge to American Consul, 1 Dec. 1898. Mrs Taylor's case is described in Sister Mary Joseph Calasanctius, Report to the Reverend Mother Superior, Feb. 1900, cited in Kelcey, 'Lost in the Rush,' (MA thesis, University of Victoria, 1989), 119.

28 Martha Louise Black, *My Ninety Years* (Edmonds, WA: Alaska Northwest Publishing 1980), 44.

29 NL, G36, reel 1, United States Consul Records, Dawson City, Yukon, Order of J.W. Good, MD, Medical Health Officer, Dawson, 15 Mar. 1899 (original emphasis).

30 Ibid., McCook to Hill, 28 July 1899.

31 NA, MG 28 I71, vol. 8, Victorian Order of Nurses Collection, Georgia Powell to Annie Pride, 10 June 1898. See also NA, MG 29 E105, Edward Lester Papers, diary entry 22 July 1898. Lester notes that the women who accompanied the Force were an unwelcome encumbrance as far as the men were concerned.

32 NA, MG 28 I71, Victorian Order of Nurses Collection, Report of Miss Powell, District 44, 1898-9.

33 YTA CR 81/45 pt. 1, file 3, Sisters of Ste. Anne Collection, W.B. Barrett, memoir, 6. See also clipping, *Whitehorse Star,* n.d., located in this file.

34 For a discussion of the private hospitals, see W.T. Barrett, memoir, 6; for earnings of private duty nurses, see NA, RG 85, vol. 657, file 3232, Smart to Major Snyder (NWMP), 5 Oct. 1902; for White's experiences, see YTA, MS 82/57 F-5, Georgia White Papers, diary.

35 YTA, CR 81/45, part 1, file 3, Sisters of Ste Anne Collection, W.B. Barrett, memoir, 6.

36 YTA, CR 81/16, vol. 75, St Paul's Anglican Church Papers, *Minutes of the Board of Managers for the Good Samaritan Hospital,* Sept. 1898.

37 YTA, CR 81/45, part 1, file 3, Sisters of Ste Anne Collection, W.B. Barrett, memoir.

38 Ethel Anderson Becker, 'A Klondike Woman's Diary,' *Alaska Sportsman* 35, 6 (1970), 36.

39 1901 census and Ferguson, *Dawson City, Yukon and Alaska Directory and Gazetteer* (1902).

40 *Klondike Nugget,* 17 Mar. 1898.

41 Berton, *I Married the Klondike,* 163.

42 For Dr Randy McLennan, see NA, RG 85, vol. 658, file 3283, Wilson to Secretary of Interior, 15 Nov. 1909 and *Dawson Daily News,* 28 Sept. 1915. For the consul's remarks, see NL, G36, reel 1, United States Consul Records, Dawson City, Yukon, McCook to Hill, 24 May 1899.

43 NA, RG 91, vol. 1, file 39, reel M2826, Articles of Corporation for the Eldorado Dome Quartz Mining Company, Dawson City, Yukon, 23 Dec. 1909.

44 NA, MG 30 E55, vol. 4, Constantine Papers, Constantine to Lieutenant Governor MacIntosh, 25 June 1896; Black, *My Ninety Years,* 68-9.

45 PABC, Add. MSS 1950, vol. 141, file 6, K.R. Genn Papers, Stringer to O'Meara, 27 July 1907.

46 *Klondike Nugget,* 27 Aug. 1898; Lulu Alice Craig, *Glimpses of Sunshine and Shade in the Far North*

(Cincinnati: Editor Publishing 1900); Ferguson, *Dawson City, Yukon and Alaska Directory and Gazetteer* (1901), 57, 66.

47 Sister Mary Joseph remembered that she shared her salary of $180 per month with the lay teacher. See YTA, CR 81/45, part 1, file 4, Sisters of St Anne Collection, reminiscences by Sister Mary Joseph Calasanz. For staffing, see CR 81/45, part 2, Sisters of Ste Anne Collection, *St. Mary's Hospital, Dawson, 1897-98 to 1947-48*, unpaginated pamphlet (1948).

48 *Whitehorse Star*, 24 Mar. 1960 (clipping) contained in PABC, Add. MSS 686, Otto Nordling Papers.

49 Ibid.

50 Becker, 'A Klondike Woman's Diary,' 18-9, 38-41.

51 YTA, MS 82/32 F-1, part 2, file 4, Winifred McLellan Papers, biographical sketch of Gordon McLellan by Walter Hamilton, n.d., and Winifred McLellan to Maggie Electa, 8 Sept. 1905.

52 Ibid., Winifred McLellan to Edna, 8 Sept. 1905.

53 Berton, *I Married the Klondike*, 15.

54 Ibid., 16-8.

55 Ibid., 13.

56 Ibid., 32.

57 NL, G36, reel 1, United States Consul Records, Dawson City, Yukon, McCook to Hill, 13 Apr. 1899; H.J. Woodside, 'Dawson As It Is,' *Canadian Magazine* 17 (Sept. 1901): 409; YTA, MS 81/37, Alexander Godfrey Papers, Godfrey to Hat, 27 Nov. 1900.

58 Berton, *I Married the Klondike*, 31.

59 Ibid. Emphasis added.

60 YTA, MS 77/51 F-59, part 2, Walter Hamilton Papers, clipping from *Vancouver Province*, 7 July 1962.

61 Ferguson, *Dawson City, Yukon and Alaska Directory and Gazetteer* (1901).

62 See Dianne Newell, 'Klondike Photographer's Lode,' *Historic Preservation* 29, 2 (1977): 15-21. Examples of these albums are: Ethel Anderson Becker, *Klondike '98: Hegg's Album of the 1898 Klondike Gold Rush* (Portland: Binford and Mort 1949); and anonymous, *The Papers and Photographs of P.E. Larss, Klondike Photographer and Miner, 1898-1904* (Juneau: Alaska Division, State Libraries and Museums 1978).

63 PABC, E/E/ L43, Guy Lawrence Papers, memoir, 21.

64 Black's *My Ninety Years* and Berton's *I Married the Klondike* both allude to Service's low profile.

65 NA, MG 30 C49, Ella Hall Papers, memoir, unpaginated, undated.

66 Ibid.

67 NA, MG 30, vol. 2, Nevill Alexander Drummond Armstrong Papers, diary entry for 14 July 1898.

68 Mary Hitchcock, *Two Women in the Klondike* (London: Putnam's Sons 1899), 166.

69 YTA, CR 81/45, part 1, file 3, Sisters of Ste Anne papers, W.T. Barrett, memoir, 9.

Chapter 6: Sterling Reputations and Golden Opportunities

1 NA, MG 29 C91, W.C.E. Stewart Papers, John McDougal to William Stewart, 10 Sept. 1899.

2 NA, MG 30 E55, vol. 4, Constantine Papers, Constantine to Lieutenant Governor MacIntosh, 25 June 1896; NA, RG 18, reel C2152, *Dawson Gaol Register* and *Whitehorse Court Docket*. See also NA, MG 30 C43, W.L. Phelps Papers.

3 NL, G36, reel 1, United States Consul Records, Dawson City, Yukon, McCook to Hill, 4 Sept. 1901.

4 1901 census.

5 Ibid.

6 NA, RG 85, vol. 658, file 3318, Report of the receipts and disbursements for the office of the Public Administrator, Dawson, 1917. See also 1901 census.

7 NA, RG 91, vol. 1, file 66, reel M2826, Smith to Henderson, 21 Feb. 1911 re the vacancy on Yukon Council 'due to the death of R.L. Ashbaugh who represented the Bonanza District';

YTA, MS 82/190 F-18, file 24, R.L. Ashbaugh Papers, Bill of Sale #5 above Hunker Creek, Annie May Enright to Roderick Ashbaugh, n.d. (ca. 1907).

8 NA, MG 29 C91, W.C.E. Stewart Papers, John McDougal to William Stewart, 10 Sept. 1899.

9 NA, RG 85, vol. 655, file 3005, Smart to Rinfret, 18 Jan. 1900.

10 YTA, MS 82/97, R.W. Cautley Papers, memoir, 52.

11 NA, RG 85, vol. 657, file 3072, Ogilvie to Smart, Apr. 1900.

12 For private surveying work, see NA, RG 85, vol. 1523, file 3303, Affidavit of John William Renell, 29 Oct. 1909; for advertisements / advertising practices, see Maria Ferguson, *Dawson City, Yukon and Alaska Directory and Gazetteer* (Seattle: M.L. Ferguson 1901); for information about Beatty, see YTA, MS 82/390 F-119, James Edward Beatty Papers.

13 Tappan Adney, cited in Margaret Archibald, *Grubstake to Grocery Store: Supplying the Klondike, 1897-1907*, Canadian Historic Sites Occasional Papers in Archaeology and History No. 26 (Ottawa: Parks Canada 1981), 37, 49.

14 NA, MG 30 E55, vol. 4, Constantine Papers, Constantine to Deputy Minister of the Interior, 4 Dec. 1896. See also J.W. Leonard, *Gold Fields of the Klondike: Fortune Seeker's Guide to the Yukon Region of Alaska and British North America; the Story as Told by Ladue, Berry, Phiscator and Other Gold Finders* (London: T.F. Unwin 1897), 132.

15 *Klondike Nugget*, 17 Aug. 1898; quotation from Archibald, *Grubstake to Grocery Store*, 37; YTA, MS 82/454, Yukon Order of Pioneers, D.E. Griffith, 'Biographical Sketch of Leroy McQuesten' (clipping, n.d.).

16 Mabel Barbee Lee, *Cripple Creek Days* (Lincoln: University of Nebraska Press 1984); 1901 census; quotation from Archibald, *Grubstake to Grocery Store*, 38.

17 For information about insurance, see 1901 census, 40, 49; for the 26 April fire, see NL, G36, reel 1, United States Consul Records, Dawson City, Yukon, McCook to Hill, 27 Apr. 1899.

18 Laura Thompson Berton, *I Married the Klondike* (Toronto: McClelland and Stewart 1985), 35-6.

19 Archibald, *Grubstake to Grocery Store*, 38; 1901 census.

20 For Christophe Authier, see NA, RG 85, vol. 658, file 3318, Report of the Receipts and Disbursements for the Office of the Public Administrator, Dawson, 1917. For Albert Lobley, see YTA, GR 82/86, vol. 1313, Department of Indian Affairs and Northern Development, Historic Sites, Victoria Faulkner files, oral interviews.

21 1901 census.

22 N.B. Stern, 'The Jews in Yukon Territory and their Cemetery,' *Western States Jewish Historical Quarterly* 14, 4 (1982): 358. See also 1901 census.

23 Archibald, *Grubstake to Grocery Store*, 69; 1901 census; Ferguson, *Dawson City, Yukon and Alaska Directory and Gazetteer* (1902).

24 NL, G36, reel 1, United States Consul Records, Dawson City, Yukon, clipping from *Yukon Sun* (n.d.), report on meeting of Finance Committee, and Thomas McGill (Salvation Army) to McGowan, 1 Dec. 1898.

25 Ibid., McCook to Moore, 31 Mar. 1899.

26 1901 census.

27 NA, RG 85, vol. 658, file 3417, Reichenbach to Major Wood, 26 Nov. 1900 and letter for petition from Dawson merchants to Minister of Justice, 25 Apr. 1907.

28 Archibald, *Grubstake to Grocery Store*, 49-50.

29 Quoted in Suzann Ledbetter, *Nellie Cashman: Prospector and Trailblazer* (El Paso: University of Texas 1993), 46.

30 YTA, MS 81/37, Alexander Godfrey Papers, Godfrey to Hat, 27 Nov. 1900; 1901 census.

31 YTA, MS 81/37, Alexander Godfrey Papers, Godfrey to Hat, 27 Nov. 1900.

32 PABC, Add. MSS 698, vol. 6, file 4, J.B. Clearihue Papers, Joseph to Annie Clearihue, 29 Sept. 1901, 26 June 1901, and 1 Sept. 1901.

33 Archibald, *Grubstake to Grocery Store*, 72.

34 YTA, MS 86/83 F-198, Isabelle Reid Papers, Isabelle Reid to Archivist, 21 Aug. 1986. See also 1901 census and Ferguson, *Dawson City, Yukon and Alaska Directory and Gazetteer* (1901).

35 YTA, MS82/190 F-18, file 13, R.L. Ashbaugh Papers, Anderson divorce case notes, 22 Jan. 1903 and 10 Aug. 1905.

36 1901 census and YTA, MS 86/83 F-198, Isabelle Reid Papers, Isabelle Reid to Archivist, 21 Aug. 1986.

37 Berton, *I Married the Klondike,* 31.

38 NA, RG 85, vol. 1523, file 3323, Yukon Lawn Tennis Club, Petition to Crown Timber and Land Agent, 15 Sept. 1900; YTA, photograph 1213, 'Outdoor Curling Rink Championship Game. J.T. Lithgow's rink v. Col. Rourke's rink,' 9 Apr. 1901.

39 Frances Dorley Gillis, 'The Lady Went North in '98,' *Alaska Sportsman* 9, 9 (1945): 12, 31.

40 YTA, MS 82/40-2, Gillis Family Papers, archivist's notes in finding aid.

41 Martha Louise Black, *My Ninety Years* (Edmonds, WA: Alaska Northwest Publishing 1980), 68, 69.

42 YTA, MS 82/32 F-1, part 2, file 4, Winifred McLellan Papers, biographical sketch of Gordon McLellan by Walter Hamilton, n.d.

43 NA, MG 29 C92, Reverend Richard J. Bowen Papers, memoir.

44 William R. Morrison, *Showing the Flag: The Mounted Police and Canadian Sovereignty in the North, 1894-1925* (Vancouver: UBC Press 1985), Chapter 3. For a more detailed discussion and interpretation of the establishment and eventual displacement of frontier justice and the miners' meeting, see Thomas Stone, *Miners' Justice: Migration, Law and Order on the Alaska-Yukon Frontier, 1873-1902* (New York: Peter Lang 1988), Chapter 2.

45 NA, MG 30 E55, vol. 4, Constantine Papers, Constantine to Lieutenant Governor MacIntosh, 25 June 1896.

46 P.C.H. Primrose, *Report,* cited in Morrison, *Showing the Flag,* 35.

47 Morrison, *Showing the Flag,* 66-7.

48 David R. Morrison, *The Politics of the Yukon Territory, 1898-1909* (Toronto: University of Toronto Press 1968), 13.

49 Ibid., 15.

50 Quoted in David Hall, *Clifford Sifton,* vol. 2, *The Lonely Eminence* (Vancouver: UBC Press 1985), 3.

51 PABC, Add. MSS 3, vol. 1, file 9, T.D. Pattullo Papers, Laurier Subscription List, 1904.

52 PABC, Add. MSS 188, file 6. See also Robin Fisher, *Duff Pattullo of British Columbia* (Toronto: University of Toronto Press 1991).

53 PABC, Add. MSS 188, file 5, George R. Pattullo Papers, J.B. to Father, 19 Jan. 1903. See subsequent letter from J.A. Ross, Dept of Interior, to George Pattullo, 4 Apr. 1903 in which Ross informed the senior Pattullo of his son's appointment.

54 See Edward F. Bush, *Commissioners of the Yukon, 1897-1918,* Canadian Historic Sites Occasional Papers in Archaeology and History No. 10 (Ottawa: Parks Canada 1974).

55 Black, *My Ninety Years,* 98.

56 NA, RG 85, vol. 663, file 3879, Cory to Rowatt, 18 Apr. 1912.

57 Quoted in Morrison, *Politics of the Yukon Territory,* 13.

58 NA, RG 85, vol. 656, file 3045, Hall to Conklin, 13 July 1898; also file 3046, Pereira to Layfield, 6 July 1898; Black, *My Ninety Years,* 72.

59 NA, RG 85, vol. 659, file 3568, Newlands to T.G. Rothwell, 5 Feb. 1902. Details of the fraud are laid out in Lithgow to Smart, 28 May 1902.

60 For Bell, see NA, RG 85, vol. 656, file 3032, Sifton to Governor General, 18 Sept. 1899. See also Smart to Bell, 29 Nov. 1899, and Sifton to Governor General, 4 Nov. 1901. For Fawcett, see Morrison, *Politics of the Yukon Territory,* 13.

61 Privy Council Orders, Mar. 1899, cited in Morrison, *Politics of the Yukon Territory,* 23.

62 NA, RG 85, vol. 656, file 3063, Bell to Ogilvie, 19 Mar. 1900, Ogilvie to Smart, 21 Mar. 1900 and 31 Mar. 1900 re William Beattie; NA, RG 85, vol. 656, file 3032, Pattullo to Sifton, 15 Mar. 1899 re Pattullo; NA, RG 85, Fol. 655, file 3005, Smart to Corey, 8 Oct. 1907, re the firing the Philip Holliday.

63 NA, MG 30 C6, George Nash Papers, Nash to 'Uncle,' 20 July 1900.

64 NA, RG 85, vol. 655, file 3005, internal memo to Rowatt, 23 Jan. 1917.

65 Ibid., Congdon to Rowatt, Apr. 1904.

66 Ibid., 'Estimate of F.A.H. Fysh, Living Expenses for one month, married man with family of three small children,' Mar. 1904.

67 Ibid., Merchants of Dawson to Governor General of Canada, 2 July 1904.

68 YTA, MS 82/97, R.W. Cautley Papers, memoir, 54; PABC, Add. MSS 1158, Ronald Weir Papers, memoir of John McGregor, 7.

69 Canada, *An Act to Provide for the Government of the Yukon Territory, 1898*; Morrison, *Politics of the Yukon Territory*, 21.

70 Morrison, *Politics of the Yukon Territory*, 24; and Hall, *Clifford Sifton*, 4.

71 1901 census, 35.

72 Morrison, *Politics of the Yukon Territory*, 35, appendices C and D; Hall, *Clifford Sifton*, 35.

73 NL, G36, reel 1, United States Consul Records, Dawson City, Yukon, McCook to Hill, 26 Apr. 1898 (re McCook's appointment) and McCook to Moore, 30 Mar. 1899 (re public reaction to Fawcett's departure).

74 Black, *My Ninety Years*, 75.

75 NL, G36, reel 1, United States Consul Records, Dawson City, Yukon, McCook to Moore, 3 Sept. 1898. See also White and McCaul to McCook, 1 Aug. 1899.

Chapter 7: Women, Men, and Community in the Klondike

1 James Weppler, *Yukon Territory: A Community of Men,* National History Sites Manuscript Report No. 9 (Ottawa: Department of Indian and Northern Affairs 1969).

2 PABC, Add. MSS 698, vol. 6, file 4, J.B. Clearihue Papers, Clearihue to Annie, 18 Sept. 1901. Similar references are made by other Klondikers in their letters home; see YTA, MS 81/37, Alexander Godfrey Papers, Godfrey to Hat, 27 Nov. 1900.

3 YTA, MS 82/327, F-59, part 2, Blanche Pépin Lambert Papers, memoir; NA, MG 29 C91, W.C.E. Stewart Papers, John McDougal to Stewart, 10 Sept. 1899.

4 YTA, CR 81/45, part 1, file 3, Sisters of Ste Anne Papers, W.T. Barrett, memoir, 9. Emphasis added.

5 Laura Thompson Berton, *I Married the Klondike* (Toronto: McClelland and Stewart 1985), 42.

6 Ibid., 46.

7 Ibid., 47.

8 Ibid., 48.

9 Ibid., 46.

Bibliography

Archival Sources

National Archives of Canada
Armstrong, Neville Alexander Drummond Papers
Black, Martha Louise Papers
Bowen, Richard John Papers
Boyle, Joseph Whiteside Papers
Campbell, A.B. Papers
Canada. Census, 1901
—. Commission to Investigate Treadgold Concession, 1903-4
—. Department of Interior
—. Department of National Revenue. Customs Port Records, 1899-1924
—. Department of Public Works Records. Supplementary Estimates, 1901-2
—. Northern Administration Branch Records
—. Royal Canadian Mounted Police Records
—. Yukon Territorial Records
Canham, Reverend Thomas H. Papers
Coffey, George Papers
Constantine, Charles Papers
Dubé, J.C.B. (Charles) Papers
Elliott, William R. Papers
Goodwin, Charles Papers
Hall, Ella Papers
International Order of Odd Fellows. Dawson Yukon Territory. Lodge No. 1, Dawson
Keir, Ernest F. Papers
Lester, Edward Papers
McDougal, John Alexander Papers
Minto Papers
Monk, Alfred Papers
Nash, George R. Papers
Ogilvie, William Papers
Oliver, Erik Alexander Papers
Phelps, W.L. Papers
St Mary's Roman Catholic Church Papers. Dawson City, Yukon
Scoins, Clayton J. Collection
Sifton Papers
Smith, Alden R. Papers
Spreadbury, Alfred Papers
Stewart, W.C.E. Papers
Waterer, Alphonso Papers

Wood, Zachary Papers
Woodside, Henry Joseph Papers
Wragge, Edmund Carlyon Papers

National Archives of the United States, Washington
State Department of the United States. Dawson City Post Files

National Library of Canada
United States Consul Records. Dawson City, Yukon

Provincial Archives of Alberta
Arndt, Harry Papers
Gunn, Peter Papers
Larose, Eugene Papers
Martin, H. Milton Papers
United Church of Canada. Alberta Conference. Dawson City Papers

Provincial Archives of British Columbia
Bell, Peter Warren Papers
British Columbia. Bennett-Atlin Commission, 1899
Browne, Guy C. Papers
Cameron, Frank B. Papers
Canada. Department of Customs, Victoria
—. Department of Interior
Clearihue Family Papers
Clearihue, Joseph Badenoch Papers
Cleveland, F.A. Papers
Corp, Ernest J. Papers
Cran, James Papers
Doig, David Papers
Envoldson, Fred C. Papers
Genn, Kenneth Reginald Papers
Gillespie, Adam Scott Papers
Goodfellow, John Christie Papers
Graham, Harry Papers
Hart, Frank William Papers
Henderson, Robert Douglas Papers
Hoy, David Henry Papers
Lawrence, Guy Papers
Lee, Norman Papers
Mahoney, Michael Ambrose Papers
Manson, William Francis Papers
Moore, T.W. Papers
Morrison, Wm. Turner Papers
Nordling, Otto Papers
Olive, W.H.T. Papers
Order of the American Boy Collection
Pattullo, George Robson Papers
Pattullo, Thomas Dufferin Papers
Rowlinson, Seymour Papers
Sheringham, Edward Durban Papers
Tuxford, George Stuart Papers

Weir, Ronald J. Papers
Wilson, Thomas Papers
Yukon Order of Pioneers Collection
Yukoner (Steamship) Papers

University of Alberta Special Collections
Eben McAdam Papers. 1859-1927

Yukon Territorial Archives
Anderson Family Papers
Ashbaugh, Roderick Papers
Baethke, Alexander Papers
Ball, Ven Papers
Ballou, William B. Papers
Banks, Henry Dow Papers
Bartsch Family Papers
Beatty, James Edward Papers
Billy Biggs Blacksmith Shop Papers
Binder, Edward Papers
Black, Martha Louise Papers
Brooks, Thomas Papers
Campbell, Stewart L. Papers
Canada. Department of Indian Affairs and Northern Development, Historic Sites.
    Victoria Faulkner Papers
Cautley, R.W. Papers
Childs, Will Papers
Church Family Papers
Coutts, Robert C. Papers
Craig, B.F. Papers
Craig, Clarence W. Collection
Craig Family Papers
Craig, John George Papers
Craig, R.B. Papers
Cresswell, R.H.S. Papers
Cunningham Family Papers
Davies, John D. Papers
Dewey, Fred W. Papers
Eskrigge, Harry Papers
Faulkner, Victoria Papers
Finch, H.D. Papers
Fitzhugh, Robert Hunter Papers
Forrest, Emil Joseph Papers
Forrest, Joseph Paul Papers
Franklin, Henry W. Papers
Garner-Knott Family Papers
Garside, Nora Papers
Gillis Family Papers
Godfrey, Alexander Papers
Good Samaritan Hospital Papers
Goulter, Ida May Mack Papers
Grace, John Papers
Greene, Joseph J. Papers

Grumann Family Papers
Hamilton, Walter R. Papers
Haugan, Gladys Simpson and Family Papers
Henderson Family Papers
Hetherington, Albert Edward Papers
Hunt, Frederick Papers
Jacard, Frank A. Papers
Johnson, Carol Papers
Jones, E.H. Papers
Jones, Elizabeth Diets Papers
Kelley, Peter Papers
Kingsley, James E. Papers
Kirk, Lilian Papers
Lambert, Blanche Pépin Papers
Lee, James Papers
Lind, John Grieve Papers
Lindsay Family Papers
Livingstone Creek Papers
MacCaul, C.C. Papers
McLellan, Winifred Papers
McMillan, John Henry Papers
McRae, James A. Papers
McRae, Fanny Papers
Marsh, Marvin Sanford Papers
Marston, Roderick Papers
May, L.B. Papers
Methodist Church, Dawson City Papers
Mitchell, Skeffington Samuel Papers
Mizony, Paul Papers
Moody, Mary D. Collection
Moore, Mabel Papers
Mosier, Charles P. Papers
Munger Family Papers
Nordling, Otto Papers
Norelius, Andrew Papers
O'Reilly, Kevin Papers
Palmer, Ralph Papers
Park, William John Papers
Pattee Family Papers
Peterson, Johannes Papers
Potvin, Annette Papers
Pratt, John F. Papers
Reid, Isabelle Papers
Ridley, Albert J. Papers
Rintoule, David Papers
Robb, Jim Papers
Roberts, Alf Papers
Rockwell, Kate Papers
St Mary's School Papers
St Paul's Anglican Church Papers
Salvation Army Collection
Schreier, Fred Papers

Schuldenfrei Family Papers
Simard, J. Arsen Papers
Sisters of Ste Anne Collection
Snow, George T. Papers
Stone, Andrew Jackson Papers
Twidell, William Papers
Tyrrell, Joseph Burr Papers
United Church of Canada. St Andrew's Presbyterian Church, Dawson City
Waddington, Cal Papers
Waddington, Margaret H. Collection
Wass, Dorothy Papers
White Pass and Yukon Route Collection
White, Georgia Papers
Whyte, Alexander Papers
Williams, Thomas Hale and Family Papers
Yakima Valley Museum
Young, Frederick Lockwood Papers
Yukon Order of Pioneers

Newspapers
Dawson Daily News
Glenora News
Klondike Nugget
Klondike News
The [Cordova, Alaska] North Star
Stikeen River Journal
Yukon Sun & Klondike Pioneer
Yukon Sun

Books and Articles
Abel, Kerry. 'William Carpenter Bompas.' *Dictionary of Canadian Biography* 13 (Toronto: University of Toronto Press 1989): 92-4
Adney, Tappan. *The Klondike Stampede.* New York: Harper and Brothers 1900
Alberts, Laurie. 'Petticoats and Pickaxes.' *Alaska Journal* 7, 3 (1977): 146-59
Allan, A.A. 'Scotty.' *Gold, Men, and Dogs.* London: Putnam 1931
Allen, Henry T. *Report of an Expedition to the Copper, Tanana, and Koyukuk Rivers, in the Territory of Alaska, in the Year 1885.* Washington: Government Printing Office 1887
Anderson, Doris. *Ways Harsh and Wild.* Vancouver: J.J. Douglas 1973
Anzer, Richard C. *Klondike Gold Rush (As Recalled by a Participant).* New York: Pageant Press 1959
Apostol, Jane. 'Charles W. Watt: An Oregonian in the Klondike.' *Oregon History Quarterly* 87, 1 (1986): 5-20
Archer, S.A., ed. *A Heroine of the North: Memoirs of Charlotte Selina Bompas.* London: Macmillan 1929
Archibald, Margaret. *Grubstake to Grocery Store: Supplying the Klondike, 1897-1907.* Canadian Historic Sites Occasional Papers in Archaeology and History No. 26. Ottawa: Parks Canada 1981
Arestad, Sverre. 'Questing for Gold and Furs in Alaska.' *Norwegian American Studies* 21 (1962): 54-94
Armitage, Susan, and Elizabeth Jameson, eds. *The Women's West.* Norman: University of Oklahoma Press 1987
Armstrong, Nevill, A.D. *Yukon Yesterdays: Thirty Years of Adventures.* London: John Long 1936

Atwood, Fred N. *The Alaska-Yukon Gold Book: A Roster of the Progressive Men and Women Who Were the Argonauts of the Gold Stampede.* Seattle: Sourdough Stampede Association, n.d.

Austin, Basil. *The Diary of a Ninety-Eighter.* Mount Pleasant: John Cumming 1968

Auzias-Turenne, Raymond. *Voyage au pays des mines d'or — le Klondike.* Paris: Calman Lévy 1899

Backhouse, Frances H. *Women of the Klondike.* Vancouver: Whitecap 1995

—. 'Women of the Klondike.' *Beaver* 68, 6 (1988-9): 30-6

Baker, David Robert. 'Decentralization and Development: The Case of the Yukon.' MA thesis, Queen's University, 1990

Baldwin, Douglas. 'Public Health Services and Limited Prospects: Epidemic and Conflagration in Cobalt.' *Ontario History* 75, 4 (1983):374-402

Banks, Della Murray. 'Woman on the Dalton Trail.' *Alaska Sportsman* 9, 10 (1945): 10-11, 25-34

—. 'Rainbow's End.' *Alaska Sportsman* 9, 10 (1945): 14-5, 21-7

Bankson, Russell A. *Klondike Nugget.* Caldwell: Caxton 1935

Banon, Mrs E.M., ed. *The Diary of Edward Magawly Banon, Klondike, British Yukon, 1897.* Newport, RI: Privately printed by Ward Printing, n.d.

Basi, Wilhelm. 'The Translated Diary of Wilhelm Basi.' *Journal of Finnish American Historical Society* 6, 6 (1971): 22-36

Basque, Garnet. 'Bennett City.' *Canadian West* 16 (1989): 40-7

Beattie, Kim. *Brother, Here's a Man! The Saga of Klondike Joe Boyle.* New York: Macmillan 1940

Beauregard, Marthe F. *Baptèmes, mariages, sepultures de Ste. Marie de Dawson City, Yukon, 1898-1956.* Montreal: Editions Bergeron et Fils 1976

Becker, Ethel Anderson. *Klondike '98: Hegg's Album of the 1898 Klondike Gold Rush.* Portland: Binford and Mort 1949

—. 'A Klondike Woman's Diary.' *Alaska Sportsman* 35, 6 (1970): 18-20, 36-7

—. 'Little Girl on the Klondike Gold Fields.' *Alaska Sportsman* 27, 11 (1962): 22-4, 34-6

Belcher, R. 'Annual Report of Inspector Belcher.' In *Report of the Commissioner of the NorthWest Mounted Police Force, 1898.* Part 3, *Yukon Territory.* Ottawa: Queen's Printer 1899

Bell, E. Moberly. *Flora Shaw (Lady Lugard D.B.E.).* London: Constable Publishers 1947

Bell, Lieutenant Edwin. 'What I Saw, Heard, and Did In and About Rampart City, Alaska.' In *Compilation of Narratives of Exploration in Alaska.* Senate Report No. 1023, 56th Congress. Washington: Government Printing Office 1900

Bell, Robert. *The Klondike Gold District in the Yukon Valley, Canada.* A paper read before the Australasian Association for the Advancement of Science. Brisbane: Government Printer 1909

Bennett, Gordon. *Yukon Transportation: A History.* Canadian Historic Sites Occasional Papers in Archaeology and History No. 19. Ottawa: Parks Canada 1978

Berg, Helen. 'The Doll of Dawson.' *Alaska Sportsman* 8, 2 (1944): 12-7

Berry, A.E. (Edna). *The Bushes and the Berrys.* San Francisco: C.J. Bennett 1941

Berton, Laura Thompson. *I Married the Klondike.* Toronto: McClelland and Stewart 1985

Berton, Pierre. *The Golden Trail.* Toronto: Macmillan 1964

—. *Klondike: The Last Great Gold Rush: 1896-1899.* Toronto: McClelland and Stewart 1987

—. *The Klondike Quest: A Photographic Essay, 1897-1899.* Toronto: McClelland and Stewart 1983

Black, Martha Louise. *Klondike Days.* Victoria: Acme Press, n.d.

—. *My Ninety Years.* Edmonds, WA: Alaska Northwest Publishing 1980

Bloss, G. 'Saga of the Klondike: The Diaries of Rebecca Ellery.' *Canadian Home Leaguer* 19, 5 (1972): 10-1; and 20, 2 (1973):4-5

Bobillier, Marcel, 'Souvenirs du Yukon, visite aux reuisseaux du Klondike.' *North/Nord* 26, 2 (1979): 44-7

Boillot, Leon. *Aux mines d'or du Klondike: du Lac Bennett à Dawson City.* Paris: Hachette et Cie 1899

Bolotin, Norman. 'Klondike Lost.' *Alaska Journal* 10, 2 (1980): 64-73

—. *A Klondike Scrapbook: Ordinary People, Extraordinary Times.* San Francisco: Chronicle Books 1987

Bostock, Hugh S. 'Prospecting on Russell Creek.' *North* 17, 6 (1970): 30-43

Bramble, Charles A. *Klondike: A Manual for Gold Seekers.* N.p., 1897

Breen, David H. 'The Turner Thesis and the Canadian West: A Closer Look at the Ranching Frontier.' In *Essays on Western History,* edited by L.H. Thomas, 28-44. Edmonton: University of Alberta Press 1976

Brennan, T. Ann. *The Real Klondike Kate: The Story of Katherine Ryan.* Fredericton: Goose Lane Editions 1990

Brooks-Vincent, Labelle. *The Scarlet Life of Dawson and the Roseate Dawson of Nome: Personal Experiences and Observations of the Author.* San Francisco: Brown, Meese and Craddock 1900

Brown, Jennifer. *Strangers in Blood: Fur Trade Company Families in Indian Country.* Vancouver: University of British Columbia Press 1980

Brown, Wallace. 'First Impressions: Through Colonial Canada with Our Pioneer Tourists.' *The Beaver* 68, 2 (1988): 4-20

Bush, Edward F. *Commissioners of the Yukon, 1897-1918.* Canadian Historic Sites Occasional Papers in Archaeology and History No. 10. Ottawa: Parks Canada 1974

—. *The Dawson Daily News: Journalism in the Klondike,* Canadian Historic Sites Occasional Papers in Archaeology and History No. 21. Ottawa: Parks Canada 1979

—. 'Policing the Border in the Klondike Gold Rush.' *Canadian Geographic* 100, 5 (1980): 70-3

Butler, Anne M. *Daughters of Joy, Sisters of Misery: Prostitutes in the American West, 1865-1890.* Urbana, IL: University of Illinois Press 1985

Callahan, E. 'A Yukon Autobiography.' *Alaska Journal* 5 (Spring 1975): 127-8

Cameron, Agnes Dean. *The New North: An Account of a Woman's 1908 Journey through Canada to the Arctic.* Saskatoon: Western Producer Prairie Books 1986

Canada. Annual Reports from Department of Interior and Royal North West Mounted Police. *Sessional Papers,* 1896-1905

—. Department of the Interior, Northwest Territories and Yukon Branch. *The Yukon Territory, Its History and Resources.* Ottawa: Queen's Printer 1907

—. Department of the Interior, Northwest Territories and Yukon Branch. *Annual Report.* Ottawa: Queen's Printer 1897

—. Dominion Bureau of Statistics. *Chronological Record of Canadian Mining Events from 1604 to 1943 and Historical Tables of Mining Activity.* Ottawa: King's Printer 1945

—. House of Commons. *Report of the NWMP, 1898.* Ottawa: Queen's Printer 1899

Carcross-Tagish First Nation (Sheila Greer). *Skookum Stories of the Chilkoot/Dyea Trail.* Whitehorse: Carcross-Tagish First Nation 1995

Careless, J.M.S. *Frontier and Metropolis: Regions, Cities and Identities in Canada before 1914.* Toronto: University of Toronto Press 1989

Carmack, George W. *My Experiences in the Yukon.* N.p.: Marguerite Carmack 1933

Carter, Charles W. 'Memories of the Alaska Gold Rush.' *Family Heritage* 1, 4 (1978): 113-7

Carter, Margaret. *St. Andrew's Presbyterian Church, Lake Bennett, British Columbia.* Canadian Historic Sites Occasional Papers in Archaeology and History No. 26. Ottawa: Parks Canada 1981

Clark, A. McFadyen, 'Koyukon.' In *Handbook of North American Indians,* Vol. 6, *Subarctic,* edited by June Helm, 582-601. Washington: Smithsonian Institution 1981

Clark, S.D. *The Developing Canadian Community.* Toronto: University of Toronto Press 1962

—. *The Social Development of Canada: An Introductory Study with Documents.* New York: AMS Press 1942

Clement, Wallace. *Class, Power and Property: Essays on Canadian Society.* Agincourt, ON: Methuen 1983

Clifford, Howard. *The Skagway Story: A History of Alaska's Most Famous Gold Rush Town and the People Who Made That History.* Anchorage: Alaska Northwest 1975

Clum, John Philip. *A Trip to the Klondike through the Stereoscope. From Chicago to St. Michael's, Alaska.* Meadville, PA: Keystone View 1899

Coates, Kenneth S. *Best Left As Indians: Native-White Relations in the Yukon Territory, 1840-1973*. Montreal: McGill-Queen's University Press 1993
—. 'Controlling the Periphery: The Territorial Administration of the Yukon and Alaska, 1867-1959.' *Pacific Northwest Quarterly* 78, 4 (1987): 145-51
—. 'On the Outside in Their Homeland: Native People and the Evolution of the Yukon Economy.' *Northern Review* 1, 1 (1988): 73-89
—. 'Send Only Those Who Rise a Peg: Anglican Clergy in the Yukon, 1858-1932.' *Journal of the Canadian Church Historical Society* 28, 1 (1986): 3-18
Coates, Kenneth, and William Morrison. 'More Than a Matter of Blood: The Federal Government, the Churches and the Mixed Blood Populations of the Yukon and the Mackenzie River Valley, 1890-1950.' In *1885 and After*, edited by F.L. Barron and J.B. Waldram. Saskatoon: Canadian Plains Research Center 1986
—. *The Sinking of the Princess Sophia: Taking the North down with Her*. Toronto: Oxford University Press 1990
Cody, H.A. *An Apostle of the North, Memoirs of the Right Reverend William Carpenter Bompas, D.D.* Toronto: Musson 1908
Cohen, Stan B. *Queen City of the North: Dawson City, Yukon a Pictorial History*. Missoula, MO: Pictorial Histories Publishing 1990
Cole, Terrence. 'A Broken Chain and a Busted Pedal.' *Alaska Journal* 15, 1 (1985): 521-4
—. 'A History of the Nome Gold Rush: The Poor Man's Paradise.' PhD diss., University of Washington, 1983
—. 'Klondike Visions: Dreams of a Promised Land.' *Alaska Journal* 16 (1986): 82-93
—, ed. *Nome: City of the Golden Beaches*. Anchorage: Alaska Geographic Society 1984
Conger, Horace. *In Search of Gold: The Alaska Journals of Horace Conger*. Ottawa: Carleton Library 1985
Constantine, Charles. *Report of the Commissioner of the North West Mounted Police, 1894*. Ottawa: Queen's Printer 1895
Cooke, Alan, and Clive Holland. *The Exploration of Northern Canada, 500-1920*. Toronto: Arctic History Press 1978
Copp, J. Terry. *Anatomy of Poverty: The Condition of the Working Class in Montreal, 1897-1929*. Toronto: McClelland and Stewart 1974
Council for Yukon Indians. *Together Today for Our Children Tomorrow*. Whitehorse: Council for Yukon Indians 1977
Coutts, Robert. 'Gold Rush Theatre and the Palace Grand.' *The Beaver* 312, 4 (1982): 40-6
Craig, Lulu Alice. *Glimpses of Sunshine and Shade in the Far North*. Cincinnati: Editor Publishing 1900
Crow, John R., and Philip R. Obley. 'Han.' In *Handbook of North American Indians*. Vol. 6, *Subarctic*, edited by June Helm, pp. 506-13. Washington: Smithsonian Institution 1981
Cruikshank, Julie. *Life Lived Like a Story: Life Stories of Three Yukon Elders*. Vancouver: UBC Press 1990
—. *Reading Voices / Dän Dhá Ts'edenintth'sé: Oral and Written Interpretations of the Yukon's Past*. Vancouver: Douglas and McIntyre 1991
Cuba, Lee J. *Identity and Community on the Alaskan Frontier*. Philadelphia: Temple University Press 1987
Cunnynghame, Francis. *Lost Trail, the Story of Klondike Gold and the Man Who Fought for Control*. Caldwell, ID: Claxton Printers 1938
Curtis, Merle. *The Making of an American Community: A Case Study of Democracy in a Frontier County*. Stanford: Stanford University Press 1959
Davignon, Ellen. *The Cinnamon Mine: Memories of an Alaska Highway Childhood*. Whitehorse: Studio North 1988
Davis, Mary Lee Cadwell. *Sourdough Gold: The Log of a Yukon Adventure*. Boston: M.A. Wilde 1933

Dawson, George. *Report on an Exploration in the Yukon District, 1887.* 1889. Reprint, White-horse: Yukon Historical Museums Association 1987

DeArmond, R.N., ed. *Stroller White, Klondike Newsman.* Skagway: Lynn Canal Publishing 1990

DeGraf, Anna. *Pioneering on the Yukon, 1892-1917.* Hamden, CT: Archon Books 1992

Denison, Merrill. *Klondike Mike: An Alaskan Odyssey.* New York: William Morrow 1943

Deutsch, Sarah. *No Separate Refuge: Culture, Class and Gender on an Anglo-Hispanic Frontier in the American Southwest, 1880-1940.* New York: Oxford University Press 1987

DeWindt, Harry. *Through the Gold-Fields of Alaska to Bering Straits.* London: Chatto and Windus 1898

Dial, Scott. 'Those Gold Rush Saloons.' *BC Outdoors* 32, 2 (1976): 12-21

Dignard, Louise. 'A Comparative Approach to the Study of Community and Work in Canadian Mining and Forestry Towns.' MA thesis, Carleton University, 1989

Doyle, Don H. *The Social Order of a Frontier Community.* Urbana, IL: University of Illinois Press 1983

Driscoll, Cynthia R. 'Brackett's Road to Gold.' *North/Nord* 27, 4 (1981): 8-15

Duerden, Frank. 'The Development of the Non-Native Settlement Pattern of the Yukon Territory.' *Canadian Issues* 2, 2 (1978)

Dunham, Sam C. *The Alaskan Gold Fields.* Anchorage: Alaska Northwest 1983

Dyer, Jerome E. *The Gold Fields of Canada and How to Reach Them.* London: George Philip 1898

Ehrlich, Lea Kajati. 'A Corking Adventure: Eugene Allen and the *Klondike Nugget.*' *Alaska Journal* 13, 4 (1983): 8-15

Elliott, George, ed. *Klondike Cattle Drive: The Journal of Norman Lee.* Vancouver: Mitchell Press 1969

Ellis, T. Mullett. *Tales of the Klondyke.* Toronto: Copp Clark 1898

Ferguson, Maria. *Dawson City, Yukon and Alaska Directory and Gazetteer.* Seattle: M.L. Ferguson 1901, 1902

Ferry, Eudora Bundy. *Yukon Gold: Pioneering Days in the Canadian North.* New York: Exposition Press 1971

Fetherling, Douglas. *The Gold Crusades: A Social History of Gold Rushes, 1849-1929.* Toronto: Macmillan 1988

Findlay, John M. *People of Chance: Gambling in American Society from Jamestown to Las Vegas.* New York: Oxford University Press 1986

Fisher, Robin. *Contact and Conflict: Indian-European Relations in British Columbia, 1774-1890.* Vancouver: UBC Press 1992

—. *Duff Pattullo of British Columbia.* Toronto: University of Toronto Press 1991

Frederick, Richard. 'Asahael Curtis and the Klondike Stampede.' *Alaska Journal* 13, 2 (1983): 113-21

Friesen, Richard J. *The Chilkoot Pass and the Great Gold Rush of 1898.* Ottawa: National Parks and Sites Branch 1981

Fry, Art. *I Found Gold: Tagish Charlie's Legacy.* Dawson: Yukon Lottery Commission 1980

Funston, Frederick. 'Over the Chilkoot Pass to the Yukon.' Canadian Historical Images on Microfiche, No. 14295. N.p. 1896

Gartrell, George Edward. 'The Work of the Churches in the Yukon During the Era of the Klondike Gold Rush.' MA thesis, University of Western Ontario, 1970

Gaster, Patricia. 'Park J. Jewell: Letters from the Yukon, 1894-97.' *Pacific Northwest Quarterly* 81, 1 (1990): 11-21

Gates, Michael. *Gold at Fortymile Creek: Early Days in the Yukon.* Vancouver: UBC Press 1994

Geological Survey of Canada. *Report on Gold Values in the Klondike High Grade.* Ottawa: King's Printer 1907

Gibbon, John Murray. *Three Centuries of Canadian Nursing.* Toronto: Macmillan 1947

Gilbert, G.W. *A Brief History of Placer Mining in the Yukon.* Whitehorse: Yukon Department of Indian Affairs 1983

Gillette, Edward. 'The All-American Route to the Klondike.' *Century Magazine* (1900). Canadian Historical Imprints on Microfiche No. 15020. Ottawa: Canadian Institute for Historical Microreproductions
Gillis, Frances Dorley. 'The Lady Went North in '98.' *Alaska Sportsman* 9, 9 (1945): 12-3, 30-2
Glanz, Rudolph. 'From Fur Rush to Gold Rushes.' *Western States Jewish Historical Quarterly* 7, 2 (1975): 95-107
Glave, E.J. 'Our Alaska Experience.' *Frank Leslie's Illustrated Newspaper* (15 Nov. 1890): 226
—. 'Pioneer Packhorses in Alaska.' *The Century Illustrated Monthly Magazine* (Sept. 1892): 672
Goldman, Marion S. *Gold Diggers and Silver Miners: Prostitution and Social Life on the Comstock Lode.* Ann Arbor: University of Michigan Press 1981
Green, Lewis. *The Boundary Hunters: Surveying the 141st Meridian and the Alaska Panhandle.* Vancouver: University of British Columbia Press 1982
—. *The Gold Hustlers.* Vancouver: J.J. Douglas 1972
Greenhouse, Brereton, ed. *Guarding the Goldfields: The Story of the Yukon Field Force.* Toronto: Dundurn Press 1987
Greever, William S. *The Bonanza West: The Story of the Western Mining Rushes, 1848-1900.* Norman: University of Oklahoma Press 1963
Guest, Hal. 'City of Gold: Dawson, Yukon Territory, 1896-1918.' PhD diss., University of Manitoba, 1982
—. *Dawson City, San Francisco of the North or Boomtown in a Bog: A Literature Review.* National Historic Sites Manuscript Report No 241. Ottawa: Department of Indian and Northern Affairs 1978
—. 'The Political Apprenticeship of T.D. Pattullo.' *B.C. Studies* 58 (1983): 327-39
—. *A Socioeconomic History of the Klondike Goldfields, 1896-1966.* Ottawa: Parks Canada 1985
Hall, David J. *Clifford Sifton.* Vol. 2, *The Lonely Eminence.* Vancouver: University of British Columbia Press 1985
Hamilton, Walter R. *The Yukon Story: A Sourdough's Record of Goldrush Days and Yukon Progress from the Earliest Times to the Present.* Vancouver: Mitchell Press 1967
Harris, A.C. *Alaska and the Klondike Gold Fields.* N.p., 1897
Harris, Cole. 'Industry and the Good Life around Idaho Peak.' *Canadian Historical Review* 66, 3 (1985): 315-43
Hartford, William F. *Working People of Holyoke: Class and Ethnicity in a Massachusetts Mill Town, 1850-1960.* New Brunswick, NJ: Rutgers University Press 1990
Haskell, William B. *Two Years in the Klondike and Alaska Goldfields.* Hartford, CT: Hartford Publishing 1898
Hayne, M.H.E. *The Pioneers of the Klondyke; Being an Account of Two Years of Police Service in the Yukon.* N.p., 1897
Heilprin, Angelo. *Alaska and the Klondike, A Journey to the New Eldorado with Hints to the Traveller.* London: Pearson 1899
Heller, Herbert L. *Sourdough Sagas.* New York: World Publishing 1967
Helm, June, ed. *The Smithsonian Handbook of North American Indians.* Vol. 6, *Subarctic.* Washington: Smithsonian Institution 1981
Henderson, Henry. *Bob Henderson's Discovery of the Klondike.* Edmonton: H.H. Hull, n.d.
Henderson, Patsy. *Early Days at Caribou Crossing and the Discovery of Gold on the Klondike.* N.p., 1950
Hewitt, William. 'Across the Chilkoot Pass by Wire Cable.' *Alaska Journal* 8, 4 (1978): 371-6
Hine, Robert. *Community on the American Frontier: Separate But Not Alone.* Norman: University of Oklahoma Press 1980
Hitchcock, Mary E. *Two Women in the Klondike.* New York: Putnam's Sons 1899
Hosely, Edward H. 'Intercultural Relations and Cultural Change in the Alaska Plateau.' In *Handbook of North American Indians.* Vol. 6, *Subarctic,* edited by June Helm, 546-52. Washington: Smithsonian Institution 1981
Hubbard, Charles G. 'Prospecting the Great Unknown: A Miners' Tale of Life on the Cop-

per River in 1898.' *Alaska Journal* 16 (1986): 148-55

Hubbard, William K. 'The Klondike Gold Rush in Literature, 1896-1903.' MA thesis, University of Western Ontario, 1969

Hunt, William R. 'Deadly Frank Canton: First Law-Man on the Yukon.' *Alaska Journal* 16 (1986): 244-9

—. *North of 53 Degrees: The Wild Days of the Alaska-Yukon Mining Frontier.* New York: Macmillan 1974

Ingersoll, Ernest. *Gold Fields of the Klondike and the Wonders of Alaska.* 1897. Reprint, Langley, BC: Mr Paperback 1981

Innis, Harold A. *Settlement and the Mining Frontier.* Toronto: Macmillan 1936

Jameson, Elizabeth. 'High-Grade and Fissures: A Working-Class History of the Cripple Creek, Colorado, Gold Mining District, 1890-1905.' PhD diss., University of Michigan, 1987

—. 'Imperfect Unions: Class and Gender in Cripple Creek, 1894-1904.' In *Class, Sex, and the Woman Worker,* edited by Milton Cantor and Bruce Laurie, 166-202. Westport, CN: Greenwood Press 1977

Johnson, Fred E. 'The Other Side of the Mountain.' *Explorer's Journal* 52, 2 (1974): 85-90

Johnson, James Albert. *Carmack of the Klondike.* Seattle: Epicenter Press/Horsdal and Schubart 1990

Johnston, Jean. *Wilderness Women.* Toronto: Peter Martin Associates 1973

Jones, H. Wendy. *Women Who Braved the Far North.* Vol. 1. San Diego: Grossmont Press 1976

Katz, Michael. *People of Hamilton, Canada West: Family and Class in a Mid-Nineteenth Century City.* Cambridge: Harvard University Press 1975

Kelcey, Barbara. 'Lost in the Rush: The Forgotten Women of the Klondike Stampede.' MA thesis, University of Victoria, 1989

Kirk, Robert C. *Twelve Months in Klondike.* London: William Heinemann 1899

Koroscil, Paul M. 'The Historical Development of Whitehorse: 1898-1945.' *American Review of Canadian Studies* 18, 3 (1988): 271-95

Krause, Aurel. *The Tlingit Indians.* Translated by Erna Gunther. Seattle: American Ethnological Society 1976

Ladue, Joseph. *Klondyke Facts: Being a Complete Guide Book to the Great Gold Regions of the Yukon and Klondyke and the North West Territories.* Montreal: Lovell 1897

La Roche, F. *Photographic Views en route to the Klondike via the Skaguay and Dyea Trails.* Chicago: Henry O. Sheperd 1897

Ledbetter, Suzann. *Nellie Cashman: Prospector and Trailblazer.* El Paso: Texas University Press 1993

Lee, Mabel Barbee. *Cripple Creek Days.* Lincoln: University of Nebraska Press 1984

Leonard, J.W. *Gold Fields of the Klondike.* Chicago: A.N. Marquis 1897, and London: T.F. Unwin 1897.

Leonard, Stephen J., and Thomas J. Noel. *Denver: From Mining Camp to Metropolis.* Denver: University of Colorado 1990

Leonoff, Cyril Edel. *Pioneers, Pedlars and Prayer Shawls: The Jewish Communities in British Columbia and the Yukon.* Victoria: Sono Nis Press 1978

Lloyd-Owen, Frances. *Gold Nugget Charlie: A Narrative Compiled from the Notes of Charles E. Masson.* Seattle: Sourdough Stampede Association 1945

Lokke, Carl L. *Klondike Saga: The Chronicle of a Minnesota Gold Mining Company.* Minneapolis: University of Minnesota Press 1965

Lotz, J.R. *The Dawson Area: A Regional Monograph.* Ottawa: Department of Northern Affairs 1966

Lucas, R.A. *Minetown, Milltown, Railtown.* Toronto: University of Toronto Press 1971

Lucia, Ellis. *Klondike Kate: 1873-1957.* New York: Hastings House 1962

Lung, Edward Burchall. *Black Sand and Gold.* Portland: Binford and Mort 1967

Lynch, Jeremiah. *Three Years in the Klondike.* London: Edward Arnold 1904

Macbeth, Madge Hamilton Lyons. *Long Day: Reminiscences of the Yukon by Dill.* Ottawa: Graphic Publishers 1926

Marks, Lynne. 'Hallelujah Lasses: Working-Class Women in the Salvation Army in English Canada, 1882-92.' In *Gender Conflicts*, edited by F. Iacovetta and M. Valverde, 67-117. Toronto: University of Toronto Press 1992

McCandless, Robert G. *Yukon Wildlife: A Social History.* Edmonton: University of Alberta Press 1985

McCann, Larry D. 'The Changing Internal Structure of Canadian Resource Towns.' *Plan Canada* (1978)

McClellan, Catherine. 'Inland Tlingit.' In *Handbook of North American Indians.* Vol. 6, *Subarctic,* edited by June Helm, 469-80. Washington: Smithsonian Institution 1981

—. *My Old People Say: An Ethnographic Survey of Southern Yukon Territory.* Publications in Ethnology No. 6. Ottawa: National Museums of Canada 1975

—. *Part of the Land, Part of the Water: A History of the Yukon Indians.* Vancouver: Douglas and McIntyre 1987

—. 'Tagish.' In *Handbook of North American Indians.* Vol. 6, *Subarctic,* edited by June Helm, 481-92. Washington: Smithsonian Institution 1981

—. 'Tutchone.' In *Handbook of North American Indians.* Vol. 6, *Subarctic,* edited by June Helm, 493-505. Washington: Smithsonian Institution 1981

McCollom, Pat. 'Klondike Outpost: Dawson City.' *Westways* (Apr. 1977): 21-3

McConnell, R.G. *Preliminary Report of the Yukon Gold Fields.* Ottawa: Queen's Printer 1900

MacDonald, Alexander. *In Search of El Dorado: A Wanderer's Experiences.* London: T. Fisher Unwin 1905

McDonald, Alexander. *The White Trail.* London: Blackie 1908

McDonald, Alice. 'As Well as Any Man.' *Alaska Journal* 14, 3 (1984): 39-45

MacDonald, Cheryl. 'The Salvation Army: Christian Soldiers in Canada.' *The Beaver* 313, 2 (1982): 22-7

Macdonald, Norbert. 'Seattle, Vancouver, and the Klondike.' *Canadian Historical Review* 49, 3 (1968): 234-46

MacGowan, Michael. *The Hard Road to Klondike.* London: Routledge and Kegan 1962

McGrath, Roger D. *Gunfighters, Highwaymen and Vigilantes: Violence on the Frontier.* Berkeley: University of California Press 1984

MacGregor, J.G. *The Klondike Rush through Edmonton, 1897-1898.* Toronto: McClelland and Stewart 1970

McKay, Mrs J.J. 'How I Went through the Chilkoot Pass in the Dead of Winter.' *The Examiner Sunday Magazine* (20 Feb. 1898): 1-2

McKeown, Martha Ferguson. *The Trail Led North: Mont Hawthorne's Story.* New York: Macmillan 1948

Macleod, R.C. 'Canadianizing the West: The North-West Mounted Police as Agents of the National Policy, 1873-1905.' In *Essays on Western History,* edited by L.H. Thomas. Edmonton: University of Alberta Press 1976

McMichael, Alfred G. *Klondike Letters: The Correspondence of a Gold Seeker in 1898.* Anchorage: Alaska Northwest 1984

McQuesten, Leroy N. *Recollections of Leroy N. McQuesten.* Dawson City: Yukon Order of Pioneers 1977

Mann, Ralph. *After the Gold Rush: Society in Grass Valley and Nevada City, California, 1849-1870.* Stanford: Stanford University Press 1982

Margeson, Charles Anson. *Experiences of Gold Hunters in Alaska.* Hornellsville, NY: C.A. Margeson 1899

Martinson, Ella Lung. *Trail to North Star Gold: A True Story of the Alaska-Klondike Gold Rush.* Portland: Binford and Mort 1984

Marvin, Frederic R. *Yukon Overland: The Gold Digger's Handbook.* N.p., 1898

May, Robin. *The Gold Rushes from California to the Klondike.* London: William Luscombe 1977

Mayer, Melanie J. *Klondike Women: True Tales of the 1897-1898 Gold Rush.* Ohio: Swallow/University of Ohio Press 1989

Medill, Robert B. *Klondike Diary: True Account of the Klondike Rush of 1897-98*. Portland: Beattie 1949

Mercier, François Xavier. *Recollections of the Yukon, 1868-1885*. Anchorage: Alaska Historical Society 1986

Miers, Henry A. *A Visit to the Yukon Gold Fields*. Ottawa: King's Printer 1901

Mills, Thora McIlroy. *The Contribution of the Presbyterian Church to the Yukon during the Gold Rush, 1897-1910*. Toronto: United Church of Canada 1978

—. 'Memorial to the Pack Animals.' *Beaver* 310, 4 (1980): 46-51

Minter, Roy. *The White Pass: Gateway to the Klondike*. Toronto: McClelland and Stewart 1987

Moberly, Walter. *Eight Routes to the Klondike*. N.p., 1898

Moore, Carolyn. 'Crisis and Opportunity: Three White Women's Experiences in the Klondike Gold Rush.' *Canadian Woman Studies* 14, 4 (1994): 53-7

Morgan, Edward E.P. *God's Loaded Dice: Alaska, 1897-1930*. Caldwell: Caxton 1948

Morgan, Murray. *One Man's Gold Rush: A Klondike Album*. Vancouver: J.J. Douglas 1973

Morrison, David R. *The Politics of the Yukon Territory, 1898-1909*. Toronto: University of Toronto Press 1968

Morrison, William R. *Showing the Flag: The Mounted Police and Canadian Sovereignty in the North, 1894-1925*. Vancouver: University of British Columbia Press 1985

—. *A Survey of the History and Claims of the Native Peoples of Northern Canada*. 2nd ed. Ottawa: Department of Indian and Northern Affairs 1985

Morrison, William R., and Kenneth Coates. 'Soldiers of the Empire: The Yukon at War.' *The Beaver* 69, 5 (1988): 229-34

Moyles, R.G. *The Blood and Fire in Canada: A History of the Salvation Army in the Dominion, 1882-1976*. Toronto: Peter Martin 1977

—. *From Duck Lake to Dawson City: The Diary of Eben McAdam's Journey to the Klondike, 1898-99*. Saskatoon: Western Producer Prairie Books 1977

Murray, Alexander Hunter. *Journal of the Yukon, 1847-48*. Ottawa: Government Printing Bureau 1910

Murray, Keith A. *Reindeer and Gold*. Occasional Paper No. 24. Center for Pacific Northwest Studies, Bellingham, WA: 1988

N.a. *Calgary Route to the Klondyke Gold Fields*. N.p., 1898

—. *The Canadian Gold Fields and Farm Land: How to Get There*. Liverpool: Allan Line Offices 1899

—. *The Gold Fields of the Klondike: Illustrating All the Incidents*. N.p., 1899

—. *Klondike up to Date*. N.p., 1898

—. 'Lifelong Klondikers.' *Canadian Geographic* 98, 3 (1979): 52-7

—. *The Official Guide to the Klondike Country*. Chicago: W.B. Conkey 1897

—. *The Papers and Photographs of P.E. Larss, Klondike Photographer and Miner, 1898-1904*. Juneau: Alaska Division, State Libraries and Museums 1978

—. *Tacoma: The Gateway to the Klondike*. Tacoma: n.p. 1897

—. *Town Hall or High School To-night, Eight o'clock: Popular Illustrated Lime Light Entertainment by Mr F.A. Allen, B.A., on Camp Life and Placer Mines on the Yellow Yukon in Search of Gold, Prairie Homes and Imperial Honours*. N.p., n.d.

Nelson, Helen, and Arnold Nelson. 'Bringing Home the Gold.' *Alaska Journal* 9, 3 (1979): 52-9

Nelson, Klondy. *Daughter of the Gold Rush*. New York: Random House 1958

Neufeld, David, and Frank Norris. *Chilkoot Trail: Heritage Trail to the Klondike*. Whitehorse: Lost Moose 1996

Newell, Dianne (MacDougall). 'Canada's Share of the Klondyke: The Character of Gold-Rush Publicity.' MA thesis, Carleton University, 1974

—. 'The Importance of Information and Misinformation in the Making of the Klondike Gold Rush.' *Journal of Canadian Studies* 21, 4 (1986-7): 95-111

—. 'Klondike Photographer's Lode.' *Historic Preservation* 29, 2 (1977): 15-21

Nicholson, Janice E. 'Conflicts of Authority: An Analysis of Relations among Authority Structures in the Nineteenth Century Gold Rush Camps.' PhD diss., York University, 1973

Norris, Frank. 'Showing off Alaska: The Northern Tourist Trade, 1878-1941.' *Alaska History* 2, 2 (1987): 1-18

North, Dick. *Arctic Exodus: The Last Great Trail Drive.* Toronto: Macmillan 1991

O'Connor, Richard. *Gold, Dice and Women.* London: Alvin Redman 1954

Ogilvie, William. *Early Days on the Yukon.* Toronto: Bell and Cockburn 1913

—. *Klondike Official Guide: Canada's Great Gold Field, the Yukon District.* 1898

Oglesby, Robert. *The Klondyke Gold Region: Account of a Six Months Trip through the Yukon Gold Fields.* N.p., 1899

Osgood, Cornelius. *The Han Indians: A Compilation of Ethnographic and Historical Data on the Alaska-Yukon Boundary Area.* Yale University Publications in Anthropology No. 74. New Haven: Yale University Press 1971

Page, Elizabeth. *Wild Horses and Gold: From Wyoming to Yukon.* New York: Farran and Rinehart 1932

Palmer, Frederick. *In the Klondike, Including an Account of the Writer's Journey to Dawson.* New York: Scribner 1899

Parrish, Maud. *Nine Pounds of Luggage.* London: Hutchman and Company 1940

Patchell, Sarah Elizabeth. *My Extraordinary Years of Adventure and Romance in Klondike and Alaska.* London: Arthur H. Stockwell, n.d.

Paul, Rodman. 'Old Californians in British Gold Fields.' *Huntington Library Quarterly* 17 (1954): 161-72

Petrone, Gerrard. 'An Iowan in the Klondike: Selections from the Diary of Marvin March.' In *People of the Far West*, edited by Horace Dodd and Robert Long. Brand Book No. 6. San Diego: Corral of Westerners 1979

Pike, Warburton. *Through the Sub-Arctic Forest.* 1896. Reprint, New York: Arno Press 1967

Piva, Michael J. *The Condition of the Working Class in Toronto 1900-1921.* Ottawa: University of Ottawa Press 1979

Porsild, Charlene. 'Lulu Mae Eads'; 'Keish'; and 'Shaaw Tlàa.' *Canadian Dictionary of Biography.* Vol. 14. Toronto: University of Toronto 1995

Portus, G.V. 'The Gold Discoveries, 1850-1860.' In *Cambridge History of the British Empire.* Vol. 12. Edited by J. Holland Rose. Cambridge: Cambridge University Press 1933

Price, Julius M. *From Euston to Klondike.* London: Sampson, Low, Marston 1898

Procter, Hazel T. 'Tenderfoot to Sourdough: The True Adventures of Amos Entheus Ball.' New Holland: Edward C. Procter 1975

Pynn, Larry. *The Forgotten Trail: One Man's Adventures to the Klondike.* Toronto: Doubleday 1996

Quinlan, Thomas A. 'The Last Stampede: Letters from the Klondike.' *American History Illustrated* 10, 7 (1975): 10-21

Radforth, Ian. *Bushworkers and Bosses: Logging in Northern Ontario 1900-1980.* Toronto: University of Toronto Press 1987

Ray, Captain P.H., and Lt. W.P. Richardson. 'Relief of the Destitute in Gold Fields.' *Compilation of Narratives of Explorations in Alaska.* 56th Congress, Senate Report No. 1023. Washington: 1900

Rea, K.J. *Political Economy of the Canadian North.* Toronto: University of Toronto Press 1968

Reynolds, Henry. *The Other Side of the Frontier: Aboriginal Resistance to the European Invasion of Australia.* Ringwood, Victoria: Penguin 1982

Riley, Bay. 'From Regulated to Celebrated Sexuality: Prostitution in Dawson City, Yukon.' *Canadian Woman Studies* 14, 4 (1994): 58

Robertson, William Norrie. *Yukon Memories: Sourdough Tells of Chaos and Changes in the Klondike Vale.* Toronto: Hunter Rose 1930

Robins, Elizabeth. *Raymond and I.* London: Hogarth 1956

Rodney, William. *Joe Boyle: King of the Klondike.* Toronto: McGraw-Hill Ryerson 1974
Romig, Emily Craig. *A Pioneer Woman in Alaska.* Caldwell: Caxton 1948
Rosborough, Alexander J. *The Mountie and the Sourdough.* Eureka, CA: Siskiyou County Historical Society, n.d.
Rosener, Charles S. 'First Jewish Services at Dawson, Yukon Territory, 1898.' *Western States Jewish Historical Quarterly* 11, 2 (1979): 145-6
Rugieri, Vincenzo. *Du Transvaal à l'Alaska.* Traduit de l'italien. Paris: Plon-Nourrit et cie 1901
Ruskin, Evey. 'Letters to Lizzie: A Koyukuk Gold Seeker Writes Home.' *Alaska Journal* 16 (1986): 120-6
Sack, Doug. *A Brief History of Dawson City and the Klondike.* Whitehorse: Yukon News 1974
Sackett, Russell. *The Chilkat Tlingit: A General Overview,* Anthropology and Historic Preservation Occasional Paper No. 23. Fairbanks: University of Alaska Cooperative Park Studies Unit 1979
Sander, Leanne. '"The Men all Died of Miners' Disease": Women and Families in the Industrial Mining Environment of Upper Clear Creek, Colorado, 1870-1900.' PhD diss., University of Colorado at Boulder, 1990
Santor, Donald, and Stewart Dicks. *The Great Klondike Gold Rush.* Scarborough: Prentice-Hall 1978
Schlissel, Lillian. *Women's Diaries of the Westward Journey.* New York: Schocken Books 1982
Schwatka, Frederick. *A Summer in Alaska.* St Louis: W. Henry 1894
Scott, Thomas S. 'Some Experiences on the Chilkoot Pass.' *Canadian Magazine* 10 (1898): 329-38
Secretan, J.H.E. *To the Klondike and Back: A Journey down the Yukon from Its Source to Its Mouth.* New York: Hurst and Blackett 1898
Senkewicz, Robert N. (S.J.). *Vigilantes in Gold Rush San Francisco.* Stanford: Stanford University Press 1985
Shand, Margaret Clark, and Ora Shand. *The Summit and Beyond.* Caldwell, ID: Caxton Printers 1959
Shaw, Flora Louise. 'Klondike.' *Journal of the Royal Colonial Institute* 3 and 4 (1899). Canadian Historical Imprints on Microfiche No. 15527. Ottawa: Canadian Institute for Historical Microreproductions
Shortridge, James R. 'The Alaskan Agricultural Empire: An American Agrarian Vision, 1898-1929.' *Pacific Northwest Quarterly* 69, 4 (1978): 145-58
Sinclair, James M. *Mission: Klondike.* Vancouver: Mitchell Press 1978
Slobodin, Richard. *Band Organization of the Peel River Kutchin.* National Museums Bulletin No. 179. Ottawa: Department of Northern Affairs and National Resources 1962
—. 'The Dawson Boys.' *Polar Notes* 5, 3 (1963): 24-36
—. 'Kutchin.' In *Handbook of North American Indians.* Vol. 6, *Subarctic,* edited by June Helm, 514-32. Washington: Smithsonian Institution 1981
Smith, J. Gordon. 'The Klondike.' *Canadian Magazine* 10 (Feb. 1898): 322-8
Snow, Jeanne H. 'Ingalik.' In *Handbook of North American Indians.* Vol. 6, *Subarctic,* edited by June Helm, 602-17. Washington: Smithsonian Institution 1981
Sola, A.E.I. *Klondyke: Truth and Facts of the New El Dorado.* London: Mining and Geographical Institute 1897
Spurr, Josiah. *Through the Yukon Gold Diggings: A Narrative of Personal Travel.* Boston: Eastern Publishing 1900
Stacey, John F. *To Alaska for Gold.* Fairfield: Ye Galleon Press 1973
Stanley, G.F.G. 'Western Canada and the Frontier Thesis.' *Canadian Historical Association Annual Report* (1940): 105-17
Stanton, James B. *Ho for the Klondike: A Whimsical Look at the Years 1897-98.* Vancouver: Centennial Museum 1970
Starr, Walter A. *My Adventures in the Klondike and Alaska.* San Francisco: Lawton Kennedy 1960

Steele, Samuel B. *Forty Years in Canada: Reminiscences of the Great North-West with some Account of his Service in South Africa.* New York: Dodd Mead 1915
Steffens, Joseph Lincoln. *Life in the Klondike Gold Fields.* New York: n.p. 1897
Stelter, Gilbert, and A. Artibise. 'Canadian Resource Towns in Historical Perspective.' In *Shaping the Urban Landscape,* edited by Gilbert Stelter and A. Artibise. Toronto: McClelland and Stewart 1982
Stern, Norton B. 'The Jews in the Yukon Territory and Their Cemetery.' *Western States Jewish Historical Quarterly* 14, 4 (1982): 356-61
Stevens, Gary L. 'Gold Rush Theater in the Alaska-Yukon Frontier.' PhD diss., University of Oregon, 1984
Stewart, Don. *Sourdough Ray.* Coos Bays: Gorst 1983
Stewart, Robert. *Sam Steele: Lion of the Frontier.* Toronto: Doubleday 1979
Stone, Thomas. *Miners' Justice: Migration, Law and Order on the Alaska-Yukon Frontier, 1873-1902.* New York: Peter Lang 1988
Stratemeyer, Edward. *To Alaska for Gold, or the Fortune Hunters of the Yukon.* Boston: n.p. 1899
Stuart, Richard. *The Bank of British North America, Dawson Yukon, 1898-1968.* Manuscript Report No. 324. Ottawa: Parks Canada 1979
Stumer, Harold Merritt. *This Was Klondike Fever.* Seattle: Superior Publishing 1978
Sullivan, May Kellogg. *A Woman Who Went to Alaska.* Boston: James H. Earle 1902
Taylor, Leonard W. *The Sourdough and the Queen: The Many Lives of Klondike Joe Boyle.* Toronto: Methuen 1983
Thernstrom, Stephen. *The Other Bostonians: Poverty and Progress in the American Metropolis, 1880-1970.* Cambridge: Harvard University Press 1973
Thomas, Lowell Jackson Jr., ed. *Trails of Ninety-Eight.* New York: Duell, Sloan, Pearce 1962
Thompson, Arthur Ripley. *Gold Seeking on the Dalton Trail: Being the Adventures of two New England Boys in Alaska.* Boston: n.p. 1900
Tikhmenev, P.A. *A History of the Russian-American Company.* Seattle: University of Washington Press 1978
Tollemache, Stratford. *Reminiscences of the Yukon.* Toronto: William Briggs 1912
Treadgold, Arthur Newton Christian. *Report on the Goldfields of the Klondike.* N.p., 1899
Trelawney-Ansell, Edward C. *I Followed Gold.* New York: Lee Furman 1939
Tremblay, Emilie. *Une Pionnière du Yukon: La première femme blanche qui franchit la Chilcoot Pass.* Chicoutimi: n.p. 1948
Tronrud, I. 'Frontier Social Structure: The Canadian Lakehead, 1871 and 1881.' *Ontario History* 79, 2 (1987): 145-65
Tupper, Sir Charles. *Charges against the Government and Its Officials in Connection with the Yukon Administration, Ottawa, 1899.* Ottawa: Queen's Printer 1899
Tyrrell, M. Edith. *I Was There: A Book of Reminiscences.* Toronto: Ryerson Press 1938
Usherwood, Stephen. 'Flora Shaw on the Klondike.' *History Today* 27, 7 (1977): 445-51
Van Kirk, Sylvia. *Many Tender Ties: Women in Fur-Trade Society, 1670-1870.* Winnipeg: Watson and Dwyer 1980
Van Stone, James W. *Athapaskan Adaptations: Hunters and Fishermen of the Subarctic Forests.* Chicago: Aldine 1974
Voisey, Paul. *Vulcan: The Making of a Prairie Community.* Toronto: University of Toronto Press 1988
Wade, F.C. 'Business Talk on the Yukon.' *Canadian Magazine* 19 (May 1902): 25-31
Walker, F. 'Overland to the Klondike.' *Alberta Historical Review* 7 (Winter 1959): 1-7
Walsh, J.M. *Report Respecting the Yukon District.* Ottawa: Queen's Printer 1898
Warner, Iris. 'Klondyke Diaries, Part IV.' *North/Nord* 24, 2 (1977): 38-43
Webb, John Sidney. *The River Trip to the Klondike.* 1898. Reprint, Seattle: Shorey Books 1968
Webb, Melody. *The Last Frontier: A History of the Yukon Basin of Canada and Alaska.* Albuquerque: University of New Mexico Press 1985

Weir, Joan. *Back Door to the Klondike*. Erin, ON: Boston Mills Press 1988

Wells, E. Hazard. *Magnificence and Misery: A Firsthand Account of the 1897 Klondike Gold Rush*. New York: Doubleday 1984

Weppler, James. *The S.S. Klondike: The Last Sternwheeler*. Ottawa: National History Sites Service 1968

—. *Yukon Territory: A Community of Men*. National History Sites Manuscript Report No. 9. Ottawa: Department of Indian and Northern Affairs 1969

West, Elliott. 'Five Idaho Mining Towns: A Computer Profile.' *Pacific Northwest Quarterly* 73, 3 (1982): 108-20

Wharton, David. *The Alaska Gold Rush*. Bloomington: Indiana University Press 1972

Wilson, Clifford. *Campbell of the Yukon*. Toronto: Macmillan 1970

Wilson, Veazie. *Glimpses of the Yukon Gold Fields and Dawson Route*. Vancouver: Thompson Stationery 1897

Woodcock, George. 'Caribou and the Klondike: Gold Miners in Western Canada.' *History Today* 5, 1 (1955): 33-42

Woodside, H.J. 'Dawson As It Is.' *Canadian Magazine* 17 (Sept. 1901): 403-13

Wright, Allen A. *Prelude to Bonanza: The Discovery and Exploration of the Yukon*. Sidney, BC: Gray's Publishing 1976

Zaslow, Morris. *The Opening of the Canadian North, 1870-1914*. Toronto: McClelland and Stewart 1971

—. 'The Yukon: Northern Development in the Canadian-American Context.' In *Regionalism in the Canadian Community, 1867-1967*, edited by Mason Wade, 180-97. Toronto: University of Toronto Press 1969

Index

Carmack), 35, 85, 87
Tlálkwshaan (brother of Keish and Shaaw
Tláa), 42
Tlingit (Natives), 24, 26, 36, 38, 40-1, 56;
Chilkat, 25, 27, 41; Chilkoot, 25; control of
mountain passes, 30; Taku, 25-6; in pack-
ing trade, 33, 40-1; relationship with
Tagish peoples, 30
Tombstone, 84
Toronto, 156, 197
Totty, Rev. Benjamin, 197; and Mrs, 141
Trails: all-water route, 4-5, 162; Athabasca
Landing, 4-5, 7; Chilkoot, 4-5, 30-1, 33,
36, 38-41, 162, 180; enterprising men on,
62; Glenora-Stikine, 4-5, 7; overland, 4-5;
sexual division of labour on, 92; women
entrepreneurs, 62; White Pass, 4-5, 38
Transience. See Persistence
Transportation: dogsleds, 93, 126; Native role
in navigation, 41, 44, 56; steamboats, 40,
43
Trapping. See Fur trade
Treadgold concession, 87
Trelawney-Ansell, Edward, 125
Turner, Jimmy, 129, 198
Turner, Reverend, 141
Tutchone (Natives), 24; Northern, 25-7, 44;
Southern, 25-6, 42, 56
Tyrrell, J.B., 141

United States consul, 134, 158, 162, 174,
187-9

Van Buren, Edith, 162
Vancouver, 12, 127
Venereal disease, 102, 180
Vice: conflict between federal and local
authorities over, 106; licensing, 102; liquor
licences, 106; NWMP tolerance of, 104,
114; prosecution of, 100, 102, 116, 123,
132-3; regulation of, 100, 102, 112, 198
Victorian Order of Nurses (VONs), 149-51.
See also Nurses

Wade, F.C., 167, 182-3, 186
Walker, Minnie, 176
Wallace, Babe, 130
Walsh, Major James, 181-2, 186
Water supply, 150
Weddings, 20-1, 138, 140, 177
White, Georgia, 69, 131, 151
White, Libby, 128
White Pass Railway, 38, 62, 131, 140, 173-4
Whitehorse, 28
Whitehorse Rapids, 144
Wildlife, depletion of, 58. See also Fur trade;
Hunting
Wilkensen, Minnie, 96-7

Wilson, Arthur, 187
Wilson, Cad, 113
Wilson, Thomas, 74
Wisconsin, 161
Women: African American, opportunities for,
65; charity work, 144; on Chilkoot, 162;
class and race divisions among, 88; codes
of behaviour for, 158; dance hall workers,
112-7; domestic duties, 90, 92; employment
opportunities, 20; entrepreneurs, 62, 64,
174, 176; Han, portrait of, 47; in laundry
work, 65-6; Native, duties of, 52; Native,
married to non-Native men, 35-6; as miners and mine owners, 74, 76, 84, 85; in
packing trade, 61-2; professions for, 150,
158; as servants, 66, 68; social hierarchy
among, 112; as Sunday school teachers,
144; work on family mining claims, 79;
working conditions of prostitutes, 119-23
Wood cutters, 70
Wood, Major Zachary, 107-8

Yukon College of Physicians and Surgeons,
152, 153. See also Doctors
Yukon Council, 102, 107-8, 110, 167, 186
Yukon Field Force, 150, 180
Yukon Tennis Club, 177

Zenaide, Sister Mary, 155
Zeno, Sister Mary, 151